Resurgent Islam
A Sociological Approach

PHILIP W. SUTTON AND
STEPHEN VERTIGANS

polity

First published in 2005 by Polity Press

Polity Press
65 Bridge Street
Cambridge CB2 1UR, UK.

Polity Press
350 Main Street
Malden, MA 02148, USA

ISBN: 0-7456-3232-7
ISBN: 0-7456-3233-5 (pb)

A catalogue record for this book is available from the British Library and has been applied for from the Library of Congress.

Typeset in 10.5 on 12 pt Sabon
by SNP Best-set Typesetter Ltd., Hong Kong
Printed and bound in Great Britain by TJ International Ltd, Padstow, Cornwall

For further information on Polity, visit our website: www.polity.co.uk

Contents

Acknowledgements

Many people have contributed to getting this book into print and we have space to thank just a few of them. First, we would like to thank all the staff at Polity Press, especially Emma Longstaff, who saw the book through to publication with alacrity, and Rachel Kerr, who recognized the need for and originally commissioned the book. Thanks are also due to the anonymous reviewers at Polity who made some useful recommendations and criticisms which have helped refine our thoughts.

We have also benefited from being able to present earlier forms of our ideas to international audiences and therefore gratefully acknowledge the support of the British Academy for an Overseas Conference Grant (No: OCG-34475) in 2002. In particular, we would like to thank the participants in conference sessions at the 2002 ISA World Congress of Sociology in Brisbane, Australia and at the 2004 International Conference on Muslims and Islam in Kuala Lumpur, Malaysia, whose feedback has helped to shape our thinking on several significant issues. We would also like to thank all of those people, too numerous to mention here, with whom we have enjoyed discussing sociology and Islam and whose influence may be felt throughout the text in a variety of different ways. Of course, any failings the book may have are entirely the responsibility of the authors.

At the Robert Gordon University, we are indebted to Julian Bell for his sympathetic understanding of our research needs and the creative balancing of academic responsibilities. The School of Applied Social Studies has also provided generous support for conference attendance, which is much appreciated. Being able to present some of our ideas to students on our Religions in Conflict course has also helped to clarify our thinking in certain contentious areas.

Earlier versions of chapters 4 and 6 appeared respectively as: Vertigans, S., and Sutton, P. W., 'Globalization Theory and Islamic Praxis', *Global Society*, 16(1) (2002): 31–46, and Sutton, P. W., and Vertigans, S., 'The Established and Challenging Outsiders? The Case of Resurgent Islam', *Totalitarian Movements and Political Religions*, 3(1) (summer 2002): 58–78 (www.tandf.co.uk).

Finally, thanks as always to Pat and Val whose limitless support helped to make the book possible.

ntroduction

From 'Islamic studies' to studies of Islam

Books about Islam are no longer relatively scarce in the West. The last decade has seen the production of a plethora of texts reflecting the growing interest in Islam among Western people and academics. Such work has moved away from an older form of 'Islamic studies' and towards connecting studies of Islam with a range of academic disciplines. It is now much easier to find books detailing the main tenets of the Islamic faith, the history of Islam, studies of Islamic states and their relationships within the international states system and, in very recent years, explorations of Islamic social movements and terrorism in the name of Islam. It is not difficult to understand why interest has grown. The Iranian Revolution of 1979, the Palestinian *intifada* in 1987–92 and again in 2000, the British 'Rushdie Affair' (1989), Saddam Hussein's invasion of Kuwait and the first Gulf War (1991), the removal of Russian forces from Afghanistan and the rise of the Taliban in 1994, *al-Qa'ida*'s attack on American targets on 11 September 2001, the invasion of Iraq in 2003 and its consequences have all been associated with Islam. These are the staging posts and defining events of recent Western engagements with Islam, which tend to reinforce stereotypical views of Islam as a violent 'religion of the sword' inevitably in conflict with the West. This is a partial view of Islam, and numerous authors have tried to redress the balance. It is therefore legitimate, amidst this embarrassment of riches, to ask why we should need yet another book on Islam.

Research into the 'Islamic resurgence' across the world has largely been conducted from within the disciplines of political science –

including Middle East Studies – international relations, civilizational analysis and history. There are numerous studies of the Islamic resurgence, many published before the *al-Qa'ida* attacks on America in September 2001, which have come to be seen as symbolizing a new era in relations between Islam and Western nations. Many of these studies have mostly concentrated on the appeal of Islam to economically excluded groups. While these groups have certainly been prominent, the tendency has been to explain the appeal of Islam by relying upon criteria of exclusion, whether in relation to the economic situation of disaffected people or by analysing the power differential or cultural differences between Muslims and the West. Thus the multitude of other groups and factors involved is overlooked. Examples of such studies include Anderson (1997), Ayubi (1991), Huband (1998), Mehmet (1990), Mortimer (1982), Paz (2001a), Roy (1994) and Williamson (1987). Particularly influential among the studies that place considerable importance on culture and cultural identification is Samuel Huntington's *The Clash of Civilizations* (1993a, 1998, 2004), which is taken up in more detail in chapter 5.

Since 11 September 2001, a wealth of material has been produced which concentrates on the political activities of terrorist groups claiming allegiance to the much wider Islamic resurgence. Notable here are Bergen (2001), Burke (2004), Davis (2003), Halliday (2002), Hiro (2002), Kepel (2004), Paz (2002), Reuter (2004) and Rubin (2003). However, the majority of these texts tend to be journalistic rather than analytical, or political rather than sociological, in their approach. This should not be read as suggesting that both sets of studies are of no value, but the argument developed throughout this book is that there is a need to build on these by integrating them within sociological theories of social change.

Sociology's contribution has tended to be at one step removed, bringing the Islamic resurgence into view as one element in theories of globalization (Waters 1998), culturalist interpretations of global/ glocalization (Robertson 1992, 1995) and as a response to the spread of Western consumerism and postmodernism (Turner 1994). Even so, these studies demonstrate that sociological analysis potentially brings something unique to our understanding of this important phenomenon by connecting Islamic history to changes in the figuration of international states, the rise of political and violent forms of Islam alongside widespread beliefs in 'civilized' values and 'superior' (and 'inferior') civilizations. In short, the absence of a thoroughgoing sociological perspective leaves our understanding of resurgent Islam relatively fragmented and therefore partial.

Situating sociology

Having surveyed the existing field, we believe that a distinctively sociological approach to the study of contemporary debates on the resurgence of Islam does add something original. Sociology is the social scientific discipline that demands that we strive for a level of detachment from personal biases and emotional and political commitments, in order that we can return to the latter 'with a fresh approach', as it were, hopefully better informed than before. One of this book's central aims is to add a sociological perspective to those that currently dominate the field to help improve understanding and explanations of the growth in Islamic faith and activism. The book does not pretend to be a comprehensive account of every aspect of the resurgence of Islam, as this would require probably several much larger texts. As a result, important consequences such as changes within gender expectations, family relations, ethnicity and national identities are only discussed where they contribute to increasing understanding about why the resurgence is happening. Instead, a series of the most significant developments that help comprehend and explain the resurgence are selected and approached from a sociological perspective, drawing on theoretical resources from within the discipline.

The book is therefore not intended to be a comprehensive review of the contribution of sociologists to an understanding and explanation of resurgent Islam and the shifting relations between Islam and the West since, say, Max Weber. Nor is it an exhaustive review of sociological studies of Islam. There is not, for instance, the scope to include the work of Ibn Khaldun (1332–1406), who has been described by Gellner (1981: 16) as the 'greatest sociologist of Islam' as well as a respected economist, historian, philosopher and political scientist. Undoubtedly the significance of Ibn Khaldun's fourteenth-century study of changing Arabian civilizations and the impact upon social behaviour has been neglected within Western accounts of sociology's heritage, but the focus on resurgent Islam within this book means that this is not the place to rectify that omission. Readers should also not expect to find extended discussions of which sociological theories are more reliable and valid than others for understanding the historical development of Islam. Instead, our aim is to tackle from a sociological standpoint some key contemporary issues relating to resurgent Islam, making use of insights and ideas from a variety of sociological sources as well as empirical studies from other disciplines. In this way, the general sociological approach adopted here will hopefully be justified by the book's contribution to an improved, more reality-congruent understanding and explanation of contemporary Islam, the long-term development and multi-faceted resurgence alongside relations with non-Muslim states and people. To this end, the discussion makes use of insights from both classical and contemporary sociological and social theory.

This book is therefore an attempt to build upon the existing literature in order to contribute to the development of a more inclusive and broader sociological framework. Hence, Western secularization theories, mainstream histories of Islam, theories of globalization and studies of civilizations and their conflictual relations are all discussed here, but from a sociological perspective that strives for a measure of relative detachment from political and normative standpoints. In taking this position, we aim to create a framework that incorporates the interrelated activities of individuals, socializing agents, social movement networks and nation-states in understanding and explaining the contemporary Islamic resurgence. This emergent framework then allows the widespread increase in Islamic beliefs and practice as well as the violent actions of radical terrorist networks to be brought within a single frame of reference.

Structure of the book

The first part of the book explores the extent of the global Islamic resurgence and some significant reinterpretations of Islamic beliefs and practices, which help to explain the growth in numbers of practising Muslims during periods of secularization, and also the high-profile, often violent actions in the name of Islam. Chapter 1 begins with an overview of the extent and variety of the Islamic resurgence in a manner designed to address the rather skewed perspective created by the focus on high-profile and violent events, which have generated a fearful, emotion-laden and often misleading account of Islam. As part of this process, myths about a homogenous Islam and its 'unavoidable' conflictual relations with the West, especially America, are exposed. Chapter 2 develops the key issues arising from this first chapter, reviewing existing attempts to understand and explain the Islamic resurgence, developing an approach that can be described as a dynamic sociology of religious and secular forms of knowledge production that concentrates on the reinterpretation of religious doctrine and practices. In chapter 3, the recent terrorist attacks against Western targets are brought into focus through the classical sociological themes of suicide (Durkheim) and the salvation beliefs embedded in world religions (Weber). The chapter reviews the contributions of such sociological traditions to our understanding and builds on existing sociological-psychological approaches, taking the group or collectivity and its interconnected relations, activities and motivations as the focus, rather than simply individuals or society as a whole.

In the second part of the book, the analysis moves outwards to take in explanations of the Islamic resurgence in theories of globalization (Waters 1998, Robertson 1992), in relations between entire civilizations (Huntington 1998, 2004) and as part of world-systems theory (Wallerstein 1974). This discussion is shaped by a critical reading and adaptation of the ideas of Norbert Elias (2000[1939]) on civilizing processes and the figurational dynamics of established–outsider relations. Chapter 4 addresses the over-reliance on variants of the secularization thesis in current theories of globalization. As a result of this reliance, the character of Islamic movements is not well understood and is too easily associated with 'exclusionary' factors according to Western criteria. As a corrective, the importance of forms of 'Islamic globalization' that pre-date the more recent Western-dominated processes is established, focusing on fluctuating political opportunity structures and the opening up of new possibilities for Islamic movements to mobilize around historical symbols and ideologies. Samuel Huntington's controversial 'Clash of Civilizations' thesis is outlined in some detail in chapter 5, and challenged by reworking ideas around state formation processes and established–outsider relations. In chapter 6, interstate relations, intra-state relations and socialization processes are brought together within a single framework, thus enabling a more comprehensive explanation of the current situation. In particular, an established–outsiders perspective is adapted and applied to international terrorist networks, the establishment of secular states, new forms of global information exchange and the unintended consequences of state policies. All of these elements have contributed to the shifting balance of power between secular 'modernists' and Islamic moderates and 'fundamentalists'.

In chapter 7, the distinctive sociological contribution to understanding and explaining the cross-cutting nature and appeal of the contemporary global Islamic resurgence is described. This chapter draws some general conclusions from the rest of the book that may help sociology to move towards a more comprehensive framework that is able to understand and explain both the basis of the broad contemporary resurgence and the motivations of militant Muslims. This concluding chapter outlines the benefits of the integrative, comprehensive framework developed in the book and points the way towards future research in this area.

1

$\mathcal{R}$esurgent Islam in a Secular World

One Islam or many?

Images of Islam in Western societies are dominated by conflict, aggression, 'fundamentalism' and, more recently, global-scale violent terrorism. The horrific images of the collapsing Twin Towers of the World Trade Center in New York in 2001 crystallized existing views of Islam as particularly prone to generate violent actions against perceived enemies. Stereotypical views which portray Islam as an inherently violent religion, a 'religion of the sword' and an increasing global threat have thus been reinforced and even extended over recent years. Concentration on such representations overlooks the much broader, peaceful growth in religious behaviour in contexts where Muslims are either the majority or a minority within nation-states. Consequently, the behaviour and beliefs of the majority of Muslims who peacefully practise their faith are largely neglected within media presentations, public perceptions and even much academic analysis. These Muslims generally have no connection or empathy with the highly publicized terrorists, yet the popular perception within the West is that terrorists and demands for Islamic states are representative of large numbers within wider Muslim communities. It is also simply false, as Bruce (2003: 234–5) argues, that, wherever they 'are found in significant numbers, Muslims always want either to take over the state or to secede from it – the goal being the imposition of the Shari'ah.' This is a gross oversimplification of the nature, depth and enormous variety within the broad Islamic resurgence, though it does typify the propensity for over-generalization in Western academic studies of Islam.

This book aims both to understand and explain the diverse Islamic resurgence and to shed light on the contemporary emergence of 'Muslim' terrorists. While there are some common causal factors underlying these two phenomena, there are also some very marked differences. To help draw this distinction, we will not be using terms such as 'Islamic fundamentalism', which is used to describe a wide variety of Muslim nation-states, Islamic social movements and individual activities. Too often such language is used emotively and leads to the stereotyping of all Muslims as fundamentalists. Esposito (1999: 226) argues that 'All "fundamentalist leaders" are lumped together, obscuring the fact that many Islamists are modern, educated people who hold responsible professional positions and participate in the democratic process.' 'Fundamentalist' is therefore an easy label to apply but it is one which misleads and confuses, not least because the roots of the term are to be found within Protestant Christianity, specifically American Protestantism (Marty and Appleby 1994). In the original context, fundamentalists sought to return Christianity to the 'fundamentals' of core doctrine against liberal reformers. Today the term has penetrated many societies and has lost much of its original meaning, making relatively detached analysis very difficult.

In his classical study of Islam, Hodgson (1974: 45) pointed out that academics have responsibility for 'selecting minimally misleading terms and for defining them precisely', such that they are not 'bias inducing'. To this end, instead of 'fundamentalism', we use the broader and more inclusive concept of 'praxis' – broadly, the fusion of theory and action – to emphasize those groups of Muslims who seek to practise their beliefs across societal spheres and who make no distinction between religion in the private and public spheres, often becoming involved in consciousness-raising activities and the promotion of Islam as a guide to all aspects of life (Vertigans 2003). Islam for these believers should be shown at the level of individual devotion and through social interactions and activities. Muhammed Qutb (1964: 9), brother of the influential radical Muslim Sayyid Qutb (1906–66), outlines the way in which praxis can be extended to provide the basis for a way of life, stating that

> Islam is not a mere creed, nor does it represent simply an edification of souls, or a refinement and training of human virtues but is rather a harmonious whole that also includes a just economic system, a well-balanced social organization, codes of civil, criminal as well as international law, a philosophical outlook upon life along with a system of physical instruction.

Radical interpretations of Islam as a way of life believe that these values cannot be achieved without an Islamic state and therefore seek to bring about the transformation of societies, often leading to political challenges to secular nation-states. Because of the emphasis upon praxis and to avoid confusion with terms such as 'Islamist', the concept of 'praxisitioners' will be used in relation to individuals and specific groups who practise their faith at individual, social and political levels (Vertigans 2003). Groups associated with violent terrorism such as Jihadi Salafist groups connected with *al-Qa'ida* are militants at the extreme end of the praxist spectrum. There is considerable debate over the extent to which these groups can be called Muslims because their views and actions are considered by many to be against Islamic teachings. However, adapting W. I. Thomas's sociological maxim (1928) that if people think something is real then it is real in its consequences, suggests that if militant terrorists think they are Muslims then it is up to theologians and not sociologists to demonstrate otherwise. By way of contrast, the overwhelming majority of Muslims whose beliefs form part of the mainstream and who do not actively seek to radically transform societies, will be referred to simply as 'Muslims'.

Like all major world religions, Islam is a complex set of relations involving both continuities and change. The meaning of religion and relations therein are open to considerable variation according to individual interpretation, social context and time period. For example, the meaning of practice and belief within Christianity differs across the world and even within a single nation-state. Very few Western observers would categorize Northern Irish Catholics and Protestants together simply as Christians, because of the historical divisions, ecclesiastic nuances, behavioural and spiritual differences and, in this instance, the religio-ethnic conflict. Ecumenicalism has not been achieved. Different interpretations also are to be found within the Islamic faith, particularly the Sunni/Shi'ite divide and between and within Muslim states. Like Christianity, but unlike Catholicism, Islam has no central authority for doctrine, training or discipline. Yet the tendency remains to discuss Islam generically as a rather more homogeneous entity. We need to avoid making religion the inevitable primary source of people's identity because it blurs the significance of other important distinctions such as ethnicity (Mabry 1998). To the list of differences we must also add the contextual variations according to nation-state, nationality and, in many instances, tribal descent and migration that have all had considerable impact upon identity formation, type of Islamic practice, beliefs and ideology and the nature and timing of the 'Islamic resurgence'.

Language is also an important difference between ethnic groups that provides a practical impediment to forging global unity. Arabic was the language of Muhammed and the *Qu'ran* but is not the universal language of Muslims. Roy (2004) estimates that Arabic speakers constitute only 20 per cent of all Muslims. Yet in the West there is a tendency to extend perceptions of uniformity, again exemplified by Bruce (2003: 228) who argues that Muslims speak the same language because 'apart from Arabs all Muslims are bilingual.' It is implausible to imagine, for example, that millions of illiterate non-Arab Muslims who communicate in their indigenous languages are also fluent in Arabic, particularly when one considers that some well-educated leaders of Islamic movements in the West do not speak Arabic. We therefore need to identify both similarities and significant differences.

Ahmed (1992) has argued that Islam is varied because the religion has been heavily influenced by the conceptions, assumptions and social practices of the places that Islamic groups conquered or where Islam was introduced. This point is developed by Macey (1999) who notes that there are intimate connections between religion and culture that can make it extremely difficult to separate the reproduction of culture from the reproduction of a particular variant of Islam. When these variations are combined, they contribute to a rich diversity of appearances, activities and interactions, as anyone who has witnessed social life in either a Muslim society or Muslim communities within Western societies would be able to testify. For example, within the Maghreb states of North Africa, there are significant variations between the Islamic resurgences taking place in the different countries, which are at least partly due to the character of the beliefs which developed within specific tribes, brotherhoods and associations and the ways in which those beliefs were transformed during the process of state formation. Each government adopted a different approach to religion within the political programmes of modernization. For example, Algeria adopted a specific interpretation of socialism and Tunisia firmly implemented a secular system, while Morocco sought to utilize the king's lineage to the Prophet Muhammed, combining religious rhetoric and symbols with a modernization strategy. Partly as a consequence of such variations, Islamic identities and movements vary across the Maghreb. Nonetheless *all* the states in the area have experienced an Islamic resurgence, albeit with the significant variations noted above. In order to understand the Islamic resurgence therefore, we need both to be able to explain the underlying social processes giving rise to Islamic growth and to remain sensitive to local variations.

Despite the reality of such variety, negative perceptions of a generic Islam remain, based around Western perceptions of Islamic 'fundamentalism'. Kramer (1996: 37) highlights this simplistic understanding when he argues that

> Islamic fundamentalism ... appears as a militant ideology, demanding political action now. Here it takes the form of a populist party, asking for ballots. One day its spokesmen call for a *jihad* against the West, evoking the deepest historic sentiments. Another day, its leaders appeal for reconciliation with the West, emphasizing shared values. Its economic theorists reject capitalist materialism in the name of social justice, yet they rise to the defense [of] private property. It[s] moralists pour scorn on Western consumer culture as debilitating to Islam, yet its strategists avidly seek to buy the West's latest technologies in order to strengthen Islam.

Such views badly misrepresent Islamic 'fundamentalism' as a generic and widespread orientation within Muslim communities and demonstrate why we need to develop more discriminating conceptual categories and terminology. Islam mobilizes a broad range of people with very different beliefs, aims and approaches to faith and social life. It is therefore irresponsible to conflate Islamic movements that participate in mainstream political processes with terrorist groups pursuing violent and armed actions against civilian populations.

Historical consensus or conflict?

Perceptions of a violent generic Islam are rooted in historical stereotypes that have been significantly reinforced since the attacks on America in 2001. Processes of stigmatization resulting from these stereotypes have been given considerable support and credence by some of the anti-Western pronouncements issued by Islamic praxisitioners over the last century. One of the most notable early ideologues was the Egyptian Sayyid Qutb, while more recently groups associated with *al-Qa'ida* must be considered in the same vein. The historic roots of such anti-Westernism can be traced all the way back to the Crusades, which occurred between the eleventh and thirteenth centuries. Although the Saracen Muslims were ultimately successful, images of Christian military expeditions and the atrocities committed in the name of religion have solidified into historical understandings of an aggressive Christianity and Western imperialism. These sentiments feed into the violent rhetoric of today's praxisitioners, who draw on the legacy of the Crusades to make sense of current events. Qutb proved to be extremely influential in using images associated with the Crusades, suggesting that conflict between Islam and the West is inevitable, not least because 'Western blood carries the spirit of Crusades within itself' (cited in Haim 1982: 154).

More recently, as explored in detail in chapter 6, Osama bin Laden has frequently evoked the Crusades in his rallying calls to arms. During the American-led attacks on Afghanistan he exhorted Muslims to oppose the American actions, which he described as 'the most ferocious, serious and violent Crusade campaign against Islam ever since the message was revealed to Mohammed' (November 2001). Following the invasion of Iraq, use of these historical events was evident when the Palestinian Sheikh Muhammed Abu al-Hudud (2003) made reference to the 'American-British Crusaders cruel attack'. Similar sentiments were also evident in President G. W. Bush's (2001b) statement following the 11 September 2001 attacks, that 'this crusade, this war on terrorism is going to take a while.' Praxisitioners were quick to latch onto Bush's remarks. For example, in March 2003, just as the American-led invasion of Iraq commenced, the Palestinian Sheikh Mudeiris (2003) stated that 'this is a Crusader Zionist war. It is not I who say this, it was the little Pharaoh [Bush] who announced it when he stated that this was a Crusader attack.' Perhaps not surprisingly, the images of the Crusades and their use within the radicals' rhetoric is much more prominent in parts of the world where they occurred and where recent Western military action has taken place. For example, the Crusades have more contemporary relevance within the Middle East than in South East Asia. International relations have also been adversely influenced by the history of colonialism, which impacted upon most majority-Muslim societies. The colonization of Muslims across the world and colonial *realpolitik* in the division of large sections of the Middle East following the end of the Ottoman Empire (1299–1918) provide a backdrop for many Muslims seeking to understand contemporary actions and relations with both Europe and the US. The legacy of colonialism helps praxisitioners to justify their beliefs and actions.

However, when a broad, long-term perspective is taken, it becomes clear that the extended periods of cooperation and peaceful coexistence, which still apply today for the overwhelming majority of Muslims and the West, are more representative of relations between Islam and the West than the relatively short-term episodes of violent conflicts. Yet it is the legacy of the latter that has come to be seen as representative in many cultural representations. Thus the influential Bernard Lewis (1990: 2) states that 'The struggle between Islam and the West has now lasted fourteen centuries. It has consisted of a long series of attacks and counterattacks, jihads and crusades, conquests and reconquests.' A 'civilizational conflict' perspective that pits one 'civilizational entity' against another over very long time periods frames such an interpretation. Today, the over-concentration on violent episodes is evident within the popular media and is contributing to the very process on which it is reporting. For many Muslims, recent actions such as the ongoing conflict over Pàlestine, the killing of thousands of civilians in Afghanistan, the invasion and occupation of Iraq and its messy aftermath and the reluctance of the West to assist Bosnian Muslims are all seen as part of the ongoing process of Western, Christian hostility to Islam, which can be traced back to medieval times. Our central aim in this book will be to demonstrate the enhanced explanatory power of an alternative sociological perspective that concentrates instead on the underlying social processes produced by the expanding figurational relations of interdependent people within Muslim societies and between nation-states.

The impact of recent world events

There have been a number of recent events that have led to a reassessment of relations between Muslim and Western people. In 1979 the Iranian Revolution had a huge impact both upon Western perceptions of Muslims and vice versa. For many Muslims it reinvigorated Islam as an ideological form, the significance of which is explored in chapter 2. The Revolution also began a painful process within sociology, as it stimulated the gradual undermining of the then dominant secularization paradigm. The long-term and widespread character of the Islamic resurgence demonstrated that the central argument of the thesis – the secularization of all modernizing societies – was becoming untenable.

There are a number of reasons why the Iranian Revolution occurred, including economic recession and political mismanagement, massive corruption and alienation of large sectors of the population, not only poorer sections but also elements within the middle and upper classes. Ironically and belatedly, political liberalization had been introduced in 1978 following considerable American pressure. This policy ultimately provided support for de Tocqueville's observation (1956 [1835, 1840]) that the biggest threat to an autocracy is when it begins to liberalize. American influence became a cause of considerable concern amongst the Iranian people, many of whom viewed the Shah as too dependent on the US. The cross-cutting nature of the Revolution is largely overlooked today as the uprising has become associated with images of the bearded *ayatollahs* led by Ayatollah Ruhollah Khomeini taking control. As the 1979 hostage-taking at the American embassy seemed to indicate, Islam had again become a threat to Western interests. Western governments quickly sought to discredit the *ayatollahs* regime, describing it pejoratively as 'fundamentalist' and aiming to isolate Iran internationally through political pressure and the imposition of sanctions. This was part of a strategy initiated by America, designed to contain Iran and prevent the Revolution from being exported to neighbouring states. It was with this intention that America supported the Iraqi dictator Saddam Hussein, most notably in the Iran-Iraq war between 1980 and 1988.

Within Western government policies there has been a noticeable absence of any real attempt to understand the underlying causes of the Iranian Revolution and the increasingly visible presence of Islam across the Middle East. The over-concentration on containment and isolation at the expense of generating knowledge and understanding has largely dominated the Western approach. Unless Western analysts, policy-makers, academics and secular Muslim governments acknowledge the important differences within Islam and the justification of some grievances then the reasons both behind the broad Islamic resurgence and rise of Muslim terrorism cannot be grasped. This can only be achieved by learning to understand the fluid and multifarious nature of Islam, what it can offer and mean to individuals, communities and nation-states, and the significance of the ensuing ideologies and actions within those contexts. It is therefore important that relationships between contexts and behaviour are identified, in other words what is it about Islam and the social contexts that has brought about the Muslim resurgence and more specifically, Islamic terrorist groups?

Similarly, the rhetoric of Islamic praxisitioners and attempts to justify terrorist atrocities also rely on interpretations of historical events and the use of stereotypes regarding 'the West'. Western actions against Muslims and associated states are considered to be a combination of the revival of both the Crusades and colonial intervention. Such mutual stigmatization represents the underlying power relations and helps to sustain one-dimensional views of the 'Other'. It is against this backdrop of reciprocal stigmatization that American-led actions in Afghanistan and Iraq are considered by millions of Muslims, highlighting the enormous challenge facing those looking to contribute to a more reality-congruent perspective on both sides.

The contemporary 'Islam and the West' paradigm

Today, the dislike and mistrust of America that were features of the Iranian Revolution are becoming increasingly widespread across Muslim nation-states and communities. As the last and now dominant 'superpower' in the world, America has become the most disliked of the Western nation-states. The roots of what Halliday (2002) describes as 'Anti-Americanism' can be traced to the post-World War II period and the divisive Cold War policies. Prior to this period, Britain was generally the most despised nation-state, as it was the greatest colonial power, imposing British rule over millions of Muslims. The British Empire controlled territories with more Muslims than any other empire, including the Muslim Ottoman Empire. Other European nation-states tended to be the most disliked in places where they were the colonialists, such as the French in Algeria. The contemporary development of anti-Americanism is crucial to understanding resurgent Islam, as perceptions of American actions and policies have contributed to the serious undermining of the capitalist system and of the appeal of the West and thus to the resulting opposition to both. Abdallah (2003) identifies a number of Muslim grievances in the Middle East that have contributed to America's attaining its special reviled status. Such grievances include the staunch American support for Israel and American policies and actions against Muslim states, when compared with the support for undemocratic Arab states. These points can be extended beyond the context of the Middle East.

From a position of initial support based upon moral and humanitarian factors, the relationship between Israel and the West, particularly America, was transformed within the *realpolitik* of the Cold War. As Saikal (2003: 89) comments with respect to the strategic partnership between America and Israel within a decade of the formation of the Israeli state, this 'may have been beneficial to domestic and Cold War politics, but only at the cost of tension and turbulence in America's relations with the Muslim world.' Financial and military support provided by America has proved instrumental in Israel's maintaining a strategic edge over its neighbours. This support and uncritical political protection at the UN following aggressive actions such as the annexation of East Jerusalem, the invasion of Lebanon, incursions into Palestinian territories and so-called 'targeted killings', allied to the apparent lack of sympathy for the plight of the Palestinians, has had a major effect upon levels of anti-Americanism. A survey of Muslims in Lebanon undertaken in October and November 2001, showed that 90 per cent were disaffected by US support for Israel and 70 per cent reported disaffection when asked about American foreign policies within the Middle East (reported in Haddad and Khashan 2002). In Saudi Arabia, a long-term US ally, a Gallup Poll carried out in 2002 (reported in Pollack 2003) found that 64 per cent of Saudis held unfavourable views of America. Within this context of antago-nism, America's ongoing monopolization of the peace process and diplomatic effort appears to be undermined by what many Muslims consider to be a conflict of interests. In blunt terms, to what extent is America able to be an impartial power-broker when it is seen to be providing unqualified support for Israel?

Other American actions also seem to be contributing to heightened feelings of revulsion: military attacks and sanctions against some Muslim states, including Afghanistan, Libya, Sudan and particularly Iraq, discrimination against Muslims inside America following the September 2001 attacks and the widely reported 'inhumane' treat-ment of Muslims at the Guantanamo detention centre in Cuba and Abu Ghraib prison in Iraq. The case of Iraq is illuminating in helping to understand Muslim views across the world. Prior to the invasion of 2003, there was considerable disquiet about American support for sanctions against Iraq, which was strengthened when the impact upon Iraqi citizens became apparent. As the global reaction to the subsequent invasion showed, there was widespread condemnation of Western actions and, not surprisingly, this was particularly noticeable within the Middle East. A poll carried out by Zogby (2003) when the occupation of Iraq had begun reported that 81 per cent of Saudis were against US policy in Iraq while 94 per cent had unfavourable opinions of US policy towards Palestinians (a rise of 7 per cent from the previous year). More generally, as al-Sayyid Said (2001) remarks, 'For the Arabs, the image of this war – that of a rich, strong super-power hitting a small country – does not lend itself to sympathy, and creates a gap that cannot be bridged by propaganda.' Just like the attacks in Afghanistan which killed several thousand civilians, con-tinuous media coverage highlighted the fact that the invasion to 'liberate the Iraqi people' was leading to many of them dying in the process.

Finally, America's support for undemocratic Muslim regimes, such as the Saudi kingdom, the Iranian Shah's repressive regime and the military dictatorships of Generals Zia ul-Haq and Musharraf in Pakistan, has been seen as contradicting the Western rhetoric of promoting democratization. American politicians frequently declare democratization to be one of the US's goals in the Middle East, but little demonstrable progress had been made between President Bush Snr's declaration for democracy in the Middle East in 1991 and President Bush Jr's 2004 'Greater Middle East Initiative', aimed at stimulating democracy, improving human rights and initiating economic reform in the region. However, the presidential elections held in Afghanistan (2004) and the Palestinian territories (2005), the Iraqi parliamentary elections (2005) and large-scale Lebanese demonstrations (2005) both pro- and anti-Syria highlight that change is possible in the region. The changes also disprove the widely held belief that Islam is inherently anti-democratic. It still remains to be seen the extent to which America will stop sustaining non-democratic regimes that serve American national interests.

A combination of these factors has led many Muslims to conclude that there has been a concerted American campaign against Islam. As Sheik Omar Abdul Rahman stated before the 1993 bombing of the World Trade Center (for which he was convicted), 'America is behind all these un-Islamic governments' with American actions designed, 'to keep them [the un-Islamic governments] strong' and to try to 'defeat the Islamic movements' (quoted in Murphy 1993: 20). The extent of anti-Americanism has been noted in the reactions to the September 2001 attacks on America. Brown (2001) reports on the scenes of celebration in Palestine, Palestinian refugee camps, Lebanon and Saudi Arabia and the nature of the media commentary in Bahrain, Iran and Iraq, which considered the attacks to be a consequence of American actions. For example, in the Bahraini *Akhbar al-Khalij*, Hafedh al-Shaykh wrote that 'the U.S. now is eating a little piece from the bread which she baked and fed the world for many decades' (cited in Brown 2001: 1). However, there was also strong public condemnation of the attacks within these same countries, exemplified by the Lebanese newspaper *al-Anwar* arguing that 'the crime is so horrendous that it is unacceptable even to the worst enemies of the United States' (ibid.). In Iran, a long-time opponent of the US, a minute's silence was observed for the victims prior to an international football match.

It also needs to be emphasized that many Muslims who hold some anti-American views are not opposed to all things American and do not advocate violence. For example, several surveys into Arab perceptions have revealed a 'strong dislike for American foreign policy, but much more nuanced, and often quite positive, attitudes toward American society and culture and toward the American people' (Tessler 2003). Opposition is often directed at American actions, especially foreign policy, and not the American people, philosophy

and values. This dual approach was found within much of the condemnation of the 2001 attacks within the Middle East. The Iranian
Keyhan International reported: 'For world public opinion the mood
of the majority . . . agreed that the United States deserved it. They
nevertheless felt pity for the ordinary American citizen who was made
to bear the burden of the criminal policies of the successive admi-
nistrations' (quoted in Brown 2001: 1). Such sentiments were borne
out in a Gallup Poll carried out in the week following the attacks on
America. Across nine Muslim countries, 67 per cent of respondents
described the events as 'morally unjustifiable' while a clear majority
also stressed deep concerns about the West, and America in particular (reported in Newport 2002). Beyond the Arab region, the media
commentary in some Muslim nations was more absolute in condemnation of the terrorists and less explicit in attributing blame to
American actions. If we also look at representations prior to the 2001
attacks it is noticeable that anti-Americanism had already been building up across the world. Since 1980 the extent of anti-Americanism
has grown within the Arab media in particular, as witnessed in the
types of headlines used, the selective reporting and focus upon negative stories related to the US (Darwish 2003). Overall, reaction to
and views of America are considerably more sophisticated than is
popularly perceived within the West.

Media representations and political attention have contributed to
the impression that opposition to America is unique to Muslim
nations and communities. It is often overlooked that anti-
Americanism can also be found within other societies and religions.
For example, it was not only Muslims who applauded the September 2001 attacks. As the Pew Center's public opinion survey showed,
anti-Americanism has spread across the world as dissatisfaction rises
over American unilateralism, the push for globalization of trade and
business and America's perceived anti-environmental practices (Pew
Global Attitudes Project 2003). Opposition to American state policies can also, of course, be found within all Western states, including
America itself.

Representations within the media have contributed to what
Halliday (1996) describes as the 'myth of confrontation'. Halliday
(1996: 6) believes that the 'myth is sustained from two, apparently
contradictory, sides – from the camp of those, mainly but not exclusively in the West, who seek to turn the Muslim world into another
enemy, and from the camp of those within the Islamic countries who
advocate confrontation with the non-Muslim, and particularly
Western, world.' Myths 'pertaining to Islam, propagated against

Muslims . . . are also taken up by Islamists to provide justification for their own causes.' This simplistic division between good and evil is replicated within the rhetoric of Western opinion-formers and radical Muslim spokespersons. In this respect clear similarities can be noted between the views of George W. Bush and Osama bin Laden. Bush refers to nations and peoples as being either 'for or against us', while bin Laden requests that Muslims choose between supporting *al-Qa'ida* and thereby Allah, or become apostates, henchmen of and collaborators with the West. There are no grey areas when such myths are used to mobilize support. Western policies in Iraq and Afghanistan and attacks associated with *al-Qa'ida* in America (2001), Bali (2002), Turkey (2003), Spain and Egypt (2004) have contributed to the spread of a 'civilizational conflict' perspective to larger groups of people, taking on the character of a central paradigm for the understanding of relations between Islam and the West.

Islamic consensus and conflicts across the world

In light of changing popular perceptions it is important to establish the extent to which these are representative of Islam in the contemporary world. Today, Islam is the fastest growing religion in the world at a time when the influence of other religions is also expanding. Evangelicalism is growing in the US and South America; the Russian Orthodox Church has undergone a revival following the demise of the Soviet Union; Orthodox Judaism is expanding in Israel and the Diaspora; radical Hinduism has become a significant force in India; and the impact of counter-secularization is growing across the world. There are over 1.2 billion Muslims spread across the world, with Muslim nation-states stretching from the former Soviet Republics to Tanzania and from Morocco to Indonesia. Across Western Europe and North America, the number of Muslims is growing quite rapidly, principally as a consequence of immigration and subsequent rates of reproduction rather than conversion. Islam is becoming increasingly visible both within Muslim and non-Muslim states as the religion becomes an important resource for the development of personal identity.

The Islamic resurgence is more than simply the growth in numbers of believers. Muslims have become more noticeable in terms of appearance, expressed beliefs and religious practices, as a collective identity as well as increased numbers undertaking the *hajj*, the pilgrimage to Mecca. One of the many ways in which the resurgence has undermined the main planks of the secularization thesis is in the increased intensity of beliefs and the frequency of Islamic practice among younger generations, who might be expected to adopt secular ways of life. As von der Mehden (1987) argues with respect to Malaysia, 'the younger generation of *abangan* [moderate Muslims] are becoming *santri* [devout Muslims].' Western perceptions concerning the impact of the resurgence are also in flux, as the terrorist attacks in American and Europe have generated a more widespread feeling that Islam, particularly radical groups, can no longer be considered a problem that can safely be left for the 'developing world' to tackle.

However, it is inappropriate to view Islam *per se* as a threat to Western 'civilization'. Obviously, some Islamic groups are attacking Western symbols, institutions and people; but it should be pointed out that even here, commentary is prone to over-generalize. For example, contrary to widespread opinion, there is no homogenous *al-Qa'ida* organization that is responsible for all terrorism associated with Islam. The groups carrying out atrocities vary considerably in composition, theology and ideologies, as well as having diverse, often vague and/or long-term objectives. They are, however, often united by their short-term approach to attack Western targets, and some groups have developed links in order to share resources, techniques and strategies, with groups associated with *al-Qa'ida* providing some coordination (Burke 2004; Reuter 2004). At this point it is worth reiterating that such extremist praxisitioners are in a small minority, yet they are considered to be representative of Muslims as such. This is partly a consequence of sensationalist media reporting, which ignores the un-newsworthy peaceful and productive social, cultural, economic and political interactions between the majority of Muslims and Western citizens and political systems.

It is equally important to emphasize that within the wider, generally peaceful majority of Muslims, there are also important variations in views on religion, economic modernization, relations with the West and the extent of their own religious practices. The latter may involve social and cultural support at community level, political and economic participation within nation-states and involvement in international or global organizations. A Muslim's commitment to faith can be limited to individuals holding the three fundamental principles (there are five for Shi'ites): one God; the existence of the Prophet Muhammed; and salvation; in addition, there are the five pillars: the profession of faith; praying five times per day; almsgiving; annual fasting; and a pilgrimage to Mecca for all those able to make the journey. Muslims will still be considered Muslims if they do *not* practise the five pillars, but not if they disagree with any of the three basic principles. Islam can also be more extensive, becoming a key component of individual identity as the religion can be interpreted to operate at the everyday level of individual behaviour and social interaction. For these Muslims, faith can be very much an individual matter, affecting their own behaviour and impacting upon other Muslims as a consequence of individual practice. Other Muslims are involved within social networks and community groups, providing relief and support to those requiring it. This is evident in the provision of food, health resources, education and accommodation by groups such as the *Jamaat-I-Islami* of Pakistan, the Muslim Brotherhood across Egypt, Syria and Jordan and Turkish *tarikats*. Often these groups have a middle-class social base and provide services to poorer members of their communities. Activities by Muslims are also noticeable within national and local politics and often include groups who also provide social welfare. Political involvement can be either directed in the case of the first two examples above or indirect through influence, patronage and lobbying in the Turkish case. Muslim representatives among professional classes are also prominent within occupational associations and include engineers, lawyers, doctors and students on university campuses.

Political activities vary considerably between and within Muslim nation-states. Religiously oriented and Islamic modernist parties participate in democracies, adopting some Western policies and forming alliances and coalitions with ostensibly secular parties. Some Muslim parties have assumed power through democratic means, such as the Justice and Development Party (JDP) in Turkey (2002 to present). In some countries, religious parties have participated within democracies but have subsequently been banned for breaching the formally secular constitution. This fate befell a succession of Islamic political parties in Turkey, including the Welfare Party, which governed a coalition in the period 1996–97, and the Algerian Islamic Salvation Front (FIS) in 1992, the latter during the cancellation of elections for 'national security reasons', at a time when it looked as if the FIS would obtain power. This action led to the Islamic alliance fracturing and the extremist *Groupements Islamiques Armés* (GIA) undertaking a campaign of armed conflict. The situation quickly spiralled into low-level warfare between the GIA and security forces during which over 100,000 people were killed. Other groups such as the Palestinian *Hamas* and *al-Jihad* have adopted terrorist tactics to address religio-nationalist concerns, including suicide attacks against

Israeli targets. Groups such as those associated with *al-Qa'ida* have also committed acts of terrorism as part of campaigns against nation-states and international institutions. In an interesting development, *Hezbollah* has expanded upon its original terrorist tactics against Israel and its allies around Southern Lebanon to become a political party participating in the Lebanese electoral system, representing and competing for the votes of the Shi'ite community. There are also signs that *Hamas* is broadening its political strategy to incorporate democratic representation, witnessed by successful participation in recent municipal elections and an intention to compete in 2005 legislative elections. Islamic groups have also taken power through military conquest, as in the cases of the House of Saud in the establishment of the state of Saudi Arabia in 1932, the Taliban in Afghanistan during the late 1990s, in the aftermath of revolution as in Iran in 1979 or following a change in policy from socialist and Arabist leanings to an 'Islamic order', which occurred in Sudan during the 1980s under the influence of Hassan al-Turabi's National Islamic Front. In these instances, largely unsuccessful and very different attempts have been made to implement elements of Islamic law based upon divinely sanctioned religious tenets associated with the words and deeds of the Prophet Muhammed and described by the generic term, *Shari'ah*.

Cross-cutting the different levels of Islamic activity and approaches are individual participation and the ways in which individuals and groups view their religion and associated behaviour. Many Muslims choose to portray their faith symbolically, for example men growing beards and women choosing, or in some cases being forced, to wear the veil. A significant number of these individuals are also becoming more involved in community, national and international organizations, whose direct action is aimed at transforming social relations beyond practical and local political levels. Within many of these groups there is a perception of Islam as a source of social order and the basis for moral rules, although again there are considerable differences concerning the extent to which this should be implemented and how. Praxisitioners consider that the influence of religion should be the dominant frame of reference for individual behaviour, communities, nation-states and international relations.

To understand the basis for religious doctrines, attention needs to be paid to the origins of Islam. Of particular importance are the revelations to the Prophet Muhammed (570–632 AD), which he then implemented across individual, family and community relations covering such spheres as morality, justice, equality, personal hygiene, war, economic practices, political behaviour, community and ultimately international relations. This form of praxis helps to explain the challenge on religious grounds to contemporary secularization by many Muslims. The success achieved by Muhammed and the expansion of Islamic influence through conversion, military conquest and political alliances have helped to legitimize Islam as an ideology. Thus, the expansion of Islam from Medina in Saudi Arabia to territory across Asia, North Africa and Europe for long periods when Muslim empires were the dominant global power remains a source of tremendous pride among Muslim groups today. Historical success has legitimized Islam as a religion that can be implemented in other societies and nation-states. Today, praxisitioners are reinterpreting Islam to address contemporary contexts and provide a comprehensive framework for life that will ultimately become the basis for Islamic government. In some respects, these radical groups share a rhetoric similar to recent government attempts in Iran, Saudi Arabia, Sudan and Afghanistan to extend the influence of religion in political, economic, social and cultural spheres. However, the radicals are more idealistic, not least because they have the freedom of opposition and not the pragmatic restraints of government.

Within Muslim societies and communities important differences can also be noted in the role of the *ulema* (men of religious learning, loosely considered as the Muslim equivalent of clergymen) and *marabouts* (Sufi leaders who, in opposition to mainstream Sunni theology, are intermediaries between Allah and believers). In societies that place greater prominence on religion within politics, such as Saudi Arabia and Iran, the *ulema* or *ayatollah*s are heavily involved within government. The Iranian *ayatollah*s are the governing representatives within the *Majlis* and the unelected Council of Guardians. The alliance between the *ulema* and the Saud dynasty can be traced back around 250 years, when Muhammed Ibn Abdul-Wahhab, the founder of puritanical Wahhabism, asked Muhammed Ibn Saud, at that time the ruler of a small principality in what became part of Saudi Arabia, for protection. Today, in terms of theological knowledge, the relatively uneducated and secular king is the supreme religious leader, yet, as the Saudi dissident Muhammed al-Massari has claimed, many consider the royal family to be debauched drunks and the *ulema* as defenders of corruption (Jerichow 1997: 119). As the king is the guardian of the two holiest Islamic sites this relationship, and the power of the royal family, causes considerable resentment, both within Saudi Arabia and beyond.

Saudi Arabia faces a central paradox within the Islamic resurgence. It is one of the most religious Muslim nations, using religion as the main tool for social control and political legitimization, sponsoring religious activity both at home to counter Arab nationalism and over-seas to promote Wahhabism in different communities, in the process countering the influence of other nation-states with Islamic creden-tials, especially Iran. Yet the regime faces one of the most threaten-ing challenges from radical Muslim groups. This challenge first came to prominence in 1979 when militants seized the Holy Mosque in Mecca and an armed conflict with government forces followed. The group called themselves the *Ikhwan*, after a fanatical group formed in the early twentieth century that aimed to return Islam to its true form of Wahhabism. The original *Ikhwan* were instrumental in the rise of King Abdul-Aziz al-Saud, and ultimately the formation of Saudi Arabia, until they began to criticize and ultimately to rebel against al-Saud for failings in the implementation of Wahhabism and were eventually crushed. The Mecca uprising, and particularly the regime's reaction, ignited inter-tribal feuding and led to Islamic protests against the House of Saud. Notably, Osama bin Laden was deeply affected by the siege.

Relationships between the *ulema* and Muslim populations also vary across and within societies. Generally the *ulema* interpret reli-gious tenets, provide spiritual guidance and are prayer leaders for the public and leading figures within their respective communities. Within many Muslim nation-states the *ulema* are employed by the government and are appointed, dismissed and paid as state emplo-yees. As Enhali and Adda (2003: 2) point out with respect to the secularism introduced following Algerian independence in 1962, 'the *ulema* . . . were turned into civil servants who contributed to strengthening the state and following its policies.' Governments expect the *ulema* to provide support and can subject them to close scrutiny. *Ulema* publicly opposing their government can be dismissed or even imprisoned. Consequently, any opposition to secularism can prove to be short-lived, and other potential dissidents are dissuaded from using mosques to voice their concerns. This relationship, in par-ticular the ways in which Islamic authorities such as the *ulema* are used to legitimize secular government policies, has somewhat com-promised the *ulema*'s role. Such *ulema* tend to play no part in radical approaches to social and political change. Of the leading Islamic figures of the last hundred years, only Ayatollah Khomeini of Iran belonged to the *mullah*s or *ulema*. However, it is arguable that his role was able to grow in prominence only on account of the relatively weak control the Shah's government exerted over religion and, in par-ticular, its decision to exile him to Iraq and France, from where he had the freedom to organize opposition to the regime.

Opposition to the *ulema* is not restricted to their relationship with the state. Contemporary praxisitioners are also often opposed to the conservatism or traditionalism of the *ulema* and *marabouts*. For example, in Senegal, praxisitioners are developing their own modern Islamic education systems and are challenging both secularism and the traditional, irreligious Sufi ways of the majority of the population (Loimeier 1996). Similar challenges to traditional religious authorities can be noticed throughout Muslim societies and communities and emphasizes that praxist Islam is not inherently traditional or conservative as is widely perceived. As Hodgson (1974: 64) remarked, many of the so-called 'traditional' thinkers are 'attacking actual Muslim custom and *tradition*'. There are increasing signs that opposition to secular regimes is growing, even within state-controlled mosques, particularly amongst younger members of the *ulema*. In nation-states where governments have less control over religious institutions, especially when there has been an increase in private mosques, members of the *ulema* are using their communications with worshippers to challenge community, state and international policies.

Given the diverse range of belief and practice outlined above, it seems that there are many ways in which Muslims can feel themselves to be making a contribution to the global *ummah* (Muslim community). Islam can thus be directed towards the transformation of the individual, bringing about change from within, from below and above, or it can be directed at the transformation of society and even the human world as such. There is little common agreement upon how this is to be achieved though, and Islamic movements can often lose sight of the wider goals as they pursue local issues. Opinions vary both about the nature of Islam and the introduction or expansion of modernization programmes and Western-style secularism. In a recent development brought about by the realization that many traditional political, administrative and economic practices were contributing to the lack of development in Muslim states, Muslim movements are rarely opposed to modernization *per se*. Gellner (1992: 22) suggests that 'a puritan and scripturalist world religion does not seem necessarily doomed to erosion by modern conditions. It may on the contrary be favoured by them.' This is possible because many Muslim individuals and movements recognize and make use of the potential offered by modern technologies and ideas to transform themselves and Muslim societies. The change in approach towards modernization helps to emphasize why many Muslims, including praxisitioners, neither hold traditional views nor behave traditionally (Kurzman 2002). Indeed, praxisitioners are not reluctant to replace tradition with modern ways, particularly science and technology, providing that these are embedded within Islamic ideology and practices. The debate within Muslim societies and between radical movements tends to concentrate on the level of modernization required and the extent to which it can be implemented with or without Western practices and philosophies. Waters (1998) makes the point that in this sense, Islamic movements are forced to engage with, rather than ignore, Western modernity.

Secularization as myth and reality

With relations apparently deteriorating between Muslims and the West, it seems reasonable to expect academic examination to contribute to the falsification of myths, opening up the diversity of Islam, exploring the cross-cutting appeal of Islam and the identification of the causes of the current resurgence. So far, this has not really happened. Not only has much of the analysis failed to illuminate levels of understanding and explanation, some of it has contributed to the solidification of myths into an academic discourse from where it permeates into common-sense understanding. The orientalist mentality described by Said (1978), though overstated, remains, despite the impact of globalization in blurring cultural boundaries. Islam viewed through a modern Western lens as an independent variable has long been held to be responsible for the socio-political and economic problems within Muslim nation-states. For instance, the influential von Grunebaum (1946: 322) argued that Islam is unchanging, associated with failure and decay as it has 'stagnated in self-inflicted sterility'. This assessment has not moved forwards in some respects; as Abootalebi (2003: 155) points out, orientalists consider that 'Islam is the independent variable that can explain the major characteristics of Muslim societies, including the lower level of socio-economic and political development.' Muslim societies are still considered to lack essential features associated with the dynamic development of the West, including rationality, liberalism and democracy, and as a consequence are considered inferior. The assumptions underlying this comparison have allowed explanations to focus on those socially excluded groups who face the harsh consequences of modernization and globalization. Such a view fails to appreciate that Islam may offer positive attractions rather than it being the case that people turn to the faith merely as a form of defensive reaction. Islam and modernity are not, as Lerner's (1958) buzz phrase 'Mecca *or* mechanization' suggests, mutually exclusive.

Explanations of the resurgence tend to share the (secular) assumption that it is largely the result of negative experiences where people are reacting to poor financial, physical or psychological circumstances in which they find themselves. Therefore, if these circumstances improve, for instance the unemployed obtain employment, then levels of religiosity will decline. Clearly these are necessary but not sufficient explanations for the current resurgence. Such accounts have strong links to the secularization thesis which stems from the mid-eighteenth-century European Enlightenment period and the later theories of sociology's founders: Marx, Durkheim and Weber. All foresaw that traditional religions were undermined by the processes of modernization and seemed likely to decline. Whether modernization was based on liberal democracy or socialism, secularization was considered a prerequisite for progress.

The sociology of religion subsequently tended to embody these assumptions (Wallace 1966; Wallis 1975; Wilson 1975). Peter Berger (1999) has recently and gracefully acknowledged that some of his earlier contributions to the secularization debate have been shown to be incorrect by social developments. What was thought to be happening in the West was transposed onto the rest of the world. Support for this thesis could be found in the secular offensives of national governments, which in turn gave legitimacy to the proposed universal application of the secularization thesis. However, in concentrating on secularization processes at governmental levels, cultural practices, counter-movements and the (lack of) impact of secular beliefs on individuals were not fully grasped. Certainly secularization processes associated with modernization have been implemented across Muslim nation-states, such as the reforms instigated by Asad in Syria, Atatürk in Turkey, Ben Bella in Algeria, Bourguiba in Tunisia, Gaddafi in Libya, Nasser in Egypt, the Pahlavi Shahs in Iran and Sukarno in Indonesia. All attempted to begin the process of stimulating secularization, though, as we shall see in chapter 6, this was attempted in diverse ways which have consequently led to varying degrees of secularism within these societies.

During the period after World War II, some states were influenced by the United States while others developed links with the Soviet Union. Some governments sought a neutral position within the emerging Cold War pattern, drawing on nationalism to mobilize the populace. Irrespective of the approach adopted, religious influence was subjected to varying degrees of state control, and secular ideologies such as nationalism were promoted. Modernization was a key objective, and, to achieve this, governments sought to eliminate religion from its powerful role, not least because religion was noticeable by its absence from the nation-states in the West that were the basis for imitation. Significantly though, this approach failed to appreciate the role that religion had played in the development of the West (Weber 1992[1904–05]) and the ways in which religion helped the populations to deal with the consequences of modernization. New ideas, beliefs and practices were introduced through a series of reforms designed to modernize nation-states. Communication and transport networks were rapidly developed, industrialization initiated, legal and financial systems modified to reflect Western arrangements, education systems introduced, economies transformed and attempts made to modernize indigenous cultures and reduce the traditionalizing influence of the family on socialization processes. However, modernization projects generally failed to achieve their promises of economic prosperity, instead becoming associated with economic failure and social problems. The majority of these governments became authoritarian and financially corrupt, distanced from the population, relying more on their armed forces and a strong state to maintain the secular system. In short, there is evidence to suggest that processes of secularization were imposed from above and have not become firmly entrenched in social and cultural life. Secularism is now often concentrated in urban areas, leaving many rural areas relatively untouched, as happened in the first modern attempt at secularization introduced by Atatürk in Turkey between 1923 and 1938.

Despite decades of secularizing offensives, religiosity has not been eradicated and throughout the latter part of the twentieth century actually grew (at varying rates) across Muslim societies and communities. Modernization and secularization often contributed not to a reduction in religious behaviour as expected, but to an increase in Islamic influence and the emergence of new religious groups and movements. When this became apparent to academics during the 1980s the popularity of the secularization thesis meant that protest was thought to be concentrated amongst the excluded, economically backward and traditionalist. Such commentary ignored that increasing problems were not just associated with the negative consequences of modernization but with key components of modernization itself. For example, the ideology of nationalism has been adopted by millions of Muslims, but support has weakened and, within Arab nations, fell dramatically after the defeat of Egypt, Syria and Jordan in the 1967 war against Israel. The rise of Islamic communities in the West, including the numbers of people converting to Islam, also high-lights serious flaws with the secularization thesis, particularly as many of these Muslims are opposed to the principles of Western philosophies (Köse 1999; Sültan 1999; Wohlrab-Sahr 1999). None-theless, the logic of secularization continues to frame many academic studies, media reports and policy formation, in spite of the growing body of evidence against it.

Linking past and present

A misunderstanding about the Islamic resurgence that prevents iden-tification of the complex reasoning behind this phenomenon relates to the widespread belief that it emerged only in the 1970s. It is there-fore considered not as part of a long-term process but as a short-term, possibly reversible, revival. This is questionable on three main counts. First, Islam never disappeared, even in arguably the most secular Muslim nation-states like Turkey. Secularization failed to replace religion in the private sphere and to varying degrees within wider social relations and cultural activities. Migrants to Western nation-states like France, Germany and the UK also retained and adapted their faith in the new, formally secular society. Islamic beha-viour arguably did become more *noticeable* during the 1970s, for example in the wearing of symbolic clothing and increasing numbers undertaking the *hajj* pilgrimage. The resurgence is therefore more about the increasing intensity of faith rather than a simple rebirth.

Second, the resurgence has been part of longer-term processes. Muslim nation-states did not experience a simultaneous resurgence. In Turkey, an Islamic resurgence was not noticeable until the 1980s, while other countries experienced an earlier resurgence with Islamic movements involved in struggles for national independence and against established monarchies. Esposito (1999: 47–8) points out that there is a long tradition of Islamic revival and reform, noting that

> during the eighteenth and nineteenth centuries, revivalist leaders and move-ments had sprung up across the Islamic world: the Mahdi (1848–85) in the Sudan, the Sanusi (1787–1859) in Libya, the Wahhabi (1703–92) in Saudi Arabia, the Fulani in Nigeria (1754–1817), the Faraidiyyah of Hajj Shariat Allah (1786–1840) in Bengal, the militant movement of Ahmad Brelwi (1786–1831) in India and the Padri in Indonesia (1803–37). . . . They diagnosed their societies as being internally weak and in decline poli-

tically, economically, and religiously. The cause was identified as Muslim departure from true Islamic values brought about by the infiltration and assimilation of local, indigenous, un-Islamic beliefs and practices. The pre-scribed cure was purification through a return to 'true Islam'.

Such a cure can be found in the diagnosis of contemporary radical Islamic movements and even among reformists. Struggles by Muslims can be identified in Iran throughout the twentieth century, and indeed across the Middle East there was a wave of religious feeling as Islam increasingly became interwoven in attempts to overthrow European domination. Throughout the early part of the twentieth century, Egyptians often provided ideological inspiration for Muslims across the world through the emergence of movements such as the Muslim Brotherhood, who were involved in anti-imperialist campaigns against the British. The influences on the brotherhood's leadership of this time included that of lbn Taymiyya (1268–1328) and his ana-lysis of the problems facing fourteenth-century Muslim societies (Esposito 2002). lbn Taymiyya's influence highlights both the impor-tance of historical theologians and the existence of similar debates about the relationship between religion and societal changes over six centuries earlier. During the creation of Pakistan in 1947, the adap-tation of Islamic slogans and symbols within the Muslim League's interweaving of religion and nationalism proved effective in mobiliz-ing support for a Muslim homeland from a receptive population.

A similar relationship between Islam and nationalism can be found within movements against colonialism in the Maghreb, the Gulf nation-states and South East Asia, particularly in Indonesia and Malaysia in the mid-twentieth century. During the 1950s and 1960s widespread disenchantment arose with liberal nationalist and colo-nial governments, and the regimes in Egypt, Libya, Sudan, Iraq and Algeria were all overthrown, with varying degrees of religious involvement. It was also at this time in Egypt that 'two ideological orientations or movements emerged, both of them populist: the Islamic activism of the Muslim Brotherhood and the Arab nationa-lism/socialism of Gamal Abdel Nasser' (Esposito 1999: 66). Both movements proved extremely influential across North Africa and the Middle East but, 'while Arab nationalism attempted to subsume Islam, Islamic activism asserted the primacy of Islam and called for an Islamic order . . . as the basis for Arab unity and solidarity' (ibid.). In Egypt, this contrast, and abortive attempts to assassinate Nasser, contributed to thousands of praxisitioners being imprisoned and some leaders executed.

Krauthammer (1990) analyses Muslim nationalist independence movements and views with concern the rise in Muslim demands for self-determination and the threat they pose. He argues that there are two phases in the development of Islamic challenges. First, 'from Morocco to Pakistan . . . [Muslims] threw off European imperialism in a process that began earlier in the century and may be said to have culminated with the revolution in Iran.' This, he argues, has been followed by a second stage that is 'the further evolution of the Islamic awakening: the demand for local hegemony by Moslem populations at the borders of the Islamic world'. Krauthammer's analysis identifies how Islamic movements can vary in objective but it still oversimplifies the extent and diversity within the resurgence. It is also incorrect to include Iran in stage one because the Iranian Revolution would arguably fit more readily within the second stage as the demand for local hegemony was a central part of the unrest. However, Krauthammer identifies important differences in the motivations behind Islamic challenges. The emergence of Jihadi Salafist groups like *al-Qa'ida* highlights the increasingly international character of movement networks, which shifts the analysis beyond Krauthammer's 'stages' and emphasizes further the variety to be found within Islamic groups.

Finally, use of the expression, 'the Muslim world' in discussions of the resurgence is also prone to create confusion, not least because, as Hodgson (1974) observed, 'it is time we realised there is only "one world".' The expression is misleading, implying as it does, a unified group of peoples and/or nations. In reality, Muslims are divided by sect, religious interpretation, nationalism, language, ethnicity and in some cases tribal loyalties. Muslim nation-states are divided on numerous grounds, including ideology, historical conflicts, diplomatic manoeuvring and national interests, and millions of Muslims live as part of a minority within societies across the world. Consequently there is a need to use the phrase with caution. This problem can be particularly acute in civilizational analyses that collapse Islamic diversity into the over-arching framework of an Islamic civilization. The tremendous variation of Muslim experiences across different contexts and time periods means that applying the concept of resurgent Islam also has to be undertaken with caution. Our usage of the term is based upon the widespread increase in religious believers and Islamic behaviour across the world, while acknowledging its different causes and effects.

If sociologists are to avoid contributing to the caricature of Islam as a war-like religion and civilization propagated by dogmatic

Muslim militants, then there is a need to work towards a much more comprehensive sociological account which focuses on the social, cultural, political and economic contexts in which Islam is embedded. In doing so, sociology may add a new dimension to wider understandings of Islam and relations between 'Islam and the West'. This means that theological issues and debates will only be discussed in this book where these are necessary to this task, as there are already numerous texts which deal with internal theological arguments (for example: Armstrong 2002; Du Pasquier 1992; Guillaume 1990; Hodgson 1974; Rodinson 1973). Our aim is to provide an approach which pulls together existing research and evidence, while locating this in a historically informed, developmental and resolutely sociological perspective.

2

The Paradox of Secularization

Introduction

In this chapter the process of developing an understanding and explanation of the multi-layered Islamic resurgence begins to move beyond
the previous flawed secularization thesis. This entails addressing why
Islam is increasing in influence, numbers and actions despite generations of secularization. As part of this process it is necessary to
explore a broad range of Muslims' socio-economic backgrounds,
which highlight the need to go beyond exclusionist criteria in
explanation-building. The breadth of the resurgence is highlighted by
Esposito (1999: 100) in relation to Egypt as he argues that 'Islamic
political and social activism in the [nineteen] nineties continued to
root itself more deeply and pervasively in Egyptian society, growing
among the lower and middle classes, educated and uneducated, professionals, students and laborers, young and old, women and men.'
This cross-cutting appeal is becoming increasingly noticeable across
many majority Muslim societies, yet the argument that Islam appeals
primarily to the poor remains. But when moderate and praxist
groups, both Sunni and Shi'a Muslims, are examined it becomes
noticeable that they are dominated by the relatively highly educated
and middle classes who seek to rally the lower classes to their cause.
This does not mean that people in the lowest socio-economic strata
are not already religious; in many instances they have adopted more
Islamic behaviour and beliefs with an increasing observance of rituals
and ceremonies. As we will see later, while a majority of Muslims
remain focused upon individual faith and involvement in community
relations, there are growing numbers previously associated with

moderate Islam who have become politicized and are being mobilized by praxisitioners. Consequently, if we are to develop a sociological approach that can both understand and explain the Islamic resurgence, then these factors need to be incorporated. The first step in this direction is to examine programmes of secularization that have been implemented in Muslim societies and have ultimately contributed to the broad Islamic resurgence and political mobilization of movements against secular influences. This analysis is not exhaustive. Instead it is designed to help illuminate the background on which to draw together existing explanations for the resurgence.

Secularizing offensives and Islamic resistance

Unlike the emergence of Christianity, which developed as a religion of outsiders and was subservient to the power of the Roman Empire, Islam quickly became an established religion in which government and religion were embedded within social, economic, cultural and political relations. As a consequence, secularization offensives within Muslim societies have often been contentious, causes of resentment and hostility. This legacy has contributed to attempts at secularization being only partially successful, commencing with processes instigated by the Muslim Ottomans. A measure of general agreement exists that under Islamic leadership, the Ottoman Empire (1299–1918) experienced considerable growth, spreading to cover a vast area stretching from the Anatolian heartlands in all directions across Europe, Asia and North Africa (the impact of the empire is discussed in more detail in chapter 4). From the seventeenth century, the long period of successful expansion began to turn into a series of regular defeats, and Ottoman territory began to be lost in battles with the emerging European powers. The remnants of the empire were finally dismembered at the end of World War I as an immediate consequence of an ill-fated alliance with Germany. During this long decline, a number of attempts at reform were made, beginning in the eighteenth century, to halt the process and enable the empire to be able to compete successfully with Western nations. These reforms tended to be imitative, as the empire was urged to accept the 'civilization of Europe in its entirety' (Saffet Paşa, Minister of Public Instruction during the 1870s, cited in Mardin 1989: 113). This resulted in the balance between religious authorities and secularists shifting towards the latter. In particular, this was at the expense of the Islamic traditionalists and *ulema*, who were gradually removed from central positions in government. As Mardin (1989: 12) argues, a process of 'depersonalization' began that was continued by republicans as more rational, impersonal and professional relations and allegiances in commerce, law and state functions emerged. Intimate socialization was replaced by Western types of affiliation as the state increasingly formalized processes of socialization. However, the Ottoman reformists were politically unable properly to challenge existing Islamic institutions, and this led to the existence of Western secular institutions without secular systems that might have challenged the traditional authorities and ways of working (Toprak 1981).

There are a number of interesting yet very different case studies amongst the nations formed in the aftermath of the end of the Ottoman Empire, including Turkey, Iraq and Syria. Other Muslim nation-states, which achieved independence after being exposed to varieties of Western colonialism included Algeria, Egypt, Indonesia, Malaysia, Sudan and Tunisia, while countries that avoided direct colonialism included Afghanistan, Iran and Saudi Arabia. The secularization processes undertaken in these different cases provide a useful illumination of the relationships between the secular established (or in the case of Saudi Arabia, the less radical established Muslims) and radical Muslim outsiders. Turkey is an important case because the Ottomans were Turks and contemporary Turkey is the most secular Muslim state, yet it has also experienced an Islamic resurgence. As the 2003 attacks undertaken by Turkish nationals outside two synagogues and the British embassy and HSBC bank in Istanbul show, there is today a radical Islamic presence there that can attack international Western symbols and institutions.

Turkey, as it is now recognized, arose after a successful war of independence during which some of the land lost after World War I was reclaimed. The head of the new state was Kemal Atatürk, who accelerated and radicalized the earlier Ottoman secular reforms, introducing Western ideas and systems designed to modernize the country. The process of secularization 'showed a clear distaste for religion' (Mardin 1990: 21), with secular values transposed from above while the state 'centre' educated and modernized. The reforms were more comprehensive than those introduced during the earlier Ottoman period, but the concentration of the reform effort on the core urban areas left the periphery relatively unchanged. This approach meant that secular values did not develop gradually to incorporate the wider population, as had happened over several generations in Western Europe. Instead, 'villages and small towns . . . continued to preserve their basic Islamic customs and traditions, and the cultural goals of secularism were only superficially fulfilled there' (Karpat 1959: 271). The centralization of power highlighted the clear shift in the power balance towards the secular reformers. Republicans became the new political leaders and tended to be concentrated within urban areas, strengthening the urban–rural split. Through a number of symbolic and pragmatic changes ranging from individual appearance to language and the introduction of the Latin script (which replaced Arabic), the split became much more visible. The wider processes of secularization did little to incorporate practising Muslims, who were derided by the newly established republicans. Yet little attempt was made by the latter to explain the modernizing programme in terms that were meaningful to the whole population. Focusing upon transforming the centre and state institutions alongside relegating religion to a private or individual matter meant that previous Islamic arrangements were not adequately replaced. To a large extent the religious traditions existing in many areas continued to be widely practised. In these areas the inter-generational socialization of Islamic norms, values and behaviour continued, though now more easily interpreted as conflicting with the perceived dominant Western ways.

This pattern of nationalist secularization proved influential throughout Muslim nations as the way to modernize and generate economic progress as it was widely thought that traditional culture was an obstacle to secularization. For example, following independence from France in 1956, Habib Bourguiba became President of Tunisia (1962–87) and implemented a rigorous secularization programme. A modern legal system was introduced, the jurisprudence of the *Shari'ah* was abolished, religious education was undermined and it was proposed – although popular opposition meant it was not introduced – to implement a legal ban on fasting during Ramadan. In Iran, following heavy British influence in the late nineteenth and early twentieth centuries, Reza Shah took control in 1925 and instigated a programme of secular modernization that was subsequently continued by his son, Muhammed. The *mullahs*' influence was undermined, religious taxes reduced and Islam came under the jurisdiction of the state. After being ousted in 1951 by a popular uprising, Muhammed Shah returned to power in 1953, and the modernization process was accelerated, with considerable American support. Industrial and commercial output increased dramatically, and state institutions expanded to meet the growing demands for health, transport, housing and education. During the 1960s, the so-called 'White Revolution' was initiated, which introduced land reforms, an expansion of social services and legal equality for women. It was during the 1960s that significant elements of the *ayatollah*s began to challenge the Pahlavi regime, with opposition gradually spreading to a cross-societal alliance that ultimately brought about the Shah's downfall. The Shah's policies had isolated large, seemingly incompatible groups such as the secularized middle class, oil workers, the unemployed, Westernized business classes and the *ayatollah*s. It is important to stress therefore that the 1979 Iranian Revolution was not an inherently anti-secular or even anti-modernist revolution, but marked a broadly based rebellion against a corrupt, inept and tyrannical ruler and regime. The theological character of the emergent Islamic Republic only emerged *after* the Shah had been deposed.

In Afghanistan, King Amanullah (1919–29) also began to secularize. He sought to enlarge his own power at the expense of the *ulema*, introducing representative government, outlawing polygamy amongst civil servants, allowing women to disregard the veil, opening girls' schools and requiring all Afghans in Kabul to adopt Western styles of dress. These reforms were not lasting. In 1929, pro-*ulema* forces overthrew Amanullah's regime (Hiro 2002). There are a number of reasons why this reform process was short-lived in comparison with the previous examples. Amanullah failed to build up a substantial and loyal modern army that could suppress opposition and the *ulema*'s power and influential social networks with the population remained strong. Afghanistan had not experienced the same history of reform as many of the other countries, although even in some of these areas the extent of reform was rather limited. Reforms introduced during the Ottoman *Tanzimat* period or, in other countries, as a consequence of European neo-/colonialism had partially implemented some modern and secular ways of thinking that meant that the changes and their impact tended to be more gradual. As such, the potential for concerted opposition in these cases had already been reduced. In Afghanistan, subsequent attempts were undertaken to implement the secular modernization of the military, civil service and education system (though Islam continued to be a strong feature of the curriculum) and to enable female emancipation. From the 1950s, modernization increasingly relied upon growing links with the neighbouring Soviet Union, partly in reaction to the alliance developing between neighbouring Pakistan and America. Again the *ulema* protested strongly against the reforms but on this occasion a modern, disciplined army had now been formed that could suppress serious opposition (Hiro 2002). This internal struggle developed into a conflict between Islamists and Marxists that escalated following the Soviet invasion of Afghanistan in 1979.

It should be noted that whilst many Muslim nations adopted Western-influenced secular modernization processes, there were still antagonisms between these nations and the West. Such antagonisms were often driven not by religious rebellion, but by political nationalist protests against inequalities and cultural imperialism, often embedded within the international politics of the Cold War period. Throughout the majority of Muslim nations, the outcome of the different approaches to secularization and marginalizing of religious authorities was broadly similar. The power balance shifted towards secularizing forces as nationalist secular elites assumed and maintained control. Arkoun (1988) argues that 'all political regimes which have emerged in Islamic societies after their liberation from colonialism are *de facto* secular, dominated by Western models, based on the Classical theory of authority and on intellectual modernity.' With the exceptions of post-1979 Iran, Saudi Arabia (to a limited extent), Turabi's Sudan and the Taliban-governed Afghanistan, secularists have been, and remain, the dominant social group and as Kepel (2004) points out, both Iran and Sudan relied on rational bureaucracies.

Yet despite decades of secularization and the dual approach to religion which represses praxisitioners whilst increasing levels of religious influence to attract moderates, the power balance is shifting once again. In part this is because 'the *intellectual* – rather than the institutional or governmental – drive for secularism has never managed to entrench itself deeply in Muslim societies' (Ayubi 1991: 55). Contrary to popular perceptions, secularization was not occurring at the local institutional and cultural-ideological levels where religious networks based around mosques, schools and brotherhoods continued. As a consequence, the adaptation of secular principles, procedures and values has only been partially successful. This is reflected in the frequent challenges to secular states by praxisitioners in various periods including the 1930s, 1940s and since the 1970s in Egypt, from the early 1970s in Tunisia, from the 1980s onwards in Turkey, between the latter stages of the nineteenth century and the 1979 revolution in Iran and throughout the twentieth century in Afghanistan.

On a first impression, this account might be read to suggest that the Islamic resurgence is principally a response to varying stages of secularization. This is only partially true. Muslim nations experienced secularization programmes during different periods, but in some Gulf states, most notably Saudi Arabia, there has been a concerted attempt to restrict the impact of secularization. This is not to suggest that Saudi Arabia is a theocracy, but that the adoption of secular modernization has been organized in quite subtle ways rather than being aggressively and overtly pursued. Urbanization and commercialization have developed rapidly since the discovery of oil, but it had been thought that a limited distribution of new wealth might help to avoid the kinds of negative consequences associated with modernization in other parts of the Middle East. Still, Islam remains prominent in Saudi Arabia and is the main institutional mechanism for social control. Religious courts and 'moral police' are integral components of the judicial system and the *ulema* remain an important element in providing the regime with legitimacy. This has bestowed the *ulema* with more power chances than in other Sunni states. However, the *ulema* are often kept under surveillance by the intelligence services and, as in other states, have been compromised by their role in supporting or being on the payroll of the state.

Like other Muslim states, Saudi Arabia has also provided financial and logistical support that encouraged Islamic radicals as a counterweight to reduce the challenge of Arab nationalism in the 1960s and 1970s (Byman and Green 1999). Partly as a consequence of this 'subdued secularization', there has been only limited secular opposition to royal rule. This scarcely noticeable secular opposition, subordination of the *ulema* who tend to support the state, the assistance given to radical groups between the 1960s and 1970s and the subsequent attempts by the regime to establish its own Islamic credentials (thus helping to legitimize the radicals' ideological position) are all factors that have contributed to the growing popularity of more radical Islamic groups. These have been able to utilize existing Islamic networks that are denied to non-religious groups and appeal to the growing numbers who are disillusioned with the perceived immorality of the royal family, political corruption and social and economic problems. The American military forces' prolonged stay in the country following the 1991 Gulf War also continued to cause rancour. There are some signs that the extent of dissent may be growing and the frequent acts of terrorism undertaken over recent years highlight that the impact of radical groups within the dissension has increased even within the *ulema*. Saudi dissident Mohammed al-Massari (in Jerichow 1997: 120) has suggested that there is an age divide emerging, with younger members of the *ulema* increasingly challenging the regime and subsequently being imprisoned. By establishing itself as a moralistic, Islamically oriented government, the

Saudi regime set the criteria on which it should be assessed, whilst providing people with the resources and educational opportunities to criticize the regime on its own terms. In light of the limited opportunities for secular opposition forces it is therefore not surprising that Islam in Saudi Arabia is becoming radicalized.

Since the 1991 Gulf War, Saudi Arabia has sought to accommodate a liberalization process to appeal to younger groups who are increasingly exposed to Western culture. Measures have included the establishment of a consultative assembly and provincial assemblies. However, attempts at liberalization are limited by corruption and vested interests within the royal family, and any movements considered to be too 'Western' would antagonize large elements of the population whose identities revolve around the puritanical ideologies that the Saudi state has helped to foster. Despite, or perhaps because of, being one of the least secular states in the Middle East, Saudi Arabia seems to be facing one of the largest threats from praxisitioners and has unintentionally been responsible for exporting terrorism, evidenced for instance by the high percentage of Saudi terrorists taking part in the 2001 attacks in America.

In summary therefore, it can be seen that Muslim nation-states have introduced a variety of approaches to secularization. Many of these have tended to subordinate Islam to state control, ever since Atatürk built upon the earlier Ottoman reforms and instigated widespread changes during the 1920s. Yet with some notable exceptions (see chapter 1), the resurgence has only recently become a broad, cross-cutting phenomenon. To begin to understand why this is so, we need to explore explanations for Islamic identification in more detail.

Explanations of Islamic resurgence

A useful starting point when trying to understand the Islamic resurgence is to examine the reasoning that exists in academic accounts. In the bulk of academic analyses of Islamic movements it is possible to notice a concentration on the idea that the unemployed, bazaaris and peasants, in addition to migrants to the West, constitute the basis for both the broad resurgence and praxist groups. This, it is argued, is a consequence of economic conditions related to processes of modernization and globalization (Anderson 1997; Ayubi 1991; Huband 1998; Mehmet 1990; Mortimer 1982; Paz 2001a; Roy 1994; Williamson 1987). Mortimer (1982: 403) exemplifies this argument when claiming that Islamic groups consist of those 'whose lives are in one way or other disorientated by rapid change: merchants and manufacturers being edged out by foreign competition or by the growth of a new capitalist class . . .'. A few examples will demonstrate the force of this line of argument.

In countries such as Egypt, which are experiencing serious economic problems, there is considerable support for this body of materialist explanation. Ayubi (1991: 86) argues that 'the main cause behind the surge in political Islam is a "developmental crisis", whereby many new social forces have been unleashed without their energies being politically absorbed and without their economic and social expectations being satisfied.' A different approach to development was adopted in Algeria, but the end result has been very similar. Maddy-Wietzman and Litvak (2003: 79) note that 'a generation of misguided, mismanaged "state capitalism" policies, the worldwide slump in the hydrocarbon sector beginning in the mid-1980s, rampant corruption, rapid population growth, and high unemployment all fuelled the breakdown of the ruling FLN (Front de Libération Nationale) regime and the Islamists' rise.' Today, after decades of massive financial surpluses and the employment of 'guest workers' to undertake jobs that the indigenous population could not or did not want to undertake, even the oil-rich states are now experiencing financial deficits and rising unemployment. For example, Hiro (2002: 399) points out with respect to Saudi Arabia that unemployment rates are officially 18 per cent – the CIA (2004) estimates this rate to be 35 per cent – and the economy is only creating 50 per cent of the jobs required for the 100,000 people entering the employment market for the first time, a problem that is likely to be exacerbated by the disproportionately young demographic distribution. Rising unemployment amongst the indigenous population has resulted in foreign workers having to return to their countries of origin and the financial problems faced by the state have led to subsidies for water, electricity and food being reduced. Unsurprisingly, such cutbacks have caused further resentment among those adversely affected. Champion (1999) has suggested that the problem is accentuated by poor planning, mismanagement and corruption, an inefficient bureaucracy, inertia, the massive costs involved in inviting foreign soldiers to defend Saudi territory from possible attack from Iraq and the subsequent liberation of Kuwait. Economic problems will be further exacerbated by Islamic terrorist attacks on Westerners employed by oil companies and the crisis this is generating within the oil industry. Consequently, the problems seem to be long-term and will require major restructuring. At present the latter appears unlikely.

Similar reasoning can also be applied to the radicalization of Muslims within the West. In Britain, Lord Ahmed (quoted in Burke et al. 2004: 9) has suggested that young Muslims are experiencing alienation based on levels of relative poverty, with unemployment rates four times higher than the national average and educational achievement 20 per cent below average. Ahmed argues that British Muslims are the country's real 'underclass'. Across majority-Muslim countries modernization has tended to be concentrated in urban areas, resulting in large-scale urbanization and migration from rural towns and villages as people are attracted by the promises of employment and a better life. Some studies have identified the impact of urbanization and migration, both from rural communities to the urban and from Muslim societies to the West, on patterns of identity formation, leaving people culturally and psychologically disoriented (Ayubi 1991; Esposito 1999; Hardacre 1993; Hiro 2002; Mardin 1989; Mehmet 1990; Paz 2001a). Huntington (1998: 11) argues that 'recent migrants to the cities generally need emotional, social and material support and guidance, which religious groups provide more than any other source.' Migrants are then likely to think about their previous experiences based around the strong feelings of what Tönnies referred to as *Gemeinschaft*-type social bonds and the relatively strong links with neighbourhood, extended families and friends. Many will compare these romanticized images with the *Gesellschaft* associations that are characteristic of Western cities with their impersonal, rationalistic and dislocated relationships, together with the often inadequate housing and the poverty which many migrants experience. Changes in physical and social environments therefore tend to produce physical and psychological consequences for the individual. In short, people may well become more religious as 'a reaction to alienation and a quest for authenticity' (Ayubi 1991: 11). In these situations, Islam is more likely to be, not 'the opium of the people, but the vitamin of the weak' (Debray 1994: 15). If so, then it can be argued that migrants can become the targets for recruitment to both secular and religious radical groups (Hiro 2002).

Alienation is also associated with the processes of secularization in majority-Muslim societies, particularly in the most vigorous attempts at establishing secular states. For instance, 'Bourguibism' in Tunisia imposed secularization from above, which led to the state taking control over religion and the country's Arab-Islamic heritage. Religious practices were downplayed and even denounced, whilst modernization and Western values were promoted within urban areas (Ayubi 1991; Enhali and Adda 2003; Esposito 1999; Maddy-Weitzman and Litvak 2003). Many Muslim societies developed a well-educated, modern, Westernized elite and other supporting socio-economic groups, which left many people not directly involved in the process feeling disenfranchised, their cultures undermined and not adequately replaced. In Europe and America alienation has been reported amongst Muslim immigrants, who face racism and have difficulties adjusting to Western modernization and its values. Paz (2001a: 8) argues that the first generation of immigrants were focused upon solving their economic difficulties and sought to assimilate into Western societies but 'the expectations of the second and third generations of immigrants were in many cases unfulfilled, reinforcing their alienation from the Western societies that surround them.'

Gradually it has become apparent to governments and academics seeking to understand and explain what is happening that the widespread Islamic resurgence is not only or even primarily about protests by the uneducated poor. Slowly, the involvement of highly qualified people, particularly in the organization of Islamic movements, has been identified (Ahmad 1991; Ayubi 1991; Euben 1999; Fischer 1980; Huband 1998; Huntington 1998; Kepel 2004; Mehmet 1990; Munson 1988; Roy 1994; Williamson 1987). However, in these accounts, the rationale used to explain the involvement of poorer socio-economic classes is expanded to include more highly educated groups. At face value this reasoning appears inappropriate because nation-states have rapidly expanded the available opportunities in further and higher education as part of their wider approaches to modernize and develop their economies and societies. Malaysia is typical of this approach, with university education considerably expanded during the 1970s, attracting many students from rural and peasant backgrounds (Nash 1991). Large numbers of individuals and their families across Muslim societies have undertaken considerable sacrifices to acquire a higher education. For many people, the sacrifices have not been rewarded, because graduates have not achieved the level of employment and accompanying lifestyles that they anticipated. In such instances, the argument regarding causes of radicalization may be quite similar to that used for relatively disadvantaged groups; Islam appeals to people who became highly qualified but subsequently fail to obtain appropriate, or indeed any employment on graduation due to the limited opportunities available in poorly performing economies. As the United Nations Development Program (2002: 2) concluded with respect to Arab countries – a conclusion that can be applied across most of the developing world – there is a 'mismatch between aspirations and their fulfilment'. Roy (1994) refers to these recruits to Islamic activism in pseudo-Marxist terms as, 'lumpen intelligentsia'.

As part of the expansion of education facilities and opportunities, Islamic students increased in significance across campuses within Muslim societies, frequently winning elections and taking control of student unions. Universities have provided bases on which to develop policies, not only for their respective campuses but also on national and international issues. For example, in Egypt, student groups associated with the Muslim Brotherhood and more radical movements like *al-Jihad*, have been highly critical of the government, notably the Sadat regime's policies, including the Camp David peace accord with Israel. The reasons for students becoming involved in Islamic politics have been linked with their social backgrounds. Hiro (2002: 75) argues with respect to Egypt that

> the majority of [Islamic] university students came from rural, petty bourgeois families who had been the traditional backbone of the Muslim Brotherhood. Alienated by Sadat's recognition of Israel, and disgusted by the rising corruption, material and spiritual, engendered by the regime's open-door economic policy to attract foreign capital and give a boost to private enterprise, this section turned against the government.

Again, it is possible to find alienation also being applied to explain the involvement of the educated. Cederroth (1996: 367) explicitly brings the two groups together when arguing that the reawakening of interest in Islam on Malaysian university campuses is part of the wider resurgence and 'has been attributed to feelings of rootlessness among the masses of migrants coming from stable, religiously orthodox environments in the rural areas.'

Another group considered prominent within Muslim movements are the owners of small businesses whose increased religiosity Fischer (1980) interprets as the 'revolt of the petite-bourgeoisie'. Paz (2003: 58) takes a different line, identifying other middle-class groups when suggesting that 'professions such as physicians, lawyers, pharmacists, engineers, academic scholars, or merchants who have suffered from the state's tendency to nationalize the economy – have found in the Islam propounded by modern Islamists, the solution to their problems.' Both arguments share the view that the lower and upper middle classes are attracted to Islam due to loss of business, the lack of economic opportunities and limited political participation. Ayubi (1991: 176) addresses such discontent more explicitly when suggesting, with respect to praxisitioners, that they are 'not rebellious because they are opposed to development (or even to an extent, to modernization) but rather because they desired it so strongly and yet could not get it. Theirs is the proverbial case of "sour grapes": they hate modernity because they cannot get it.'

Considerable importance can also be attributed to identity formation in the appeal of Islam (Ayubi 1991). Muslims experiencing periods of alienation, instability, threats to livelihoods and uncertainty are able to gain a more secure sense of identity through Islam, particularly through involvement in movements that can offer social relationships and support networks. Bassan Tibi (1988), an Arab Muslim political sociologist, has argued that if there is an identity crisis amongst Muslims then it is as a consequence of Westernization. People are turning to Islam in the hope of a better future and as the basis for identity. This could be seen to apply most notably for younger Muslims, who could be seen to experience what Erikson (1968) refers to as 'identity crisis', as they seek to negotiate the transition from childhood to adulthood in changing circumstances and with their future status not clear. During this stage, individuals become more conscious about identification and the types of people they want to become. Erikson argues that ideology and social relationships play key roles in processes of identification, helping people to identify beliefs, attitudes and values and therefore bring about a sense of unity. In this sense, Erikson argues that individual development is based upon the way personal experience interacts with the social context. It can be argued that, in many situations, Islam provides adolescents with some key characteristics of identity formation, also offering an explanatory framework that incorporates models of beliefs and behaviour. Through membership of movements individuals are then able to form social relationships that provide comradeship and support in religious contexts.

Many of these explanations explicitly or implicitly attribute central importance to modernization and the upheaval brought about in peoples' livelihoods and identities or in the broken promises of educational systems or migration. Paz (2002: 73) specifically addresses these issues, arguing that the roots of Islamic terrorism lie 'in the inability of many individual Muslims to cope with the technological, cultural, social or economic aspects of Western modernization'. Ayubi (1991: 176) provides a more detailed discussion, arguing that

there are similar socio-economic conditions under which all radical Islamic movements function; in a way, they are all a manifestation of, and a reaction to, a developmental crisis in the Muslim part of the Third World. They have all appeared in an environment of rising expectations, poor achievements and frustrated hopes. They are almost all movements of the upwardly mobile, formally educated and recently urbanised youth, who were 'released', often mobilised, but not completely assimilated and rewarded by the national State, because of incomplete industrialisation and unfulfilled modernization.

Consequently, Ayubi concludes that people do not become what he terms 'Islamic militants' because of their opposition to rapid development or modernization. On the contrary, these Muslims' beliefs are a reaction to development being *too slow* and not providing them with the benefits achieved by others. In these contexts, Muslims are seen to turn their backs on capitalism and modernization and accept radical Islam as 'a community-building movement, seeking to keep the noxious effects of the market, which is identified with secularist immorality, out of the community of believers' (Keyder 1988: 13).

In a similar vein, it is also considered that Islam is opposed to the wider processes of globalization. Rubin (2003: 1) argues that in 'the majority of [Middle Eastern] regimes, opposition movements and intellectuals in the region are consciously anti-globalization.' This view accords with the views of some globalization theorists, who suggest that since the 1970s globalization has entered an intensified phase, leading to the conclusion that processes of globalization constitute one significant factor in explaining the Islamic resurgence (Waters 1998). Clearly, if the resurgence began prior to this period, then we need to be cautious about according too much weight to globalization *per se* in our explanations. This is an issue dealt with in much more detail in chapter 4, which demonstrates that the relationship between Islam and globalization is more complex than may at first sight appear.

Similarly, as Gellner (1992) has argued, there is no inherent or inevitable incompatibility between Muslims and modernity. Mabry (1998: 87) argues 'that in the event of modernization, the presence of Islam does not demand the rise of fundamentalism, nor provide an impervious shield to secularization. The politics of industrializing Indonesia and Malaysia demonstrate that disparate Muslim communities do not necessarily merge into homogeneous nations of Islam.' As Toprak also observes in relation to the social background of MPs from the Turkish religious party (NSP) of the 1970s, these were 'well educated, professionally successful, presumably of middle or upper-middle income' and, as such, 'do not fit the image of the stereotype religious fanatic' nor the 'category of men who have been adversely affected by modernization and turned to religion as a means of registering their own discontent' (1984: 130). Even groups such as *Jamaat-I-Islami* in Pakistan favour modernization as the best way to improve socio-economic conditions and promote technological development. They, like other radical groups, do however make a clear distinction between *modernization* and *Westernization*, arguing that modernization does *not* have to be accompanied by secularization and the resulting marginalization of religion, which generates the erosion of family ties and declining moral standards. Contrary to some views therefore, both Islamic moderates and praxisitioners endorse modernization, though not necessarily Western ideas and ideals of 'progress'.

Turner (1994: 78) has moved the analysis of the relationship between Islam and modernization a step forward, arguing in relation to 'fundamentalism' that 'both Islam and Christianity can . . . be analysed as a value-system which actually promoted modernization because modernization was an attack on magical beliefs, local culture, traditionalism, and hedonism. Fundamentalism is . . . the cultural defence of modernity against postmodernity.' Many Muslims and Christians utilize technological innovations and modern communications but feel increasingly threatened by the relativistic postmodern emphasis on cultural and moral diversity that is seen to turn theology into a series of narratives. Gülalp (1999: 23) has also argued that the resurgence in Turkey is related to a 'global crisis of modernism and the rising challenges against the universal myths of Western civilization'. Secularism is now being questioned as one element in the postmodernization of Western culture (Crook et al. 1995). However, these comments overlook some significant aspects of modernity that praxisitioners remain opposed to, not least the challenges posed by rationalization and secularization and the ways in which modern science tended to undermine religious knowledge. Whilst Gülalp rightly identifies the significance of the postmodern undermining of the Western Enlightenment paradigm *in the West*, the Islamic emphasis upon spirituality and irrefutable truth is, as Turner notes, vehemently opposed not only to postmodernity, but also to the scientific philosophy of modernity. In some ways, the idea of a universal postmodernity shares the same universalistic assumption of the secularization thesis, namely that Western experiences and intellectual debate will be similar across an increasingly globalized human world. It does not seem particularly appropriate to translate the intellectual crisis in some parts of Western academia onto millions of Muslims whose main concern is unlikely to be philosophical relativism.

What seems to attract a measure of broad agreement across the range of explanations is that many Muslims are becoming more religious as they encounter periods of economic uncertainty, limited employment prospects, cultural displacement, psychological alienation and, in many instances, poverty. For most Muslims who are part of the resurgence, the increase in levels of religiosity results in greater emphasis upon religion in their private lives, stricter adherence to the 'five pillars' and regular observation of rituals and ceremonies. Islam is providing a range of functions ranging from spiritual and practical support to explanations of current affairs. But after reviewing the explanations three major questions arise.

First, why is the widespread Islamic resurgence a relatively recent phenomenon? Second, why are groups of people who are *not* adversely affected by economic development (and underdevelopment), or indeed who seem to be prospering, turning to radical or activist forms of Islam? Third, why is the piety of the majority of Muslims concentrated within the private sphere? In other words why have these Muslims not become praxisitioners despite encountering many of the same experiences as their more radical peers? These questions arise because similar causal relationships have been invoked to explain a generic resurgence, with little recognition that anomalies exist which require a more discriminating approach. Gülalp (1999: 34) observes the failure of many studies 'to note that while neither immigration nor urban poverty and *anomie* are new phenomena, the growth of Islamism . . . is. Working classes or other urban poor elements [in Turkey] were always primarily composed of recent immigrants yet they did not use to subscribe to Islamism until the 1980s.' Therefore it is likely that there is much more to the resurgence than those features associated with social exclusion. In the remainder of this chapter and following chapters, we begin the process of addressing why there has been a relatively recent resurgence that seems capable of attracting relatively highly educated and prosperous social groups. Why the majority of Muslims' religiosity remains predominantly within the private sphere is addressed later, particularly in chapters 4 and 6.

Nationalism and other ideologies

Informed speculation on the future of the Islamic resurgence takes two broad forms. Either the resurgence will be a relatively short-term phenomenon related to stalled modernization processes, or the phenomenon may become much more deeply rooted and will result in more Islamic revolutions. Sayarı (1984: 120) provides a good example of the first line of thinking:

> the primordial loyalties of the Middle Eastern peoples [and other Muslim societies], based on kinship, religion, ethnicity and regional or tribal affiliations, would be considerably weakened, if not entirely replaced, by new ties of identity based on new forms of social differentiation and political cleavages, and therefore, that their societies would come more and more under the influence of such secular ideologies as nationalism or socialism.

In the twentieth century, some majority-Muslim states, such as Turkey, adopted a secular nationalist ideology. This ideology was heavily influenced by the nationalism that had evolved within the West and was promoted at the expense of religion. The new Turkish government sought to build upon the unity that developed during the Young Turks' Turkification programme towards the end of the Ottoman Empire and the fight for independence. However, the gradual manner in which nationalism emerged in the West during the eighteenth and nineteenth centuries, and in particular the ways in which religion was utilized as a basis for unity, were overlooked as secular Muslim regimes aimed to develop national identities almost overnight.

In many Muslim societies under European colonial rule, nationalism emerged as part of struggles for independence. Such nationalist ideologies were influenced by long-term exposure to Western political and philosophical ideas and beliefs. Religious symbols and slogans were often incorporated in anticolonial opposition and this helped to mobilize popular support for independence, transcending the local sectarian, ethnic and tribal differences. Such a process was witnessed to differing degrees in Algeria, Indonesia, Malaysia, Morocco, Pakistan and Tunisia. In Egypt, the Muslim Brotherhood, which, during the leadership (1923–49) of its founder, Hasan al-Banna, and until it was banned in 1954, was probably the most influential Islamic movement of the era. Although branches of the Brotherhood were established in other Muslim nation-states, their primary focus was on evicting the British from Egypt. This central aim led to the Brotherhood's involvement, albeit limited, in the coup leading to the Republic of Egypt being proclaimed in 1953. In Sudan, the Muslim Brotherhood was also actively involved in the anticolonial movement, but as Sidahmed (1997: 97) has pointed out, a 'Sudanese nationalism' did not fully develop. Although, a 'nationalism movement' did emerge, based around anticolonialism it was divided by sectarian, regional, tribal and partisan loyalties that were to play a major part in the ensuing, long-running conflict following independence.

Following independence, nationalism became strongly associated in nation-states with the secularization processes outlined above, which formally divided the *umma* into distinct territories with different, often competing territories. Governments sought to build upon the national consciousness that had often developed in revolutionary periods. Secularizing offensives meant that governments chose to break substantively with the past, deciding instead to subjugate religion to state control. The potentially fruitful combination of Islam and a nationalist ideology was often not realized. This is particularly noticeable for nation-states such as Iraq, Syria, Lebanon and Jordan that were created by the allies who divided the defeated Ottoman Empire's territory after World War I. The lack of unity and shared history between the disparate groups living within the new nation-states meant that it was difficult to engender national identities as the primary source of allegiance to replace previous loyalties of religion, tribe and locality. Nationalism was therefore imposed from above and failed to displace religion as the primary loyalty of many Muslims. Following independence, some nation-states did attempt to make use of Islam as one significant source of unity in attempts to engender nationalist consciousness in the new states. Morocco identified three sources of national allegiances: Islam, Arabism and Moroccanism (Mezran 2001). In contrast, neighbouring Algeria adopted socialism, secularism and *étatism* as the main elements of national identity, with Islam relegated to a secondary position and under control of the state. As Deeb (1997: 122) argues, 'The Algerian state spoke for Islam but Islam did not speak for the Algerian state.'

In multicultural societies such as Indonesia and Malaysia, in which the majority of the population are Muslims (estimates suggest that Muslims constitute around 90 and over 50 per cent of the respective populations (Cederroth 1996)), governments have faced a dilemma over the extent to which religion should be a cornerstone of national identity. Indonesia's constitution allows the state to be governed by religion, though this is stated in a very broad way that gives equal rights to the main religions. Such a position has enabled a loose form of national identity to emerge that incorporates the different religions and considerable variations within the religions across the 300 inhabited Indonesian islands. By comparison, following Malaysian independence in 1957, Islam was declared to be the state religion, but this was largely a symbolic status and the constitution also protected the rights of the other acknowledged religions. But whilst Islam was identified as the Malaysian state religion, in reality this meant little to Muslims, who were significantly disadvantaged in comparison with the Chinese, and many Muslims sought more religious laws and control. Ethnic riots erupted in 1969, instigated by the predominantly Muslim Malays, leading to the government restructuring the economy, opening up more opportunities for Malays in higher education, enhancing funding for Muslim projects and banning most political activities (Cederroth 1996; Kepel 2004). Islamic political activity was permitted however, and this was to prove influential in the long-term development of radical forms of Islam and the emergence of the *dawkah* group aimed at making 'better Muslims'. Religious freedom for Muslims, particularly on the expanding university campuses, has contributed to stronger connections between Islam and Malay nationalism, making it more difficult to develop a cross-ethnic nationalism which could include the Chinese and Indian populations.

Nationalism within the Middle East has been further complicated, as the Moroccan example shows, by Arab nationalism, which was once dominant across the Arab nations. The popularity of Arab nationalism is associated with Gamal Abdel Nasser, President of Egypt between 1954 and 1970. In Egypt, 'Nasserism' developed and came to be associated with anti-imperialism, pan-Arabism, republicanism and state socialism. Nasser sought to unify the Arab nation-states and used nationalist rhetoric to highlight their similarities and foster unity and, in doing so, helped to generate feelings of cultural superiority. Arab nationalism was popular across the Middle East. The Gulf kingdoms, especially Saudi Arabia, sought to undermine it because of the republican and socialist emphasis of Nasserism, which they perceived threatened their own status and position. Defeat alongside Jordan and Syria in the 1967 Six Day War against Israel, and subsequent loss of territory, had a significant negative impact upon the popularity of Nasser, Arab nationalism and morale of Arabs. Yet despite these events and local and regional conflicts which militated against any wider unity, Arab nationalism still has a part to play in the region, bringing together people who share a common language and many cultural similarities. The 1973 war with Israel and the show of collective strength by Arab nations in the oil crisis of the early 1970s managed to restore some pride in the ideology. In turn, this has since been undermined by the reliance upon American-led forces to repel Saddam Hussein's invasion of Kuwait and, later, the invasion of Iraq by an American-led coalition. Disunity is also fostered by the lack of a coherent and cohesive opposition to Israel and support for Palestinians. It can be concluded that the power and influence of Arab nationalism before 1967 is unlikely to return, certainly in the short term, not least because there has been a widespread perception that nationalist programmes alone will not address the problems that the region faces.

Islam has however continued to play a part in nationalist movements in more recent years, most notably in Bosnia during the 1990s. Bosnia is interesting because contrary to popular opinion, the conflict with Christian Croats and Serbs was not primarily based on religious antagonisms. Bosnian Muslims were not radical and indeed were generally relatively relaxed in their religious practice, partly as hitherto they had been lacking the combination of key ingredients observed behind resurgences elsewhere, such as religious education, impoverished lower classes and problems associated with Western-influenced secularization including dislocation and alienation. However, amidst the threats and attacks by Serbs and Croats, Muslims began to unite around Islam as the key source of their national identity, albeit based more upon cultural relations than religious activity. Religion became the unitary factor for them because it was the one aspect that was shared and through which they differed from Serbs and Croats (Iveković 2002). The relationship between Islam and nationalism was strengthened when the West's refusal to supply arms led the Bosnian Muslims to request assistance from across the Arab nations and South East Asia. A rapid process of de-secularization amongst the Bosnian Muslims quickly followed as the fabric of normal social life was destroyed in the conflict. Islam thus provided Muslims with spiritual comfort and guidance, while religious movements and Muslim nation-states provided financial and material support (Iveković 2002). For the first time in decades, women began to wear the veil as a symbol of the greater levels of religiosity both physically and psychologically, as Islam became immersed within a nationalist struggle. The West's refusal to supply arms contributed to feelings of anti-Westernism amongst Muslims and was instrumental in the re-mobilization of a limited number of Afghan Arabs, who were to prove unpopular among the Bosnians. These Arabs had fought with the Afghan *mujahideen* against the Soviet Union during the 1980s, and many would later return to Afghanistan during the period of the Taliban regime.

Today, Islam continues to play a central role in nationalist movements, particularly within Chechnya and in South East Asia. In Kashmir for example (Rao 1999: 74), socio-economic stratification and inequalities exist between Muslims and the dominant Hindus. Both groups had shared a 'largely joint cultural identity', but as disagreements grew over the distribution of resources they began to emphasize differences that enabled distinctions to be more apparent and focused upon 'the only part of this [joint] identity which was potentially divisive: religious identity'. In this manner, ethnicity and religion became sources of identification that in other contexts would have been more class-based and have become interwoven with nationalism. In the case of Kashmiri Muslims, this has meant the pursuit of independence from Indian control.

Irrespective of the extent to which Islam has been integrated within nationalist movements, it has invariably been subordinated to differing levels of secularism. The length of time that this relationship has been in place, often beginning when independence was achieved from colonial control, has become a key factor behind the contemporary character of the broad Islamic resurgence. Whilst independence and the formation of modern nation-states have been achieved at varying times, the respective governments have since had significant time to make a noticeable difference to the lives of the population. Important improvements have been made in areas such as income, life expectancy, transport systems and communications. Increasingly though, these advances are being offset by problems associated with secular regimes, in particular the growing gap between rich and poor and rising levels of corruption, which are leading to considerable resentment and anger (Dekmejian 1994; Esposito 1999; Hiro 2002; Mezran 2001). Reported corruption is probably most noticeable in Saudi Arabia, where it has been estimated that the House of Saud, incorporating thousands of princes, in a population of 22 million (World Bank 2003), has drawn off around 40 per cent of oil income, equating to around $160 billion (Hiro 2002). Growing corruption is also seen to be part of a general decline in social morality as people compare their government's rhetoric with actions. Because of Saudi Arabia's self-declared and heavily promoted position as the guardian of sacred Islamic sites and the irreligious behaviour of Saudi princes – including gambling, drinking alcohol and associating with prostitutes – Muslims both within and beyond Saudi Arabia, have come to see the regime as hypocritical.

As we have identified, secularization and attempts to create national identities have been associated with numerous problems. But we also need to stress that these processes have achieved some successes. Millions of Muslims have become embedded within national communities, united geographically and sharing a common history.

Many of these Muslims would defend the secular state against invasion and potentially radical Muslim revolutions. Considerable progress has been made towards modernization; economics and politics are dominated by secular groups whose methods and ideas have penetrated state systems and institutions from penal codes to education; Islam is, almost without exception, subservient to the nation-state. But across Muslim societies, secular nationalism has failed to incorporate dissatisfied groups and social classes. Wider populations have not embraced the secular ideology of the political and socio-economic elites, with large sections continuing to identify with Islam. In Algeria during the 1980s the distance between the elite and the masses produced widespread opposition against the government that utilized religious symbols to help mobilize support (Stenberg 1996; Volpi 2003). Turner (1994: 89) points out that, 'at the ideological level, Islam has been able to fill the gap (or at least the experience of a gap) between the promises of Westernization and/or Marxism and the actual reality of social change at the everyday level.' Zubaida (1989: 40) has argued that this is because 'Islam in its political and progressive form is more accessible to the people, springing as it does from their historical cultural roots.' Arguably, the secularizing offensives of nation-states bypassed Islam, thus it is not surprising in light of the religion's political component, stemming from its origins, that many Muslims turned to Islam as a challenging ideology.

The foregrounding of Islam as an ideology is based on the implementation of revelations from Allah during the early periods of the Muslim empires and the formation of the *ummah* during the time of Muhammed (570–632 AD). For many Muslims the achievements of the past have provided legitimacy for Islam as a contemporary ideology, which maintains its relevance today in the form of an Islamic internationalism and under some interpretations as a state ideology. Sayyid Abul A'La Mawdudi (1983), the extremely influential Islamist, argued against Muslim nationalism in Pakistan. Based upon his interpretation, Islam is a universal ideology that cannot be used to underpin nation-states. Such a perspective has been adapted by many praxisitioners who are increasingly critical of nation-state ideologies, which they perceive to be distortions of Islam in so far as nationalism is promoted at the expense of the primacy of the global *ummah*. For these Muslims, the *ummah* must be the primary source of Islamic identity and should not be undermined by divisive nationalism or ethnic identifications. Islamic internationalism can also be seen less dramatically within the wider resurgence and the closer affinity that Muslims feel for other Muslims, particularly in times of crisis. Such feelings can be observed in attitudes towards the plight of the Palestinians and expressed anger over the American-led invasion of Iraq and atrocities committed against Bosnian Muslims. The expansion of the mass media in Muslim societies, including the effects of satellite technology (see chapter 4) has had a major impact in blurring national boundaries, developing international Islamic identifications and contributing to changing perceptions of the *ummah*.

Internationally, Islamic interpretations and behaviour have also been influenced by Saudi Arabia. Since its formation in 1932, the Saudi monarchy's central role as the custodians of holy places, protecting the international Muslim community's most important religious symbols, has become central to the state's ideology. Islam became the defining characteristic of Saudi nationalism. Nevertheless, the primary allegiance of many Saudi Muslims is to Islam, not to the Saudi state. Saudi nationalism has only weakly penetrated civil society. Indeed, for praxisitioners the existence of a national state on the land where Muhammed was born and the expansion of Islam began, is viewed as an obstacle to achieving the *ummah* and is incompatible with Islamic universalism. As we shall see in chapter 6, this has had a large impact on attempts by the regime to make use of Islam to bolster its legitimacy in order to counter the threat of Arab nationalism, which has had damaging unintended consequences.

Pressure from Muslims on nation-states that have based their legitimacy on incorporating Islam can also be seen in the formation of Pakistan (translated as 'land of the pure') and its emphasis on creating a state 'wherein the Muslims shall be enabled to order their lives in the individual and collective spheres in accord with the teachings and requirements of Islam as set out in the Holy *Quran* and the *Sunna*' (Constituent Assembly). In 1949 a resolution was passed which declared that, 'sovereignty over the entire universe belongs to God Almighty Alone' and therefore power exercised by Pakistani governments can only be 'within the limits prescribed by Him' (Constituent Assembly, 1949). Subsequently, Pakistan was declared an Islamic Republic and the capital city named Islamabad to emphasize symbolically the new nation-state's religious centre, integrated with the modernization of society. In the process, it was intended to assimilate the multi-ethnic population into the national ideology, including recent migrants who had left India due to partition and moved to Pakistan because of their religious identity. However, Islam was unable sufficiently to underpin a national identity amongst the population and could not overcome the linguistic and cultural distinctions and economic inequalities between the separate Eastern and

Western areas, which in 1971 developed into open warfare. At the time of the war, Islam was not a major political force on either side. West Pakistan was governed by Bhutto's socialist manifesto, although later concessions to Islam were made to try to legitimize the failing regime. In East Pakistan, opposition was mobilized around ethnic nationalism. These divisions led to East Pakistan gaining independence and being renamed Bangladesh, with considerable assistance from India. The new nation-state adopted Bengali nationalism as its ideological cornerstone, rather than Islam.

In comparison with Saudi Arabia, Pakistan was attempting to create a much more modern Muslim state within new boundaries and against a backdrop of previous colonial control. Pakistan's first permanent constitution, agreed in 1956, reflects this, with the emphasis being placed on secular laws and administration within a broad and rather flexible, non-binding Islamic ideology (Ahmad 1991). Since then, the interaction between modernization programmes and Islam has been varied. For instance, there was a weakening of the connection when General Muhammed Ayub Khan took power in 1958 and introduced a comprehensive reform programme which entailed the reorganization of the state, economy and religion. Following another military coup in 1977, General Zia ul-Haq sought to strengthen the relationship between the state, modernization and religion, introducing an alternative Islamification programme, including Islamic legal and economic reforms. In contrast, Saudi Arabia has utilized Islamic traditions and conservative Wahhabism within its contemporary ideology (Mortimer 1982). In both cases, the contradiction between employing Islam as the cornerstone of state nationalism when for many Muslims it should be the source of a universalizing Muslim identification has not been resolved, leaving a gap which has been exploited by radical forms of Islam.

Balancing the explanatory account: Islamic attractions

Thus far the focus has concentrated upon views of the resurgence and Islamic reactions to the detrimental effects of secular modernization. As we have already mentioned, many of these factors are commonly associated with the resurgence. But these accounts overlook the highly positive features of Islamic beliefs and practice for adherents and the manner in which groups like the Muslim Brotherhood and *Jamaat-I-Islami* have identified the perceived crisis within Islam to be a Muslim problem that needs to be addressed through greater piety and spiritual intimacy (Werbner 2003). In other words, they argue that there needs to be a greater observation of religious practices. Islam can also be seen to address social inequality and injustice whilst promoting creative solutions to social welfare provision. In this way the religion makes a positive contribution to everyday life, individual experience and community cohesion. Further legitimacy is conferred by the communal actions of businesses and groups like the Muslim Brotherhood and Turkish *tarikats*. Islamic banking and a broad range of businesses, including supermarkets, petroleum, construction, media and private healthcare, have grown across Muslim societies, employing thousands of people and providing services to many more. Religious groups and movements, often linked to Muslim businesses, have become cornerstones of communities, providing mosques, schools, community centres, healthcare, housing and employment opportunities. Kepel (2004) points out how the practical services are inculcated with morality. For example, when faced with Egypt's overcrowded transport system, the *Gamaat Islamiya* provided minibus services for female students. When this became overwhelmingly popular, access was restricted to women who were veiled. In the West, groups like the Deobandi, Barelwi, Tablighi and Tijan Brotherhood have provided charity and sought to develop strong communities that preserve and adapt Islamic customs and support networks, generating a sense of unity. Such activities strengthen the beliefs of Muslims receiving and providing services. It is important to stress that these groups and movements are not inherently connected to political violence or terrorism, though this is not unknown. Many people across the world are well aware of the militant acts by *Hamas* in Palestine, but the movement's 'peaceful face' as provider of crucial social services, food, shelter, jobs, security and education is less well known (Abu-Amr 1994; Juergensmeyer 2003). In Lebanon, *Hezbollah* have also combined violence with the provision of social welfare services (Esposito 1999; Hamzeh 1997) that has contributed to the transition to democratic politics and the organization's continued existence following the withdrawal of the Israeli army from Southern Lebanon in 2000. In providing welfare services that nation-states cannot, Muslim groups are helping to reinforce the legitimacy of Islam in areas where secular governments are weak.

Since the 1970s, radical Islamic awareness has been galvanized by a series of events that have contributed to raising levels of religious pride and strengthening the appeal of Islam as a contemporaneously relevant ideology. Particular importance is attributed to the invasion of Afghanistan by the Soviet Union in 1979. The manner in which

Muslims across the world reacted to the conflict proved inspirational for internationalist Islam and provided Afghans with financial support and a source of fighters. The role of the international allegiance of Muslims in forcing the withdrawal of the Soviet Union from Afghanistan in 1989 made a huge impression on Muslim levels of pride. The legacy of war against the Soviets also played a major role in the contemporary rise of radical Islamic terrorist groups. Recently, Afghanistan has again played a part, albeit unintentionally, in the mobilization of Muslims who were dismayed by American attacks on the nation-state and in particular the perceived indiscriminate killing of several thousand civilians. The presence of hundreds of thousands of American troops in Saudi Arabia following the first Gulf War has also been seen negatively, given that Saudi Arabia has sacred meaning for Muslims as the birthplace of the Prophet Muhammed and the place where the *Shari'ah* and *ummah* were first introduced. Saudi Arabia had also contributed earlier in a different way when it was part of the embargo by oil-producing nations in 1973, which led to a tremendous rise in oil prices and helped to instil a greater sense of pride in ethnic and religious loyalties that had been undermined following conflict with Israel. The long-running Palestinian–Israeli conflict and the US-led coalition's invasion and occupation of Iraq have also proved instrumental in raising an internationalist Islamic consciousness.

Perhaps the most significant single event of the late twentieth century has been the Iranian Revolution, which helped to change perceptions of Islam in the West as well as inspiring many Muslims in other countries. Many Muslims were impressed by the contribution of their much-derided religion in overcoming the largest army in the region, denouncing Western interests and securing power. Admiration for the revolution was widespread amongst both Sunni and Shi'ite populations, leading to many secular governments sharing Western concerns about the possibility of more Islamic revolutions. The popularity of radical forms of Islam received a boost, with many militants emboldened by the outcome of events in Iran. Zubaida (1989: 40) elaborates on this effect, noting that the

Islamic Revolution . . . was populist and anti-imperialist. . . . For some it seemed that, unlike the 'imported' ideologies of Marxism or nationalism, Islam in its political and progressive form is more accessible to the people, springing as it does from historical cultural roots. Political Islam acquired many recruits, a political respectability and viability, it became firmly established in the mainstream.

The influence tended to be greatest where people were most desperate, in contexts that were considered to legitimize radical action. In Kashmir, *Jamaat-i-Kashmir* became influential in the political struggle for independence, interweaving nationalism with Islam. During the 1980s and early 1990s *Hezbollah* proved extremely effective under Iranian sponsorship, undertaking terrorist activities against foreign forces and representatives. *Hezbollah* attacks against Israeli forces were instrumental in Israel's decision to withdraw from Southern Lebanon. The success of *Hezbollah* was lauded across the Middle East, arguably inspiring Palestinians to radicalize their protests following the stalling of the Israeli–Palestinian peace process. Nevertheless, and notwithstanding recent terrorist attacks against Western targets across the world, fears regarding the potential overthrow of secular regimes have proved to be misplaced. Radical Islamic activity has not been transformed into social revolutions in even those states, such as Algeria and Egypt, which have been considered under the most serious challenge (Reed 1993; Wright 1992).

Why then has there been no wider Islamic revolutionary transformation of nation-states? There are numerous reasons for this. First is the significance of Shi'ism within the Iranian Revolution (the Lebanese *Hezbollah* are also Shi'ites), and in particular features like the authority of the imams and the emphasis upon martyrdom that played a large part in mobilizing opposition and undermining the military. Second, the lack of theological unity between Sunnis and Shi'ites has often prevented greater cooperation across national boundaries and weakened the potential for the Iranian Revolution to be exported. Third, ethnic, regional, tribal and ideological divisions among opposition groups have frequently prevented opposition within nation-states from working together. Fourth, the power of governments and widespread suppression of Islamic movements has restricted opportunities for the mobilization of popular opposition. Fifth, the pragmatic use of religion by secular states (which has unintentionally contributed to greater radicalization) has on occasion given the impression of greater official religiosity and Islamic presence within national polities, and in the short term this has helped weaken the appeal of praxist movements. Sixth, the relative success of secularism within many societies has meant that there is some stability, and while many people are discontented, others feel successfully integrated into the modernizing societies. Nationalism has been embedded within key elements of majority-Muslim societies and there is sufficient loyalty to secular values, despite its well-documented problems. Many Muslim states also consist of diverse ethnic groups and minority groups such as the Turkish Alevis and Pakistani Baluchis who support the secular state, not least because of the protection it provides.

Key differences can also be noted when pre-revolutionary Iran is compared with other Muslim nation-states. In 1979, Iran had a unique set of circumstances that other countries have not mirrored. With time, it has also become apparent to many that the Iranian Revolution is failing to deliver on its promises. Non-Iranian Shi'ite praxisitioners argue that this is due to Iran compromising its commitment to the *Shari'ah*, whilst Sunni groups see that the inadequacies of Shi'ism have contributed to this failure. Perhaps a key feature is that there is not the widespread popular feeling of desperation required to transform the Islamic resurgence into revolutions elsewhere. However, as Hassan (2002: 234) remarks, 'the declining support for radical and militant movements is paradoxically further radicalising these movements and transforming them into more violent and secretive organisations . . . fuelled by a sense of desperation.' Certainly in situations such as the occupied Palestinian territories, overwhelming feelings of despair, powerlessness, frustration and anger are contributing to a growth in violent activity. Contrary to Hassan's analysis, such activities in the occupied territories led to increased support rather than being a reflection of unpopularity, although there are signs that the considerable death toll, economic stagnation and lack of progress towards peace and a Palestinian nation-state are dividing public opinion on the effectiveness of the second *intifada* (Vertigans 2004b). To varying degrees, similar feelings can be found within other extreme national and international praxist groups whose actions tend to alienate the majority of the people whose support they need to gain greater political participation. Kepel (2004: 207) has raised similar points, arguing that violence during the 1990s showed 'structural weakness, not . . . growing strength'. There is some validity in this assessment, but whereas Hassan is referring to 'fundamentalists', Kepel discusses the demise of the Islamist movement (an incompatibly broad coalition, as discussed in chapter 1). This assumption is based on diverse and unconnected events that include: the 2001 attacks on America, the failure to turn the secular Bosnian Muslims into an Islamic state, the lack of revolutions in Egypt and Algeria and the 'postmodern' coup that led to the Refah Party (a moderate religious party in Turkey) resigning from government. Kepel argues that these events are connected to the atrocities committed by the GIA during the Algerian civil war. But as he also acknowledges, state repression of 'Islamists' has played a major role in the current weakness of the groups, within Egypt in particular. This is very different from proving that Islamism has declined. It may simply be the outcome of draconian measures that have done little to address the underlying causes. Islamism in these contexts has been constrained rather than eradicated. The inclusion of Refah within the broad movement is rather confusing, not least because the party possessed many of the democratic principles that Kepel believes are now in demand across Muslim societies. Indeed, in the unlikely event that free elections are held across the Middle East in the near future, it is not difficult to see parties similar to Refah gaining power. The subsequent electoral success of one of Refah's successors, the JDP, in 2002 further weakens this argument. Whilst Kepel is obviously correct that since the Iranian case, Islamic revolutions have signally not taken place, Islamic resurgences, which radical groups are very much part of, have, contributing to societies becoming fractured along religious and secular or Western lines.

Conclusion

The contemporary Islamic resurgence can be seen as a multi-faceted and quite diverse phenomenon, which, though clearly associated with global transformations is also connected, often in fairly direct ways, to the social, economic and political changes experienced in majority-Muslim societies and communities in minority-Muslim nation-states. In particular, the combination of endogenous and exogenous factors has led to the marginalization of Islam from the emergent national public spheres. Nonetheless, Islam did not simply disappear, but remained firmly rooted within the private sphere and Islamic institutions, from where, with the exception of Afghanistan, Iran and Sudan, it has not been implicated in state problems such as rising unemployment, social dislocation and exclusion, alienation and corruption. Such problems have instead come to be associated with secular governments and ideologies, including nationalism. This has meant that the popularity of Islam as an oppositional ideological position is related to its marginalization. As an ideology untarnished by involvement in the creation of serious social problems, Islam is coming to be seen through the historical lens of its former successes.

The paradox of the secularizing offensives in majority-Muslim societies is that, despite attempts to reduce the influence of Islam and to separate state institutions from religious authorities, the process of marginalization has, over the long term, effectively provided new forms of legitimacy for Islamic solutions and activist Islamic groups. The current situation is also leading to reinterpretations of Islam and re-readings of Islamic tenets in the light of contemporary problems and concerns. Chapter 3 deals with some particularly significant developments which may help to explain better some of the most violent manifestations of Islamically oriented terrorism.

3

Sacrifice and Salvation in 'Islamic Terrorism'

Sacrifice, salvation and suicide

Western commentators appear to reserve their strongest words of condemnation for the violent attacks with murderous intent on civilian targets by terrorists who, in the process, intentionally kill themselves. Such acts have often been described as unjustified, irrational and, quite literally, inexplicable. Sometimes these are individual acts (though pre-planned with others), as seen in many Palestinian and Lebanese *Hezbollah* suicide bombings, but some of these acts are planned *and* committed by groups of terrorists acting in concert, as in New York on 11 September 2001. It is understandable that in the wake of such bloody acts, the subsequent journalism and academic commentary tends initially to be highly emotive and to concentrate on the mental states of the individuals involved. However, it is now legitimate to ask whether existing sociological traditions have anything to offer in our attempts to understand and explain the character of individual and collective suicidal attacks such as these and many others.

This task seems particularly relevant given the centrality of the classical sociological themes of suicide (Durkheim 1987[1897]) and religious salvation beliefs (Weber 1992[1904–05], 1966[1922]). The organized and increasingly group nature of this form of terrorism and the explicit link to religious beliefs expressed by the perpetrators make it highly unlikely that explanations can be restricted to individualistic psychological-motivational studies. Any understanding of individual motivation in this context would also need to be sensitive to collective religious beliefs, political ideologies and reinterpretations of these in particular social and historical contexts (Salib 2003). On the other hand, since the pioneering work of Durkheim and despite numerous empirical 'tests' of his theory, the sociological study of suicide has not expanded to become a significant specialism, leaving a gap made glaringly obvious in the current period. It appears that Durkheim's critics have done their job too well in effectively removing the study of suicide from mainstream sociological and social theory. Such a sociological vacuum has left the field open to approaches that focus on individual motivations or variable analyses based on the identification of possible suicide 'risk factors'. Such approaches cannot provide satisfactory explanations of contemporary 'Islamic' suicidal terrorism that the terrorists themselves refer to as martyr attacks.

Instead, what is now required are studies which are able to move between individual psychological states, motivations and psychic 'triggers' and the macro-sociological focus on suicide rates at the national societal level. We could say that what is required is a sociological psychology which takes the group or collectivity and interconnected relations as its focus, rather than the individual or society as a whole. This level of analysis could provide a potentially productive bridge between individualistic and societal approaches. This chapter makes a tentative contribution towards such a reorientation. Such a move *would* deal with motivations, particularly salvation beliefs, but within the context of shifting social figurations. To help achieve this, a brief review of Durkheim's ideas follows in order to set the scene for a wider discussion of collective suicidal terrorism, which draws on the theme of salvation beliefs in Weberian scholarship.

Durkheimian resources

As is now well established, Durkheim identified two poles around which a typology of suicide can be constructed. The first pole, social integration, covers egoistic and altruistic suicides, whilst the social regulation pole covers anomic and fatalistic suicides. Social integration refers to the relative strength of the social bond between individual and society and the connection of individuals to socially given norms and values. Social regulation refers to the way that society places limits on human desires and prevents them from becoming destructively uncontrolled. Essentially, regulation consists of the balancing of desires and goals with the approved social means for expressing and achieving them.

Taking both poles into account, Durkheim's typology allows macro-level comparisons to be made within and between societies to identify the social conditions and institutions that may contribute towards or reduce suicide rates. A few examples will help to bring out the potential utility of this scheme for understanding contemporary suicidal terrorism as well as pointing up some of its limitations.

Social integration and suicide

The individualistic form, egoistic suicide, occurs when the social bond between the individual and society is not strong enough to produce in people sufficient solidaristic energy. This can be seen in Durkheim's comparison of Catholicism and Protestantism in Europe. Religion is a fundamental social institution that connects individuals to something 'outside of themselves' via the sharing of religious beliefs and involvement in collective ritual practices, and in this sense religion is a key source of social integration. Durkheim's well-rehearsed argument is that Catholicism is a relatively stronger integrative religion than Protestantism, due to its collective form of worship and group-based rituals, compared to a more individualistic form of worship and religious observance in Protestantism. In addition, Durkheim notes that Protestantism allows for a 'spirit of free inquiry', which undermines the effectivity of traditional beliefs in binding people to society. Numerous empirical studies or 'tests' have questioned Durkheim's central finding that Catholicism is a more integrative religion than Protestantism in relation to the Netherlands, Prussia and Switzerland (Day 1987; Halbwachs 1978 [1930]; van Poppel and Day 1996). Halbwachs questions whether religious influence can be separated out amongst the diverse range of possible causal variables, thus challenging Durkheim's methods and conclusions. A further criticism is that, because Catholicism holds a stronger view than Protestantism of suicide as a sinful act, an affront to God's gift of life, the potential social stigma for families of suicidal individuals tends to put more pressure on coroners to reclassify suicides as accidental deaths or to return open verdicts. If so, then Durkheim's comparison of the official statistics is built on shifting sand and his conclusions are invalid.

Nevertheless, there remains some support for Durkheim's general thesis that suicide rates vary with the level of social integration, notwithstanding the empirically based and methodological criticisms of the centrality of religion as an independent integrating factor (Breault 1986; Trovato and Jarvis 1986). More recently for example, in the immediate wake of 11 September attack on the World Trade Center, one study found a short-term lowering of suicide rates in the UK, suggesting that external threats to society tend to foster in-group solidarity and strengthen social integration (Salib 2003). Such a finding may also be seen as evidence of the globalizing potential of modern mass media, which promotes a wider sense of shared interests and a common fate.

Egoistic suicide can be seen as the consequence of changes which erode social bonds, leaving the individual poorly integrated especially at the key points at which he/she experiences 'society', namely those institutions that promote feelings of sociality, reminding individuals of their place in the wider society. Of course, Durkheim points to a variety of other institutional points of attachment (family, marriage, political groups), which perform this function, but the same point applies. If rates of interaction are low and common values, beliefs and sentiments not held, then social bonds are loosened, the beneficial effects of group membership are lost and destructive individualism asserted. In these conditions, higher suicide rates could be expected as a proportion of the population loses a meaningful experience of life and is then 'freed' from social restraints and able to take his/her own life.

At the other end of the integrative pole lies altruistic suicide. Altruistic suicide occurs when the felt social bond is so strong that the experience of individuality is seriously undervalued, such that people will commit sacrifices for the interests of the group, even to the extent of sacrificing their own lives. Therefore, altruistic suicide is not brought about because the individual feels that he/she has the personal right to take his/her life (as in egoistic suicide), but because society demands it of them. Examples would include *suttee*, the practice of Indian women committing suicide on the funeral pyre of their husbands, and *seppuku*, Japanese ritual disembowelling. In European societies, Durkheim provides the example of military suicide, in which soldiers intentionally give their lives in battle for the benefit of the group. Davies and Neal (2000: 38–9) point out that *suttee* was more common among warrior castes as a parallel demonstration by widows of the bravery and self-sacrifice of their warrior husbands. Similarly, *seppuku* is a samurai practice, an element of the traditional array of customs associated with knights and, in a greater variety of forms in modern times, the Japanese military.

There is an issue with such suicides as to what extent they can be seen as 'genuine' suicides rather than, say, merely a willingness to be killed in battle. For example, it might be said that

> Today when a terrorist from a culture that is neither Christian nor indi-vidualist dies by driving a truckload of explosives into the midst of his enemies and blowing himself up, Westerners are apt to call it suicide. Such a phenomenon is not suicide but it does underline the close connections between a willingness to die in battle and altruistic suicide in the military that was emphasized by Durkheim. (Davies and Neal 2000: 39)

In short, military altruistic suicide can refer not to willing death on the battlefield, but rather, to voluntary death. 'Altruistic suicide is not a matter of calculation. Indeed, that is what makes it suicide. Altru-istic suicide is an end in itself, unlike the death of the kamikaze pilot which is the unfortunate by-product of some other purpose . . .' (ibid.). Such a definition would also rule out 'suicide' bombers, the *al-Qa'ida* activists who flew planes into the twin towers of the World Trade Center, Tamil Tiger attacks in Sri Lanka, Northern Irish Repub-lican hunger strikers and so on. This way of defining terrorist actions as outside of Durkheim's classification of suicides is untenable and unproductive. For instance, 'genuine' military suicides may also be the unfortunate by-product of some other purpose, such as an attempt to demonstrate dissatisfaction with military life or express feelings of emotional emptiness. Conversely, violent terrorist actions may well be 'ends in themselves' in so far as people volunteer to commit suicide in this way in order to experience the 'felt joy of sac-rifice', with the killing of civilians itself a by-product of this desire. If military sacrifice and altruistic suicide are indeed very close (ibid.), then maybe this is because military sacrifice really is a form of altru-istic suicide in the way that Durkheim described. Wherever people's individuality becomes submerged beneath the needs of the group, leading to suicide, we should consider these as altruistic suicides.

Durkheim (1987 [1897]: 217–40) subdivides altruistic suicide into three sub-types: obligatory; optional; and acute altruistic suicide. Obligatory suicides are defined as those engaged in because the action is seen as the individual's duty, often in response to an episode of social shaming which demands a suicidal response from those who are so shamed. Obligatory suicide shades into Durkheim's second type, optional suicide. The latter are those which, although not part of a strictly defined social duty, nonetheless derive from socially created options conveyed to group members from an early age. In this way, those opting for suicide do so to achieve high (perhaps the highest) esteem bestowed by their group, and hence suicide takes on a positive value. However, it may be surmised that in relation to Islamically oriented suicidal terrorists, Durkheim's third type – acute-altruistic suicide – may provide the best 'fit' within his scheme. Indeed, Durkheim argues that such a suicidal type often occurs at times when the individual renounces life 'purely for the joy of sacrifice' (Durkheim 1987 [1897]: 223). As we shall see later, many of the statements and actions of recent Islamic terrorists seem to fit this description very well. Durkheim gives the example of suicides within religious cults when people come to perceive their individual life as unimportant in relation to the experience of a higher divine power or to be engulfed within that power.

In summary, egoistic and altruistic suicides involve changes in the balance of individuality and conformity which lead either to not enough or to too much social integration. As ever, Durkheim is trying to establish that for successful social life, people need to achieve a workable balance between individual self-experience and self-expression and social integration, which is broadly in line with his concept of human nature as '*homo duplex*', or 'two parts' consisting of individual and social elements of the self.

Social regulation and suicide

At the pole of social regulation, Durkheim points to the social framework of rules through which the expression of felt desires is balanced alongside the available means to express them. In anomic suicide, social regulation is relatively weak and individuals experience a very flimsy institutionalized framework of rules to guide everyday behaviour, leaving them not knowing 'how to go on'. This basic uncertainty develops into a morbid fear and dread of life that becomes literally unbearable, and in this situation suicide becomes an option as a source of relief from the terrors of social life. The acute form of anomie can be produced during rapid social change such as economic booms or slumps, which affect the stability and even relevance of institutionalized social norms. Once such a system of norms is upset, the individual's memories, social skills and abilities become worthless and society fails to provide a predictable social environment, leading to the inability to achieve a balance between wants and desires and the means to achieve these. In contrast, chronic anomie occurs when societies are in a continuous process of change that does not allow a stable framework of norms to develop and take hold. Arguably, modern capitalist societies could be seen as chronically anomic in so far as they are based on the 'Constant revolutionising of production, uninterrupted disturbance of all social conditions ever-lasting uncertainty and agitation . . .' (Marx and Engels, 1983 [1848]: 83). In this way, anomic suicide is symptomatic of capitalist economies.

At the other end of the regulative pole is fatalistic suicide. This occurs when social rules become so invasive and constraining as to close off any possibility of positive change. Though an analysis of this type is badly underdeveloped in Durkheim's work, he does use the example of the suicide of slaves as an example of a group which can see no way out of their situation, such that suicide provides the only form of escape. It is therefore possible to envisage fatalistic suicide as emerging within the context of a highly asymmetrical power relationship when subordinated and oppressed groups may come to perceive their position as irretrievable using legitimate means. We may also tentatively suggest that such fatalism may partly describe the perceptions of some suicidal terrorists at least in relation to their assessment of the enduring life chances of the group rather than the individual. Palestinian terrorist groups surely come close to expressions of such fatalism, given perceptions of hopelessness in relation to the overwhelming power imbalance in relation to that of the Israeli state and its international supporters. This sense of des-peration has been graphically illustrated within Victor's analysis (2004) of female bombers. For example, in a reflective comment that picks up not only on the Israeli occupation, but also on the position of women within Palestinian society, Mabrook Idris, the mother of the second *intifada*'s first female 'martyr', Wafa Idris, remarked that 'she was young, intelligent, and beautiful, and had nothing to live for' (ibid.: 41).

For suicide rates based around too little or too much social regu-lation, Durkheim posits the idea that such rates are not directly related to poverty or to the material conditions of disadvantaged groups but are just as often found among higher-status groups. This clearly shows that the suicide rate in a society is closely tied to people's attachment to social norms and is a genuinely *sociological* problem rather than a psychological one based on the study of indi-vidual motivations, or an economic problem rooted in relative dep-rivation and material inequalities. Using literary, historical and clinical examples, Durkheim argued that 'egoistic suicide was asso-ciated with apathy, altruistic suicide with passionate or deliberate

determination and anomic suicide with irritation and disgust.' This
is because

> For the egoistic suicide, life 'seems empty' because thought, by becoming
> self-absorbed, no longer has an object; the altruistic abandons himself to
> enthusiasm, religious, moral or political faith or the military virtues and
> almost by definition sacrifices himself [sic] while for the anomic, lost . . .
> in the infinity of desire, passion, no longer recognizing any bounds, no
> longer has any aim. (Durkheim cited in Lukes 1973: 213)

Discussion of Durkheim's typology often overlooks or does not
develop his argument that mixed 'types' are possible, when social
causes can be demonstrated to converge. Thus he refers to
'egoistic–anomic' suicide, which he considered to have a particular
affinity because they were essentially two different aspects of a single
social state. He also refers to 'anomic–altruistic' and 'egoistic–
altruistic' suicides (ibid.: 213). Once we accept this mixing of fundamental social causes, then Durkheim's scheme makes a potentially
valuable sociological contribution as one important element in a
larger programme of research in relation to suicidal terrorism in its
various forms, including that connected with an Islamic orientation.
Such a project would analyse the changes, both to social rules (regulation) and the production of social solidarity (integration), relating
these to types of suicidal terrorism. When social change, conflict or
economic development leads to the disruption of both regulative and
integrative social institutions, then this convergence may lead to differing types of suicides.

As an illustration, one recent study has used Durkheim's idea of
'mixed types' in the analysis of Palestinian suicide bombing against
targets in Israel, suggesting that many of these actions are best seen
as 'fatalistic–altruistic' suicides (Pedahzur, Perliger and Weinberg
2003). That is, although such suicidal, self-less acts were primarily
motivated by acute altruism, elements of fatalism, a strong sense of
hopelessness and a perceived inability to change the current situation
were also evident. This argument can be connected to the heightened
experience of Palestinian in-group solidarity bound up with an asymmetrical power relationship, made more concrete by the more powerful group's (Israelis') recourse to violence through the apparatus of
the state. In such a situation, and although clearly the Palestinians
are not totally powerless, suicidal forms of terrorism become meaningful actions. As Reuter (2004: 169) says, 'the struggle begins to
count for more than life itself', with the individuals carrying out
attacks having been socialized to adopt relatively low levels of indi-

vidualism and dominant social goals (Saghieh 2002). Acknowledgement of such meaningful violence in terrorist groups does not of course condone it, but it does take us some way towards explaining why such acts occur and helps us to understand why groups of people are able to countenance and justify them to themselves. Arguments in this vein have the potential to produce much more balanced and evidence-based conclusions than the popular media representations of suicidal terrorism as the work of 'madmen', 'criminals' and weak-minded individuals who have been 'brainwashed' by their leaders (Sofsky 2002). As the psychologist Ariel Merari argues in respect of Palestinian terrorists, militant groups 'cannot create suicidal bombers, but merely reinforce existing predispositions' (cited in Reuter 2004: 10). This is also noticeable in the backgrounds of many suicide terrorists associated with *al-Qa'ida* who were self-consciously motivated to undergo military and terrorist training and, although influenced by militant preachers, initiated contact with the militant movement. In summary therefore, Durkheim's work on suicide seems to be far from exhausted and forms one branch of a sociological perspective capable of understanding activism within contemporary terrorism.

Durkheim's critics

Over the twentieth century there was of course intense criticism of Durkheim's original study, from the perspectives of interactionism, phenomenology and ethnomethodology. From these perspectives, Durkheim's analysis can be seen as positivist and reductionist, relying too heavily on the now suspect official statistics. Such critique also raises issues of the reliability of data and the validity of cross-cultural comparison. Durkheim's concentration upon social-structural factors meant that individual motivations and other subjective elements such as perceptions, beliefs and attitudes were not adequately addressed, and this has led to later studies paying more attention to the accounts of suicidal individuals, for instance through the accounts of relations and friends, suicide notes and coroners' reports. Interpretivists such as Douglas (1967) have argued that in studying suicide, sociologists should try to get as close as possible to the inner world of the suicidal person, through diaries, life histories and 'real world' experiences, rather than focusing on suicide rates, which are better seen as artefacts or, in today's terminology, 'social constructions'. The latter critique reached its logical conclusion in the ethnomethodological position, with Atkinson (1978) arguing that suicide statistics, like crime statistics, are merely the end product of a complex social process involving the construction of the meanings of particular suicides, which Durkheim's study simply failed to consider, but which form the subject of future research.

These criticisms have resulted in the majority of subsequent sociological suicide studies focusing upon the micro level of social reality (Gibbs 1994; Gove 1973; Stack 1990; Thorlindsson and Bjarnason 1998). However, such a move has tended to limit the sociological imagination and effectively excluded analysis of social processes, which bring together interstate dynamics, group-level actions and micro-level analysis from the understanding and explanation of suicide. This helps to explain the paucity of sociological research into the current wave of suicidal terrorism, which is desperately in need of just such an evidence-based, relatively detached intervention to balance some of the more individualistic, journalistic and pseudopsychological attempts at explanation. The remainder of the chapter seeks to continue to build on the beginnings of such a project by drawing selectively on Weber's work on Islam and Islamic history, whilst also examining Islamic tenets and their reinterpretation amongst terrorists including Jihadi Salafist groups associated with *al-Qa'ida*. In order to demonstrate how useful such a perspective might be, it will be necessary to examine some of the latter group's documented statements, which may help to locate their suicidal actions within the wider social, political and historical context.

The suicidal acts of 11 September

The 11 September 2001 attacks in America as well as the bombings in Kenya and Tanzania (1998), Yemen (2000), Bali (2002) and Morocco and Istanbul (2003) have collectively resulted in the deaths of over 4,000 civilians and were not carried out by single individuals operating alone. Instead, these acts of terror were planned and carried out by groups of activists who also took their own lives in the process. They were not individual suicides. These acts were therefore collective or group suicides, not individual acts of self-immolation. In relation to Durkheim's typology of suicide, they are much more difficult to categorize and raise some significant questions. It is very difficult to classify them simply as either egoistic, altruistic, anomic or fatalistic suicides as their collective nature takes them beyond Durkheim's original scheme, which was designed to capture the social forces operating to produce a certain level of suicide in differing societal contexts. However, his conceptual framework and the overlapping nature of suicide categories still provide a useful base from which to examine the underlying reasoning for the attacks. Given the levels of long-term planning over extended time periods and their careful and deliberate execution, these acts may be understood as purposive and intentional, value-rational actions.

If this is so, then the question becomes one of tracing out the figurational dynamics (Elias 1978) which have generated the conditions in which the political demands of the terrorists are made and which give their motivating ideals and beliefs a meaningful context. To carry out such acts with no prospect of survival for oneself demonstrates a conviction that the act or its consequences must take precedence over one's own self – a submergence of the self into the act or a submergence of the self within a higher purpose. One suggestion that has been proposed to help explain suicidal Islamic terrorism is the demand of Islamic beliefs themselves, or some dogmatic interpretation of Islam, which then provides a religiously oriented motive to carry out attacks, despite their suicidal consequences. This is the import of Richard Dawkins's (2001) argument in the immediate aftermath of 11 September 2001, leading him to wish for an end to religions altogether as a way of removing such overly strong, fanatical motivational forces. Dawkins pleaded for recognition of the benefits of a more 'rational' approach to human behaviour, suggesting that rewards in the afterlife may have played a significant part in motivating the attackers. However, this philosophically idealist account of terrorist activities (terrorists hold wrong-headed religious beliefs) and its similarly idealist solution (religious beliefs must be removed) fail to appreciate the significance of praxis, the fusion of beliefs and actions, in terrorist actions.

In an interesting account of the 'warrior charisma' developed by the native American Cheyenne, Turner argues that religious institutions can be important in the 'regulation of the scope and nature of violence' (2004: 261). The reputation of the Cheyenne was that they were ruthless in battle, prepared to engage in ritualized suicide. Unarmed 'suicide boys' initiated Cheyenne attacks on the enemy by attempting to 'tear them apart with their bare hands' (ibid.: 258); others then tied themselves to stakes, inviting enemies to kill them. Such suicidal behaviour was part of a ritualized sequence designed to strike fear into the enemy by means of the Cheyennes' bravado and unconcern for their own lives. However, the preparation of warriors and fighters for their roles in battle required more than simply imbibing religious beliefs and ideology. Turner argues that it was the disciplined *physical* training of the embodied self that was required of Cheyenne warriors, who thought of themselves as 'already dead' before going into battle, which enabled individuals to engage in extreme (by today's standards) violence on behalf of the group. Given that Cheyenne warriors were trained to think of themselves as already dead, Durkheim's mixed category of fatalistic–altruistic suicide seems appropriate as a description. The deaths of such warriors had, in a sense, already happened, their individuality had already been submerged within the higher needs of the group even before going into battle. Turner's argument here is that the training which produced such fatalism involved disciplined embodied practices and not simply ideological indoctrination in the transformation of character. The same process of embodied self-production can be seen to have taken place in the Afghanistan training camps of *al-Qa'ida* and other militant groups (Burke 2004). In concentrating on the production of a contemporary 'warrior charisma' through physical discipline and bodily training as well as educating adherents in radical interpretations of Islam, such camps demonstrate that 'religious experiences [are] crucial to sustaining violent but spiritual personalities' (ibid.). In order to examine this type of explanation more closely in relation to Islam, there is a need briefly to rehearse some significant features of the historical development of Islamic theodicy.

In contrast to Dawkins's pro-science–anti-religion analysis, Fuller (2001) argues that suicidal violence is not the unique preserve of the religiously motivated, thereby rejecting the view of these attacks as uniquely 'Islamic'. The incidence of suicidal attacks for political, philosophical and financial reasons, as well as Turner's arguments above, tend to support this claim. However, there is a danger that focusing upon suicidal terrorist attacks in general should be allowed to mask a better understanding of the specific type(s) of 'Islamic terrorism' seen in recent years. Alongside previous terrorist acts associated with *al-Qa'ida* and which developed in impact and velocity from the first attack on the Twin Towers in 1993 and the bombing of *USS Cole* in Yemen in 2000, those of 11 September 2001 and subsequent high-profile attacks in Bali, Morocco and Turkey have been legitimized by a wide-ranging and radical interpretation of Islam, described in the previous chapters. Only by examining this radical interpretation and its transmission, which distinguishes these attacks from types of secular suicidal terrorism, can they be properly understood.

In particular, attention needs to be paid to the concept and practice of religious salvation, though it is plainly unhelpful, not to say naïve, of Dawkins to consider suicidal terrorism as simply the outcome of the intentional 'brainwashing' of sexually frustrated men (Dawkins 2001). Even on its own terms, this fails adequately to consider the number of married hijackers and ignores their demonstrable educational achievements and intellectual capabilities, thus making it less likely that they would be so easily 'brainwashed' in the manner often used to explain behaviour that does not fit within Western, rational, 'civilized' parameters. Dawkins's argument also fails to explain the specific timing of these attacks and why they should happen at this time.

In order to address such questions, it is important that social scientists generally and sociologists in particular start to examine terrorist activities within their wider historical, social and international contexts (Halliday 2002; Saikal 2003; Vertigans 2004a; Vertigans and Sutton 2001). As an initial way into these complex debates, a useful starting point is to take seriously the pronouncements and reported comments of Osama bin Laden, the aircraft hijackers themselves and their supporters in relation to their expressed beliefs in salvation. The next section therefore analyses the actions and stated aims of the terrorists within the framework of Max Weber's investigation of salvation beliefs and their relationship to 'this-worldly' activity, in order to address the problem of what motivations may stand behind the most notorious and arguably symbolic attacks: the suicidal actions of 11 September.

Weber on Islam and salvation beliefs

Weber's analysis of types of salvation beliefs can be gathered from his studies of the world religions (1966 [1922]). Although Weber's sociology of religion did not systematically examine Islam, it is possible to extract some sense of his basic characterization and this section explores both his typology of salvation and his account of the significance of Islamic historical development for later developments. According to Weber, ancient Islam was not a religion of salvation, though the pure form later gave way to salvation ideas during the Middle Ages. Although Meccan Islam was monotheistic and rejected magic, Weber argued that an ascetic ethic capable of guiding conduct in everyday and economic life, of the kind associated with

Calvinism, did not develop, due to the character of the social groups which acted as carriers for Islamic beliefs. First, warrior bands adapted Qur'anic monotheism to the demands of their lifestyle with the result that the quest for salvation became interpreted in terms of the *jihad*, or holy war, with warriors promised salvation if they died in battle. Second, the growth and expansion of the mystical Sufi brotherhoods (*c*.700–800) produced an interpretation of Islam that relied on a perception of believers as vessels of divine power, leading to a passive acceptance or restfulness rather than an engagement with this-worldly matters (Goldman 1991: 42). Indeed, this-worldly engagement was seen as giving in to the world and its profane demands. So, with these two group carriers, Islamic salvation beliefs produced either a passive attitude to the world or support for warriors in Islamic wars of conquest. Weber argued that in terms of historical significance, 'the warrior seeking to conquer the world' was the 'primary carrier' or representative of the world religion of Islam (Weber 1966 [1922]: 132).

Despite the usual complexities and historical detail of Weber's analysis, his discussion of the ethics of salvation religions contrasts two broad alternatives, two ways of feeling a certainty of grace for believers within religions of salvation. First, a perception of oneself as the *vessel* of godly power points in the direction of mysticism and restfulness in the 'bosom of God', leading to an attitude of resignation and acceptance. Second, salvation can be secured through a conscious perception of the self as the *tool* of godly power, with God working in and through the self, with the self becoming an agent of God's purposes. While the first interpretation would tend not to support actions to transform a corrupt world, the second certainly could do so. When connected to Islamic history and its warrior basis, it is easier to see how an interpretation of Islam as lending support to violent terrorist activities could be constructed, thus identifying the Islamic faith itself as a causal factor in providing the motivation for such attacks.

Nevertheless, Weber's discussion of the world religions identifies Christianity as the prime source of salvation beliefs leading towards asceticism and an active engagement with the world. As is well known, he identifies the Protestant ethic as a major source of motivation for the ethical support of capitalistic economic behaviour, tracing this ethic to Calvinist beliefs in predestination which result in intense 'salvation anxiety' produced by a lack of certainty in who were the elect, those destined for salvation in the afterlife. This concept of salvation anxiety could not, according to Weber, be applied to ancient Islam, as this form initially developed a tendency to withdraw from the world with the ethical concept of salvation being 'alien' to it (ibid.: 262). This changed after Muhammad's flight (*hijra*) to Medina when the religion became transformed into a national Arabic warrior religion with a belief in predestination manifesting itself during battle.

The belief in predestination therefore *was* present in Islam, but Weber points out that this did not lead to an ascetic engagement with the world as in the Protestant sects. In Islam, 'The religious fate of the individual in the next world was held, at least according to the older view, to be adequately secured by the individual's belief in Allah and the prophets, so that no demonstration of salvation in the conduct of life is needed' (ibid.: 204). Unlike Calvinism therefore, Islam did not lead to salvation anxiety as salvation was assured for all true believers. The anxiety-stimulated this-worldly activity which formed an 'elective affinity' with the spirit of capitalism, promoting capitalistic economic behaviour and development, was absent in Islam. Weber argues that as Islam became increasingly urbanized, the doctrine of predestination also lost its significance as it produced no guide for everyday conduct. He also cautions against seeing salvation beliefs in general as simply the preserve of disprivileged classes. Salvation beliefs are not limited to such social groups and therefore do not constitute a 'slave revolt in morality' (ibid.: 115). This is so because salvation has often also been offered to the wealthy. However, Weber (1985: 27) also argued that, 'other things being equal, classes with high social and economic privilege will scarcely be prone to *evolve* the idea of salvation' [emphasis added]. This meant that a 'theodicy of disprivilege' *arose* amongst poorer classes who found solace through believing that they would receive their rewards in heaven. It is this latter line of thought that can be seen to have penetrated much of the secular analysis of the contemporary Islamic religious resurgence.

The framework of analysis for understanding Islamic resurgence has been expanded to incorporate the insurgency of the 'disprivileged' as their poor or deteriorating conditions of existence effectively counter and nullify the other-worldly promises of theologists. Such a position neglects and is not able adequately to explain the appeal of radical forms of Islam to highly educated and often relatively successful Muslims whose education and success have been, at least partly, within secular educational and economic systems. In the case of terrorists associated with *al-Qa'ida*, some of whom were relatively well or highly educated and came from prosperous backgrounds, the secular stereotype of the 'excluded fundamentalist' or the 'materially deprived' and therefore strongly motivated with little to lose, becomes untenable. This is borne out by the statements issued by *al-Qa'ida*, particularly the comments made by bin Laden, which do not address the issues of wealth distribution, poverty reduction or tackling the problems of the 'world's poor' (Halliday 2002: 50). Instead, bin Laden's statements are political in character, focusing on the 'US military presence in Arabia; US support for Israel; its continued bombing of Iraq; and its support for regimes such as Egypt and Saudi Arabia' (Bergen 2001: 242). Israeli occupation of Palestinian territories can also be added to this list of grievances. The underlying motivation for the suicidal attacks can only begin to be understood when the appeal of a religious ideology to those actually involved is grasped within the context of expanding social interdependencies and shifting figurational forces at an increasingly global level.

The radical Islamic interpretation of suicidal terrorism

Clearly, there are problems within Weber's historical analysis of Islamic development, not least with significant elements of his characterization of Islam (Turner 1993) and his argument regarding Islamic warriors as the primary 'carrier groups' of Islam. This argument grossly oversimplifies the wide variety of interpretations amongst cultural, ethnic, tribal, linguistic and political groups. It is not recognized as the primary characterization of even the ancient forms of Islam (Turner 1993) and certainly is not applicable to later social structures. However, there remain some extremely fruitful insights to be gleaned from Weber's work that may help in understanding and explaining recent Islamic suicidal terrorist attacks. In particular, Weber's identification of the existence of an Islamic warrior tradition that portrays warriors as 'agents of God' raises the significance of *jihad* as potentially legitimizing violent actions to transform the world by promoting 'this-worldly' activity in the pursuit of salvation. This usage does chime with the reinterpretations within some militant groups. The construction of a radicalized version of Islam has promoted an activistic association with the warrior tradition and *jihad* which for some, including senior figures within the Taliban, leads to the view that a leader like bin Laden 'is not a terrorist, he is a holy warrior' (Qari Din Muhammed Hanif, Taliban Minister of Planning, reported in Bergen 2001: 176). The statements of some of the terrorists and their supporters demonstrates that they see themselves as being trained as tools of, or warriors for, Allah, exemplified by bin Laden's response to a question concerning previous attacks on America associated with *al-Qa'ida* in 1997: 'We, by the grace of God, are dependent on Him, Praise and Glory be to Him, getting help from Him against the US . . . we are fulfilling a duty which God, Praise and Glory be to Him, decreed for us' (bin Laden 1997).

It should be stressed that this radical interpretation and militaristic training remain the province of a minority within Islamic groups, because the majority of Muslims continue to hold beliefs privately or practise collectively and peaceably. Even within radical Islamic groups themselves there is a lack of unity, including differing interpretations of the *Shari'ah*, disagreements about the extent of the implementation of Islamic law, the balance between the traditional and the modern in society, the reliance upon Islamic methods and practices compared to those associated with the West and the thorny problem of how to transfer the beliefs of individuals and groups into society-wide norms and values. These differing viewpoints and disagreements can be seen in the groups associated with *al-Qa'ida*, which are only united by a very broad ideological position, the identification of common enemies and some general, rather vague aims. In common with other types of social movements, internal disputes around ideological positions and strategy inside the militant movement are wide-ranging, covering fundamental issues such as the nature of *jihad*, literally translated as 'effort', which can be concerned with disseminating 'the word of God and to make it supreme, and to remove all the impediments to Islam – through tongue or pen or sword' (Mawdudi 1986: 58). Within this definition there is considerable debate concerning what is permitted, most pertinently whether *jihad* legitimizes the killing of civilians as well as military personnel. The majority view within Islamic scholarship is that killing civilians is not acceptable, but groups associated with *al-Qa'ida* clearly believe that it is. Osama bin Laden (1997) stated that 'We declared *Jihad* against the US government, because the US government is unjust, criminal and tyrannical. We do not have to differentiate between military or civilian. As far as we are concerned, they are all targets, and this is what the *fatwa* [against US] says.' A *fatwa* subsequently issued (bin Laden 1998) stated that it was 'the individual duty of every Muslim who can do it . . . to kill the Americans and their allies – civilian and military'. Of course sociologically, the theological accuracy or purity of such beliefs and arguments is not directly relevant to understanding and explanation; what matters most is that the terrorists *believe* they are undertaking a legitimate *jihad* and that the call for *jihad* is not simply demanded by *mullahs* or *sheiks* but is based upon the idea of 'divine justice'. As bin Laden argued, 'Allah has ordered us to make holy wars [a type of *jihad*] and to fight to see to it that His word is the highest and the uppermost and that of the unbelievers the lowermost. We believe that this is the call we have to answer regardless of our financial capabilities' (Miller 1998). This statement stresses not only the significance of *jihad* and the ability to legitimize it through Allah's testimony but highlights, as indeed does the background of bin Laden and many other terrorists, that this interpretation appeals to a constituency well beyond the disprivileged and materially poor. As *al-Qa'ida*'s al-Zawahiri (2001a) points out, militants hold values that exceed personal material interests and loyalties as they 'have abandoned their families, country, wealth, studies and jobs in search for jihad arenas for the sake of God.'

The significance of the Islamic concept of *jihad* has quite rightly received much attention after 11 September 2001. However, discussions of this concept have often being undertaken in isolation from the wider developing international relations, with the consequence that the terrorists' actions are at best only partially understood. *Jihad* needs to be grounded within the appropriate interpretation of Islam, particularly as part of 'this-worldly' activities, because interpretations of Islam can provide guidelines for a comprehensive way of life that does not clearly differentiate between the sacred and profane. In this sense, it is contrary to Weber's Islamic typology because such an interpretation provides a way of life for Muslims, offering a much more comprehensive behavioural framework than even Calvinism, as it incorporates economic, cultural, political, social, legal and moral spheres interwoven with theology. Crucially for praxisitioners, this framework does not just provide guidance for actions in relation to existing social structures, but also establishes criteria for the transformation of these through the process of a 'ceaseless striving to reshape self and society so as to attest to your witnessing' (Murad 1985a: 5). It is this interweaving of all spheres of life that lends credence for radical praxisitioners in being legitimately part of terrorist attacks against Islam's enemies.

Routes to salvation through 'this-worldly' activities

For praxisitioners, time spent in 'this-world' is to be used primarily for the purposes of Allah, which means implementing, or at least aiming towards, the *Shari'ah* or Islamic law. *Jihad* is one way of bringing this about, and many praxisitioners focus upon the religious nature of their 'this-worldly' activities as signs of their devotion to Allah or to improve their chances for the 'other-world'. Of all 'this-worldly' activities, it is paradoxically giving up one's life for Allah and preparing for this that are considered both to show the most devotion, and to improve the chances of salvation. As one of the most influential Islamists of recent times, Mawdudi (1986: 58) remarked 'the aim is to live a life of dedication to the cause of Allah and, if necessary, to sacrifice one's life in the discharge of this mission.' In these instances the praxis of militant Muslims can be aimed at becoming a *shaheed*, a martyr. The terrorists and their supporters clearly consider that in the case of attacks against America, the loss of the lives of those directly involved was necessary. For such Muslims, 'those who die in the way of Allah attain a life, for themselves and their community and their mission, which transcends their death', 'And say not of those slain in God's way, "They are dead" nay, they are alive but you perceive it not' (Murad 1985a: 18, the latter part of this quotation taken from the *Qur'an* 2: 154). In Mitchell's study of the Muslim Brotherhood in Egypt, carried out before the broad and radical contemporary resurgence, one respondent replied in a discussion about martyrdom that 'it is the shortest and easiest step from this life to the life hereafter' (1969: 208). These sentiments are widely held within militant praxist Islamic groups.

The disjunction observed by radical Muslims between existing social reality and their theological ideology leads to 'profane' actions being directed towards salvation and the sacred realm. Islamic terrorists argue that the basis for these actions is grounded within both religious tenets and historical precedents, even though Jihadi Salafist groups like *al-Qa'ida* are very much a product of contemporary times. For instance, if we again use the 11 September attacks as an example, in the instruction letter (Paz 2001b) issued to the perpetrators, reference was frequently made to meeting the dress, Qu'ranic recitations and standards of courage set by their Islamic predecessors. The majority of contemporary Christians and more moderate Muslims do not address the gap between theological interpretations and reality because they consider that religious doctrines place greater emphasis upon salvation based upon private faith and practice. As a consequence, the majority of mainstream followers of both religions consider access to the hereafter to be possible through limited public acts of worship and moral behaviour in the private sphere. Praxisitioners strongly contest this limited interpretation of salvation and therefore, as with all the major theologies, the meaning of central tenets is contested. For instance, the Qur'anic belief that 'Allah will make those who believe and do good enter gardens beneath which rivers flow; and those who disbelieve, enjoy themselves and eat as the beasts eat, and the fire is their abode' (*Qur'an* 47: 12), does not establish how the 'believer does good', nor is there any universal agreement upon what this means for achieving salvation. How salvation is interpreted will depend upon the individual or the group's view on what constitutes 'doing good' and the extent to which Islamic practices should be fully implemented.

For moderate Muslims, 'doing good' could be limited to adhering to the 'five pillars', but for praxisitioners seeking to implement Islam in its totality, the requirements of Islam are based upon seeking to implement Allah's Word, which according to leaders like bin Laden (1997) can include, 'a duty [to kill Americans] which God, Praise and Glory be to Him, decreed for us'. Within this radical, activist interpretation is the view that achieving salvation is dependent on the individual undertaking actions that will help to promote Islamic influence. In this sense the eternal fate of the Muslim is interwoven within social relations and activities in which he or she is immersed and feels under pressure to change. It is within this context that the suicidal actions of the terrorists should be considered, as these acts were not designed simply to take American lives, although this impression is widespread. They were a means towards a radical Islamic end of achieving a global *ummah* (Islamic community), which remains a long-term goal. As part of that process, the acts were designed, at least in part, to highlight American weaknesses and demonstrate the potential for Muslim successes. It is within this perspective that they should be viewed, as part of a longer-term strategy to raise the consciousness of all Muslims and develop the struggle against the West.

This means that the focus needs to be extended beyond praxisitioners' negative motivations, such as a hatred of America and Israel and the desire for revenge. Again, bin Laden provides some illuminating thoughts in this direction when he discusses previous atrocities against Americans, highlighting the significance of salvational sacrifice as a positive action both for the terrorist and for the Islamic cause. In 1997 he explained that

We look upon those heroes, those men who undertook to kill the American occupiers in Riyadh and Khobar (Dhahran). We describe those as heroes and describe them as men. They have pulled down the disgrace and submissiveness off the forehead of their nation. We ask Allah, Praise and Glory be to Him, to accept them as martyrs.

On the connection between suicidal terrorism and the individual's salvation, he went on:

> We see that getting killed in the cause of Allah is a great honor wished for by our Prophet (PBUH). He said in his Hadiths: 'I swear to Allah, I wish to fight for Allah's cause and be killed, I'll do it again and be killed, and I'll do it again and be killed'. Being killed for Allah's cause is a great honor achieved by only those who are the elite of the nation. We love this kind of death for Allah's cause as much as you like to live. We have nothing to fear for. It is something we wish for.

In these illustrations, the terrorist acts are explained not as egoistic suicides in the Durkheimian sense and also forbidden by Islam, but as actions *for* God, which should be widely respected as such. So while suicide is a major sin, the *Qu'ran* and *ahadith* can be used to support, and ultimately theologically legitimize, what Zeidan (2001: 20) refers to as 'the voluntary sacrifice of oneself in the cause of Islam ... with the objective of defending Muslims and hurting their enemies'. As with many interpretations of Islam, opinion amongst praxisitioner groups varies over the extent that the nature and subject of terrorist attacks impacts upon the right to call the outcome a 'suicide' or a 'martyrdom'. For example, the death of civilians creates divisions between religious leaders about the perpetrators' claims to what the assassinated *Hamas* leader Abdul Aziz Rantisi termed 'self-chosen martyrdom'. Although again if the attacks are to be permitted by religious groups, specific conditions (such as a reaction to Israeli acts of violence) have to be met. *Hamas*'s condemnation of the 11 September 2001 attacks was based upon the belief that the attacks contravened Islamic tenets (Davis 2003; Juergensmeyer 2001; Reuter 2004; Vertigans 2004b; Victor 2004). Clearly groups associated with *al-Qa'ida* believe that attacks on civilians are justified and focus on making links between the individual sacrifices of Muslims as part of a process for achieving salvation. The sacrifices are also designed to raise respect for Muslims after generations of subjugation, help instil pride in Islam, raise awareness that a radical alternative is possible and to mobilize support. Highly effective action can be and has been taken against the oppressors, and as in the case of 11 September

2001, small groups of praxisitioners can effectively strike at their symbolic heart.

Poles apart: regulation and integration for *al-Qa'ida*

'Islamic terrorist' actions highlight the interrelationship between Durkheim's two poles of social integration and regulation within contemporary activities as well as illustrating the significance of political socialization. In Muslim societies as elsewhere, socialization processes have undergone some significant changes in recent times, including an increasing role for systematic education amid the spread of mass media and new forms of media. These are contributing to the development of an audience that is better informed about both local and global events and problems. Technological change, shifting political opportunity structures and the deregulation of financial systems are providing radical groups with heightened power chances and in the case of groups associated with *al-Qa'ida*, opportunities to undertake violent actions. These factors are also contributing to a widespread lack of regulation at key points both within nation-states and globally, because technological advancements, allied to a better-educated populace, have severely restricted the possibilities for states to curtail internal and cross-national dissent with impunity. For radical outsider groups which are not integrated into existing secularized or 'moderate' political systems, this developing climate gives new hope for the political socialization of wider populations.

Thus, the relative lack of intra- and interstate regulation is in turn contributing to more limited social integration, allowing radical alternatives the space in which to operate and organize. This does not mean that the imposition of draconian restrictions on human rights or a tightening of controls on the political activities of militant groups will destroy Islamic radical networks. A long-term solution will necessarily have to address the social conditions that have led to the formation of such networks in the first place. Simply imposing tighter regulation without tackling underlying causes would probably result in further resentment amongst moderate Muslims and help to recruit more to the radical cause. From a national and secular perspective, suicidal terrorists may appear to be normless, but at the group level they possess very strong values and coherent practices which regulate their behaviour and provide the basis for their actions.

In many cases the key institutions of social integration such as education systems, family, mass media and peer groups are not providing cohesive experiences of society nor able to establish people's expected places within it. Individuals as members of opposing social groups are attached neither to the societies in which they reside nor to mainstream social rules. Conversely, these socializing institutions are providing people with the skills, knowledge and in some cases the messages that challenge societies and promote radical social change. For example, Muslim states have employed radical Islamists within educational institutions, often as part of a strategy to use religious authorities as cultural support for social change. However, this policy is contributing to the stronger integration of groups of praxisitioners around radical Islamic tenets that ultimately challenge secular states. Therefore, the changing loyalties and levels of integration are significant elements to an understanding of the attacks on America as well as those in other parts of the world. Suicidal terrorism is largely the product of altruism and a strong sense of group membership, with greater emphasis upon the social group than the individual self. Yet, paradoxically, the prospect of salvation, of gaining the ultimate reward for the individual, lends religious approval to the individual's highest spiritual ambition.

Conclusion: salvation for Islamic radicals

As established above, and contrary to Weber's perception, salvation *is* one of the core principles within the Islamic faith but it is open to widely divergent interpretations. For praxisitioners – and the suicidal terrorists are amongst the most radical of these – salvation is a proactive concept to be achieved through seeking to bring about the *ummah,* the global Islamic community. Thus, actions that aim to address this also improve the individual's possibilities of achieving personal salvation. It is this interrelationship between the social and individual and the sacred and profane that lies at the core of the terrorists' activities. Using the reasoning provided by *al-Qa'ida*-related groups, it can be seen that the 11 September 2001 attacks had a number of objectives: to humiliate America, to challenge Western capitalism, to lift feelings of shame perceived to be caused by secular offensives, to highlight the potential for Islamic resistance and in the process restore pride in Islam and to raise awareness of distinctively Muslim solutions to social and political problems. As Halliday (2002) has also noted, strategically there are important underlying reasons for the attacks, linked to attempts to undermine existing Middle Eastern regimes. From the Durkheimian perspective, the attacks can be seen as altruistic in intent because the terrorists consider that the social benefits of their actions are greater than any individual loss of life. However, prominent Muslim scholars, groups associated with *al-Qa'ida* and bin Laden, have all, and often in the same sentence, stressed the relationship between terrorism and personal salvation. For example, in the statements released by the satellite TV channel al-Jazeera in October 2001, bin Laden remarked, 'When God blessed one of the groups of Islam, vanguards of Islam, they destroyed America. I pray to God to elevate their status and bless them.' Here, he is arguing that the ultimate motivation to undertake God's work is individual salvation and in this sense could be described as 'acute' altruism, with believers experiencing the 'felt joy of sacrifice'. However, this is only a partial explanation, because the acts were not just for the experience of a higher power, nor to be engulfed within that power. The individuals involved were not comprehensively integrated into Western social relations and activities, partly because these ways conflicted with their own beliefs. But as individuals, they belonged to a group and held values that provided integration both at a social and a theological level. Arguably, they were too integrated within the group, to sacrifice their own lives for what they considered to be the greater good. But again we have to return to the fact that these were not unconditional sacrifices, but ones undertaken egotistically to assist in achieving eternal life for themselves. In this sense, reference can be made to one of Weber's two alternatives in his discussion of the ethics of all salvation religions, because the terrorists clearly had a conscious perception of the self as a tool of godly power, acting as agents to help achieve God's purpose.

Weber appears to be correct, in that radical Muslims do not experience 'salvational anxiety' in the same form as among early Protestants and Calvinists. But the terrorists did not believe that 'no demonstration of salvation in the conduct of life is needed' (Weber 1966 [1922]: 204). On the contrary, they believed that they possessed greater control over their own destiny, because whilst Allah is omniscient, individuals are given freedom to act and need to undertake His [sic] Word in 'this world' to affect the decision to be made on the Day of Judgement. Consequently, the conduct of the terrorists' lives, the social relations and activities in which they were involved and the suicidal manner in which they died were all directed towards achieving salvation.

It seems likely that the military response to 11 September 2001 will serve to strengthen the radical interpretations of Islam propounded by praxisitioners. As Sulaiman Abu Ghaith made clear in an *al-Qa'ida* statement, in the longer term the relationship between terrorism and suicides will continue: 'The Americans should know that the storm of plane attacks will not abate, with God's permission. There are thousands of the Islamic nation's youths who are eager to die just as the Americans are eager to live' (Halliday 2002: 235).

Such statements hold out the prospect of salvation for those who strive for and give their lives to the cause of worldwide Islam and it looks set to continue to provide a meaningful framework for militants. In the present period, a series of factors are combining to allow and contribute to support for terrorism. Retrospectively, many people have interpreted these developments to provide greater legitimacy both for *al-Qa'ida*'s statements that sought to rationalize the 11 September attacks, and in many cases the attacks themselves. Such factors include *al-Qa'ida*'s own strategy, Western attacks on Afghanistan, the American-led invasion and occupation of Iraq, the lack of progress on achieving Palestinian independence and Israeli actions in Palestinian territories.

In a recent Gallup Poll which surveyed 10,000 people across nine Muslim countries (Green 2002), a notable finding was a very widespread hostility to the West and America in particular, which was seen as, 'ruthless, aggressive, conceited, arrogant, easily provoked and biased [in its foreign policy]'. In an interesting comparison, 67 per cent of respondents thought that the 11 September 2001 attacks against the USA were morally unjustified, whilst a higher percentage, 77 per cent, thought that Western military action in Afghanistan was unjustified. Terrorist figures such as Osama bin Laden and the hijackers, and in other contexts like the Palestinian suicide bombers, can be seen to have gained respect, admiration and legitimacy, to be held up as heroes and as martyrs for significant minorities of Muslim populations. Nonetheless, what such polls seem to demonstrate is that there are large sections of these populations which see violence on the part of 'Islamic terrorists' and Western states as unjustified, and yet they remain caught up in social dynamics and conflictual relations that are, in most respects, out of their control. With current theories of globalization suggesting an intensification and speeding up of transnational interchanges, the feeling that the 'juggernaut of modernity' (Giddens 1999) is running out of the control of even the most powerful states in the global system looks set to spread to larger numbers of people in both Western and majority-Muslim countries.

The kind of reflexively organized individuality noted by writers such as Giddens is understandable in this context as people turn their own lives and bodies into projects to be worked on. However, if so, then individual life – and death – projects may take on a renewed significance in making meaningful the individual's existence and worth in the face of impersonal global forces.

4

slam and Globalization

Introduction

The sociological study of the world religions has, in recent years, been increasingly influenced by theories of globalization, many of which take a broadly 'Eurocentric' view of the process, arguing that globalization processes have their origin or centre in the advanced industrial societies of the West. This is especially so in relation to attempts to grasp emergent religious 'fundamentalisms', but particularly those 'fundamentalist' movements that draw on or situate themselves within the Islamic faith. Seen in this way, 'Islamic fundamentalism' appears to be a defensive reaction to the dislocations and uncertainties produced by Western economic, cultural and militarily enforced globalization, which generates fears of cultural destruction and an intensified need for belonging. This kind of analysis can be described as a 'reactionary' interpretation of Islamic social movements, in so far as Islamist movements, both moderate and radical, are seen primarily as *reactions to* the impact of externally generated processes of global social change. Whilst not entirely inaccurate, such an interpretation remains partial and ultimately somewhat misleading, as it does not adequately take into account the perspective of participants within the Islamic resurgence and the way they perceive their own activity.

In this chapter, sociological theories of globalization are reviewed and evaluated by bringing them into contact with the history of Muslim societies and the pronouncements, ideas, arguments and activities of Muslims and Islamic movements aiming at individual and social change. The intention here is to provide a more balanced view of the current global situation which will help explain some of the mutual suspicions and hostilities between Western and Islamic views of what globalization means.

Globalization and fundamentalisms

In the expanding literature on contemporary globalization in the social sciences, religious movements are often seen as traditional or reactionary counter-movements, triggered by the globalization process, in so far as this process is essentially a form of 'Westernization' rooted in the further spread of capitalism and its consumer culture (Juergensmeyer 2001). This characterization particularly applies to 'Islamic fundamentalist' movements, which are seen as forms of resistance, opposed to the global spread of Western values, culture and conspicuous consumption (Robertson 1992; Robertson and Lechner 1985; Waters 1998: 2). For Bauman (1998: 3), globalization and fundamentalisms of all kinds are intimately connected:

> An integral part of the globalizing processes is progressive spatial segregation, separation and exclusion. Neo-tribal and fundamentalist tendencies, which reflect and articulate the experience of people on the receiving end of globalization, are as much legitimate offspring of globalization as the widely acclaimed 'hybridization' of top culture – the culture at the globalized top.

Radical Muslims also conflict with modernists *within* Muslim or formerly Muslim countries, many of whom adopt or aspire towards Western lifestyles and modes of behaviour. So, although the 'fundamentalist' response is thought to be related to, or bound up with globalizing processes as Bauman suggests, its intent, at least explicitly, is to resist or counter the long-term process of Western capitalist globalization, instead promoting communal alternatives. As already seen in previous chapters, rather than simply opposing globalization processes from the perspective of traditional ideologies and localized, community-based alternative positions, contemporary radical Islamic groups are self-consciously or 'reflexively' advancing the cause of an alternative form of globalization from the currently dominant, and made to seem inevitable, Western capitalist one. Islamic praxisitioners, particularly those drawn from educated and bourgeois groups, have a much more sophisticated interpretation of globalization than many modernist (and postmodernist) theories allow for, thus calling into question the characterization of contemporary Islamicist ideologies as traditional or reactionary in any simple way. These movements are not counter-movements in the sense of being reactionary and opposed to the globalizing trend (Antoun 2001). Rather, they are themselves *part of* the globalizing processes which they seek to direct, drawing on particular forms of informational and cultural exchange for support. Therefore they must be accorded more significance within theories of globalizing processes.

Islamic movements in theories of globalization

Contemporary globalization theories in the social sciences fall into three broad types (Kilminster 1997) taking in, to varying degrees, the political, economic and cultural realms (Held et al. 1999; Waters 1998). Political economy theories, based around Wallerstein's ambitious 'world-systems' approach (Bergesen 1980; Chase-Dunn 1982; Wallerstein 1974, 1980, 1989), focus on capitalist expansion and the development of a three-part international system of core, peripheral and semi-peripheral nation-states. Whether this really constitutes a theory of globalization is not entirely clear however, as Wallerstein argues that his world-system is 'not a system "in the world" or "of the world." It is a system "that is a world". Hence the hyphen, since "world" is not an attribute of the system. Rather the two words together constitute a single concept' (Wallerstein cited in Frank 1995: 164). This means that there may be and certainly have been several 'world-systems', which have constituted 'worlds in themselves'. This concept is therefore dissimilar to many other theories of globalization, which see the process as gradually taking in the whole human world so that no societies exist outside. Despite this, the basic neo-Marxist theory of an expansive capitalism moving outwards from the West has been highly influential and remains persuasive as one fundamental aspect which is necessary for understanding the present situation.

In response to what was seen as the economic reductionism of this perspective, there have arisen several 'culturalist' readings of contemporary globalization processes (Robertson 1992, 1994; Robertson and Lechner 1985; Roudometof and Robertson 1995; Waters 1998). These not only correct the exclusive emphasis on the economy but also advance the argument that globalization is *primarily* a cultural phenomenon. The idea that counter-movements, including 'fundamentalisms', form an integral part of globalizing processes is particularly evident in culturalist approaches. One aspect of these arguments is that the potentially unifying but uniformizing spread of global capitalism stimulates and promotes reaction and resistance at local and even national levels as fears of cultural dilution or foreign cultural domination grow. However, as Roudometof and Robertson (1995) have pointed out, globalization paradoxically leads to *intensified* local diversity. Corporations have to strive to fit their products and services into pre-existing cultural frameworks of meaning in order to be successful, hence Robertson's introduction of the term *glocalization*, designed to catch this subtle shift in interpretation of the likely consequences of globalizing processes. Glocalization is defined as 'the simultaneous adaptation of cultural items into different locales via the utilization of local practices and traditions' (Robertson 1995: 284). Nevertheless, this adaptive process can still be seen as the exploitative commodification of indigenous cultures, thus providing a stimulus to traditional, religious or communal ideologies as forms of resistance.

Waters (1998: 9) sees culture as the globalizing medium and most significant force because its constitutive symbolic exchanges 'liberate relationships from spatial referents' and, unlike the material exchanges of the economy on the one hand, and political exchanges on the other, symbolic cultural exchanges annihilate space and transcend the constraints of geography. Thus, 'it follows that the globalization of human society is contingent on the extent to which cultural arrangements are effective relative to economic and political arrangements' (ibid.). In Waters's scheme, 'material exchanges localize; political exchanges internationalize; and symbolic exchanges globalize' (ibid.). This is an unashamedly Western version of contemporary globalization in the sense that the key processes emanate from European expansionism. As he puts it, 'Globalization is the direct consequence of the expansion of European culture across the planet via settlement, colonization and cultural mimesis. It is also bound up intrinsically with the pattern of capitalist development as it has ramified through political and cultural arenas' (ibid.: 3). This means that every social group must now establish its position in relation to the West – they must 'relativize' themselves and their position. Turner's argument (1994) that the shift towards postmodern culture in the West has been the spur for intensified Islamic resistance also suggests that developments at the cultural level may have been most significant.

A third perspective on globalization stems from the figurational or 'process sociological' approach of Norbert Elias (de Swaan 2001b;

Goudsblom 1996; Kilminster 1998; Mennell 1990; Wouters 1990). This approach concentrates on the 'figurational compulsion' (Kilminster 1997: 259) of increasingly interdependent nations and the role played by interstate violence, drawing attention to changes in the formation of identities and behavioural codes. The significance of the figurational paradigm lies in its attempts to connect the dynamics that operate at the regional, national and global levels with processes of self and collective identity formation and changing behavioural codes. In this way process sociology attempts to move beyond the political economy and culturalist models, which give primacy to economic and cultural exchanges respectively. One possible weakness in such theorizing, however, has been the relative marginalization of the role played by social movements and other collective actors in producing intentionally directed social change. Although not a fatal flaw, such an omission needs to be rectified if 'Islamic' social movements are to be properly understood.

In all three mainstream sociological theories of globalization reviewed above, the role of religiously oriented Islamic movements is currently under-theorized. In both Bauman's (1998) and Beck's (2000) overview texts, for instance, there is no indexed reference to Islam at all. In many cases Islamic movements are seen simply as movements of reaction. In Wallerstein's world-system theory, religious and ethnic movements are seen mainly as defensive reactions to the increasingly global spread of the capitalist world-system. Beck (2000: 33) summarizes Wallerstein's position well: 'The universalization and deepening of the capitalist logic engenders resistance on a world scale, which includes anti-Western, anti-modern, fundamentalist reactions, as well as the environmental movement or neo-nationalist currents.' This is an unsatisfactory position that does not advance our understanding of the vibrancy and variety of Islam or the commitment demonstrated by praxisitioners. Of course, anti-Western sentiments are expressed in Islamicist rhetoric, but to see these as either of recent origin or simply as reactive is only possible when seen from the perspective of Western processes of globalization intruding into local and relatively static forms of Islam.

In a similar vein, culturalist theories of globalization tend to see religious 'counter-movements' as forms of resistance to capitalist expansion, but also point out that the various 'fundamentalisms' show up the inadequacy of political economy approaches to globalization. To understand the Islamic resurgence, for example, we need to know much more about Islamic cultures which would help us to understand why resistance is so strong in some areas and not in

others, or why some groups adopt Western, modernist behavioural codes and others do not. Nonetheless, despite the laudable aim of avoiding Eurocentrism, Islamic 'fundamentalism' still presents problems of analysis for cultural theories of globalization. This difficulty persists because there has not been enough reference to empirical research findings on 'fundamentalisms', with the argument being made by inference to a generic model of fundamentalism. We need to break down the present over-generalized view. Rather than being a simple resistance to the globalizing forces of capitalism and consumer culture for instance, Islamic movements can be seen as incorporating an ideology that self-consciously promotes alternative religious and cultural forms of 'directed globalization'.

In relation to the Islamic resurgence, Waters (1998) points out that since the 1970s, Islam has become available to people across the world rather than being tied to a territory or particular community, precisely because we live in a globalizing cultural regime. He sees Islamic fundamentalism as the best example of the relativizing effect of globalization because, until the onset of the latest accelerated globalizing phase from the 1970s, secular social and political issues had come to dominate Islam. However, globalization has injected new life into Islamic fundamentalism and made possible a pan-Islamic movement via 'transfers of money, military intervention, terrorism, mass-mediated messages, and *hadj* pilgrim[age]s' (ibid.: 132). There is an important appreciation here of the impact of globalized forms of information exchange and the spread of mass media, also noted by Turner (1994) amongst others. This is an important insight that helps to explain the changing forms of socialization that produce a more reflexive, comparative historical understanding of present global and national situations. It is important to remember though, that Islam has for centuries been geographically widespread, in so far as there have been Muslims in many parts of the world over this much longer time-scale. As Held and colleagues (1999: 415) note, beginning in the sixth century AD and spreading widely by the eighth century AD, Islam 'can perhaps be thought of as the first globalized world religion'. What marks the current period out as novel is the development and increasing use of global forms of communication to unite disparate groups and forge a collective, global Islamic identity.

The figurational approach tends, for the most part, to see social processes operating 'behind the backs' of those caught up in them, and this applies particularly to global processes that are beyond the control of any group or single nation-state. This does not imply chaos or total randomness though, as social processes can be seen as forms of structured change, amenable to social scientific analysis. Despite this, there is something of a lacuna in relation to the intentional actions and plans of those groups and movements aiming to exert a measure of control over these processes or even alter their direction. This is a criticism of Elias's work itself, which has been remarked on by Haferkamp (1987) and van Krieken (1998). Though globalizing processes probably are unintentional much of the time, the argument developed here is that in the perceptions of Islamic praxisitioners, their own recognition of unintentional global processes provides a stimulus to action, not an attitude of acceptance or passivity. We could say that, whilst social scientists are still trying to understand globalization, Islamic praxisitioners are actively trying to shape it.

It is understandable in the present period that the concept of globalization is a contested one. As Kilminster (1997) argues, globalization is an emergent concept, around which previously existing theoretical disagreements have clustered. It might even be said that theoretical work and the inevitable controversies around globalization processes are necessary at this time in order to generate working hypotheses to direct future research. Given this diversity, it may be better to make use of insights wherever we find them, in the expectation that globalization is constituted by economic, cultural and figurational processes, and cannot be reduced to any one of these. The rest of this chapter examines the case of the (increasingly global) Islamic resurgence in relation to globalization theories in order to enhance our understanding both of Islamic movements and globalizing processes. In particular, we can learn something of the character of Islamic movements by focusing on particular groups whose location and lifestyles have brought them into contact not only with the processes of globalization, but also with differing interpretations of those processes. Such groups inevitably develop not only their own way of understanding the present situation, but are often familiar with Western theories which purport to do the same. This means that they do not simply react to real world events and processes of change, but are bound up with such change and with modes of understanding it. For this reason, the focus upon the resurgence needs to acknowledge that Islam appeals beyond the narrow parameters of the excluded and marginalized to incorporate the growing numbers of well-educated people, intellectuals and members of the bourgeoisie (Ayata 1993; Lubeck 2000; Mitchell 1969; Saikal 2003; Vertigans 1999, 2003).

Global interpretations of resurgent Islam

Currently competing views of globalization share a presumption that this process is, at root, Western and that those who oppose it are reacting to its threats or a felt loss of control, whether on the socio-cultural, economic or political level (Halliday 1996: 125–6). Using globalization theories to explain the recent moderate and radical Islamic resurgence, it could be argued that immersion within the global system has created perceived threats to economic livelihood, political status or cultural lifestyle that have led to those threatened increasing levels of individual religiosity and/or adopting an alternative radical Islamic ideology as a defence mechanism. When alternative ideologies are religious, Western-influenced academics often draw upon the secular sociological tradition as explanation for the spiritual appeal of such ideologies, which provide meaningful frameworks in times of rapid change (see for example, Ayubi 1991; Hiro 2002; Lewis 2002; Mehmet 1990; Roy 1994; Sakallıoğlu 1996). They also point to the loss of control over national affairs as one reason for the character of contemporary Islamic 'fundamentalism'. It is possible that this line of reasoning *can* partly explain the attraction of Islam in some countries, particularly in relation to peasants and bazaaris who have been exposed to the threats generated by intensified global competition. However, this kind of perspective cannot explain why the Islamic resurgence is happening in countries where both secularization and immersion within global processes have been occurring for generations.

Similarly, the idea of an accelerated globalizing phase (Giddens 1999; Harvey 1991; Waters 1998) cannot simply be applied to the Islamic resurgence because this does not address the long-term, diverse and, for praxisitioners, all-encompassing nature of Islam based upon historically derived tenets. Rather than relativizing themselves in relation to other social groups, praxisitioners seek to universalize, based on their own perceptions of 'Truth' that are grounded in interpretations of Islamic history. In addition, although the latest phase of globalization commenced during the 1970s (Waters 1998) in the West, the impact in other parts of the world was neither immediate nor generic. Finally, whilst the effects of globalization have been increasingly noticeable throughout Muslim societies in recent years and religious behaviour has increased in visibility, it can be seen that the development of growing levels of religiosity has been part of a much longer process involving several generations, operating through changing processes of socialization. As discussed in chapter 1, there are numerous examples of nation-state-specific resurgences through-out the nineteenth and twentieth centuries, related to local and national issues.

Current globalization theories cannot therefore explain the attrac-tion of Islam to those who are not, and do not feel, threatened. They fail adequately to incorporate the implications of an ideology based upon global conquest that is rooted in a history of successful expan-sion and immersion within processes of globalization that preceded the development of the West. Many Muslims embrace globalization but not the currently Western-dominated practice and interpretation of it. Focusing on social groups' perceptions of the current global situation can illuminate some neglected aspects of global processes and provide evidence for a revaluation of Western theories of Islamic 'fundamentalism' and the broader resurgence. If we are to begin to understand the reasoning behind the Islamic resurgence we must move beyond the contemporary time-frame established by many recent studies to highlight instead the importance of historical con-texts that form the reference points for contemporary actions and beliefs. In the process we attempt to move forward the debate on the development and impact of globalization. To this end, particular attention will be placed on the most global Muslim empire, the Ottoman, in order to rectify the partial picture of global systems and to identify some of the key factors behind both its demise and the concomitant rise of Western nation-states within global relations.

Historical context of global Islam

When examining the history of Islam it quickly becomes apparent that the majority of Islamic history has been characterized by periods of rapid growth both in terms of territorial expansion and numbers of believers achieved by successful conversions, military expeditions and making new alliances. The process began with Muhammed, who implemented revelations he received from Allah and provided guid-ance for all spheres of life. This new comprehensive religious ideol-ogy was initially practised in Mecca (until Muhammed was forced to leave) before gradually becoming dominant over wider areas. Social relations and forms of cohesion were transformed as the close familial and tribal ties were weakened when believers' primary loyalty became based upon solidarity and the concept of the *ummah*, a universal community based upon religion. The *ummah* was originally formed as a single community of people from Medina 'presenting a united front to the outside world' (Rodinson 1973: 152). It was to develop into an international community extending beyond the Arabs to non-Arabs who shared an Islamic consciousness and certain rituals like the 'five pillars'. Non-Muslims were originally included but the *ummah* gradually became religion-specific when it began to revolve around the concept of *tohid*, unity based upon the Oneness of Allah and 'lack of distinction or discrimination on the basis of colour, race, nationality or ethnic background' (Ahsan 1991: 22). The extent to which this and the merging of religion and politics were achieved within Islamic empires is extremely questionable. Indeed, Keddie (1994) has argued that the latter was more a 'pious myth than reality for most of Islamic history'. Even during the period of Muhammed, whilst unity was often based upon the Muslim cause, his pragmatism and existing tribal and ethnic power, economics, skill and gender differentials and cultural and societal dynamics meant that important distinctions, as Ahmed (1992) has noted, were always present and were subsequently adopted as traditional Islamic practices. However, as Hassan (2002: 89) remarks, 'over time the *ummah* became a state of mind, a form of social consciousness, or an imagined community.' The tensions between this religious unity and cultural diversity remain, indeed the tensions have been exacerbated by communication technologies which have highlighted differences and show that perceptions of the *ummah* are very much tied into the social relations of the period. Despite these variations, Muslims today 'are increasingly returning to the sources of this early period for guidance as to where "real" Islam can be found' (Mandaville 2001: 72).

Following the death of Muhammed, Islam continued to spread across the Arabian Peninsula into Africa, Asia and Europe during the time of the three great dynasties, the Umayyads of Damascus (661–750), the Abbasids of Baghdad (750–1517) and the Ottoman Empire (1299–1918). Islam was able to gain geographical dominance in power, economic and cultural relations, leading Pieterse (1997: 181) to suggest that, 'Cosmopolitan Islam, extending through caravan and maritime trade, through diasporas and settlements, through knowledge networks and through military expansion, has given shape to the historical dynamics of globalization, of which world capitalism is one manifestation.' Such dominance provides legitimacy for contemporary radical ideologies that argue for the reintroduction of the *Shari'ah* and stress primary allegiance to the *ummah*, which has remained influential across Muslim societies but is often just one source of identity.

The rule of the Ottoman Empire can be traced to the eleventh century when Turks (Turcomans) gained control of Baghdad. The fortunes of the Turcomans were transformed with the emergence of Osman (1280–1324) and the Osmanli (Ottoman) dynasty he was to establish. A period of rapid expansion followed until the beginning of the fifteenth century when the Mongols successfully defeated the Anatolian army. However, the Mongols quickly left the territory and after an internal power struggle, the Ottomans again assumed control. In 1453, led by Mehmet II, the Ottomans defeated their Byzantine adversaries and took possession of Constantinople (later renamed Istanbul).

Military conquest of the surrounding areas of Greece, Bosnia-Herzegovina and part of Albania quickly followed. Sunni Islam as a key component of the empire was increasingly emphasized, particularly when Shah Ismail Safavi (ruled 1501–24) founded the neighbouring Persian dynasty and made Shi'ism the official state religion. The connection between the Ottomans and Sunni religion was strengthened in 1516 when Sultan Selim I added Egypt, Syria and Mesopotamia to the empire. The Ottomans now possessed many of the important Islamic cities and also captured the title Caliph ('successor' to the Prophet Muhammed) from the Egyptian Mamluks. Although the sultan was not qualified to adopt the title (not being a direct descendant of the Prophet), the two titles quickly became synonymous and the Ottomans were now considered legitimate defenders of the Sunni faith. The empire continued to expand, and by the sixteenth century most of the Middle East, Asia Minor, North Africa and substantial parts of southern Europe were dominated (Davison 1990; Heper 1985; Weiker 1991). Without question, the Ottomans were the leading global power. It should be noted, however, that the Ottoman Empire was never an Islamic 'state' in the Qu'ranic sense, as the geographic dispersion of multi-ethnic and multi-religious subjects spread across three continents prevented this (Turan 1991: 32). At no stage was the empire exclusively governed according to the *Shari'ah*.

Decline of empire

Whilst the exact date of the Ottoman decline is difficult to pinpoint precisely, a period of slow retraction occurred during the seventeenth century. The failure, and then decimation of their entire army, during the siege of Vienna in 1683, was a symptom of changing fortunes. During the following three centuries of decay, territories were lost, starting with Hungary in the seventeenth century, Greece, Algeria,

Bulgaria and Bosnia-Herzegovina in the nineteenth and Crete, Libya and Albania early in the twentieth century. The remaining Arab nations were lost following the Ottoman defeat alongside Germany in World War I.

Throughout the period of decline, Western influence in the empire increased. There are numerous reasons both why the West came to gain so much control and why the Ottoman Empire declined. The same dominant globalization paradigm that accounts for the contemporary resurgence can also be applied to explain the defeats that ultimately led to the end of empire. Obviously these defeats were against the emerging global powers that were developing rapidly across Europe and were instrumental in the ultimate break-up of the empire. But as a causal argument it places too much emphasis on the development and implicit superiority of Western-led globalization and neglects the underlying reasons why the European rivals were able to replace the empire as the dominant global force. A broader range of explanations is therefore required and can be divided into two categories, one based upon problems caused by external forces, notably the pervasive development of Western nations in global relations. As Ahmed (1992) argues, within global relations the capitulations (meaning trading privileges, which retain contemporary significance for mobilizing opposition to the EU) offered to other nationalities for imports and exports ultimately reduced Ottoman sovereignty. The second set of explanations concentrates upon the empire's inability to retain its global presence due to internal problems.

The emerging and increasingly successful Western nation-states were instrumental in creating nationalist identities, initially amongst Christian communities within the empire. Such strengthened nationalism caused tremendous internal challenges and led to the Ottomans expending considerable resources in trying to deal with the related problems (Dunn 1989). Global developments such as the discovery of the Americas led to the influx of cheap silver and partly contributed to massive inflation that the Ottomans were ill equipped to deal with. Prices of raw materials and goods rose dramatically and cheaper products and produce were imported, including coffee and sugar, which had previously been exported. In addition, the development of navigation and shipping meant sea trade around Africa led to the traditional silk routes through the Middle East and Central Asia being circumvented. These changes were happening when warfare was being modernized and required greater financial commitment for weaponry and maintenance of the armed forces at a time when the Ottomans were facing serious monetary and financial

problems. Dunn (1989) has shown that the empire lacked the necessary educated personnel and expanding tax revenue to enable greater
expenditure upon the rapid industrial developments that were producing ever more weapons in Europe of increasing power and velocity. The decline of the empire and advances made by the European
nation-states within global relations were therefore at least partly
possible because of the Ottomans' internal problems.

At a military level, the Ottomans were less efficient and effective
fighting units, relying increasingly upon less experienced cavalrymen.
Key corps and government posts became nebulous, and corruption
rose. At the highest strategic level, the quality of the Sultans' leadership also deteriorated. This stemmed from the decision to stop frat-
ricide against the brothers of newly enthroned sultans, following a
public outcry after the killing of nineteen brothers on the accession
of Mehmed IV (ruled 1648–87). Instead the new sultan's male rela-
tives were allowed to live but were confined within apartments, which
were widely referred to as 'cages'. Successors to the sultanate were
now determined by age and not ability. The isolation of the sultan's
sons within 'cages' meant that future sultans no longer gained administrative and military experience. Consequently the sultanate had less
direct contact and thus control over the provinces and led to newly
enthroned sultans being ill equipped and ill suited to rule. Without
the necessary skills and experience, the sultanate had to rely increasingly on self-centred court officials, who became extremely influential. And because the officials' economic and political interests were
based upon the *status quo*, these vested interests prevented the
implementation of reforms. For example, any significant movement
towards Western-style secularization was prevented, not least by the
sultans and their advisers, who considered this process would ultimately cause irrevocable damage to their claim that they had a divine
right to rule. Other central factors included the relative lack of interest that the Ottomans had in trade, which enabled Europeans quickly
to gain footholds in import and export markets to the extent that the
empire became dependent on their goods and services. And finally,
after a considerable period of success, rooted in Islamic doctrine, it
seems that the empire became complacent and accepted its dominance
as a divine right and was therefore culturally and psychologically ill
prepared for the challenges of the emerging rival global system. Consequently, the decline of the Ottoman Empire was multi-faceted, and
involved 'economic, military, social, administrative and psychological problems' (Davison 1990: 16; see also Dunn 1989; Lewis, B.
2002; Lewis, G. 1974; Rustow 1965).

Reform: empire and nation-states

Following a shattering defeat by the Russians in 1774, a number of changes were introduced by the Ottomans to try to reclaim past glories and prevent the pervasive European penetration. However, these changes simply mimicked the distinctive Western methods that were perceived to provide the Europeans with an advantage but were not considered to be rooted in Christianity. Because the West had proved militarily superior the Ottomans copied their techniques, tactics and tools. Prussian military advisers arrived in the 1830s and a military academy was established. A medical school and civil service were all created, and Western dress became mandatory. Generally the reforms tended to be isolated to particular spheres and the majority of the subjects remained unaffected (Davison 1990; Peretz 1988). The family, elders and community continued to be the major socializing agents and maintained the equilibrium. Unity was achieved though 'the bond that held the Moslem masses . . . and the rulers together was religious uniformity, not political consciousness' (Kazamias 1966: 40).

The *Tanzimat* period, which began in 1839, saw the reform process accelerate and key elements of Islamic law were replaced by new European-style laws, including commercial, civil, criminal and eventually constitutional regulations. Some of the sultan's powers were delegated, newspapers were permitted and secular education was introduced (Davison 1990; Peretz 1988; Rustow 1965). Attempts were made to move education from a system designed 'to induct the masses of the people into the Ottoman Islamic culture' (Kazamias 1966: 31–2), to a Westernized curriculum. However, this policy created a learning dualism because religious schools continued to teach and the two systems were rigidly kept separate, with both seeking dominance (Geyikdağı 1984).

As levels of criticism of the rulers grew and pressure increased for the adoption of a constitutional monarch, Sultan Abdulhamid dissolved parliament (1878) and ruled dictatorially. As Lewis (2002: 53) remarks, 'the cumulative effect of reform and modernization was, paradoxically, not to increase freedom but to reinforce autocracy.' During the earlier reforms, Islam had diminished in power because religion did not accord with the established European secular patterns. The substantial influence of the *ulema*, which provided legitimacy for the ruler's claim to be the temporal and spiritual representative of the people, was gradually reduced because the sultans increasingly emphasized their temporal roles. The previous division of power left the socialization of believers in familial, education and legal spheres to the *ulema*, but following the reforms this role was gradually transferred to the state (Toprak 1981). Surprisingly, the higher *ulema* continued to support the sultans even though the early modernizing undermined their own positions. Generally the *ulema* were dependent upon the rulers for whatever power and prestige they had left and, consequently, the higher *ulema* throughout the empire rarely provided leadership in resistance struggles (this is generally also true for Muslim societies under Western colonialism). Those religious figures that did become involved in revolutionary movements tended to be at a lower level, were removed from social and economic contact with the elite and were in close contact with rural or urban masses (Baier 1984; Kazamias 1966). Growing secularization also undermined the dual function that Islam had performed for the rulers of both control and cohesion (Toprak 1981), with the gap between the Muslim masses and elite growing.

In 1908 popular opposition was sufficiently influential to reduce the sultan's authority and install a government consisting of the Committee of Union and Progress (CUP), better known as the 'Young Turks'. The Young Turks accelerated the secularization process by introducing more non-religious education, courts and military institutions. The marriage contract was removed from religious control to secular law, although marriages remained arranged. Education and employment opportunities for women improved (especially during World War I when there was a labour shortage). Secondary and University education (not compulsory) were restructured, teacher training was improved, particularly in rural areas, and there was a growing intent to reform religious schools in accordance with the perceived demands of modernization (Geyikdağı 1984). Ultimately the secular reforms were doomed to failure because the government was unable to defeat the different nationalist challenges, was uncertain about how to achieve structural modernization, could not address the tensions between intended new ways and traditional institutions and left the majority of the population outside the reform process. As the highly influential social commentator Ziya Gökalp (Berkes 1959: 278) remarked at the time, 'one portion of our nation is living in an ancient, another in a medieval, and another in a modern age. How can the life of a nation be normal with such a threefold life?'

Following the Ottoman defeat in 1918 alongside Germany in World War I, the victorious allies proposed the Treaty of Sèvres that effectively meant the end of empire. Large parts of what is today recognized as part of Turkey were divided between Greece, Italy and France and the Kurds and Armenians who gained independence. The Ottoman delegates signed the treaty (supported by the sultan who obtained the role of figurehead), creating much opposition among the emerging Turkish nationalists which led to the War of Independence. In October 1922 an armistice was agreed which confirmed the nationalists' victory, and in July 1923 the Treaty of Lausanne was signed which recognized today's Turkish boundaries.

As outlined in chapter 2, the Turkish nation-state has, since independence, experienced mixed fortunes in its attempts to modernize. Some Muslim governments adopted similar practices while others developed different economic and political strategies that were also designed to strengthen the nation's position in global processes. The overwhelming majority of the strategies have been secularist. With the exception of some oil-producing nations – although even these countries are now experiencing problems – governments' policies have generally led to the growth of debt and failure to establish themselves as major influences in global markets. For many Muslims, these examples increasingly highlight a basic incompatibility between the Islamic heritage based upon unity, support and success and their current local and national experiences and understanding of the state's structures, policies and relative global position. These believers compare their experiences of economic, political, cultural, social, moral and legal spheres and the condition of the secular state in the global system with their own perception of the earlier historical successes and future potential based on Islam. This provides a 'double-legitimacy', as Islam has been involved in historical successes and is not associated with current problems.

Nevertheless, this ideological legitimacy has been available to explain the failures of the secular state and global processes since at least the eighteenth century; indeed for some praxisitioners it began following the death of Muhammed, when Islam was being gradually eradicated from influence within state institutions. It is only recently that praxism and the broader resurgence have become so influential across societies. Consequently these phenomena cannot just be explained by recent immersion in globalization processes, which preceded the resurgence in some cases by centuries, nor by accompanying modern Western secular values, which have been gradually introduced since the eighteenth century.

Contemporary and historical aspects of resurgent Islam

The role of Islam within nation-states has continued, ranging from the state-sponsored emphasis on social control and cohesion to revolt. At an individual level, levels of practice have expanded beyond the private sphere to become a popular ideological framework of reference. There has been a widespread growth in believers that cannot be explained simply by the growth in population because as Özcan (1993) has shown with respect to Turkey, the growth in religiosity exceeds the population increase. Younger populations have often questioned the Islamic interpretations and practices of their parents that they consider to be weak and lacking piety (Vertigans 2003). There has consequently been an inter-generational growth in religiosity.

This growth is not simply a negative defensive reaction to globalization and thus limited in appeal to the socially excluded. Muslims are not against globalization *per se*, not least because earlier periods of Islamic success were grounded within globalizing processes. Instead, different perceptions exist about how to approach globalization, from adopting Western discourses and institutions without reservation through to synthesizing Islamic and Western ways. Contrary to much popular opinion, most praxisitioners are not anti-globalization activists and have adopted an approach of 'counter-globalization in which Islam rather than Westernization is to be the dominant force' (Paz 2002: 69). For these Muslims, Islamic values can provide the foundations for bringing about intentionally directed global changes. As Azzam (1977: 8) suggests, for many believers, 'Muslim culture profits from all available sources, local and international, but its unique characteristic is that it has grown from the foundation of the Quran and Sunnah.'

The disparity identified between national and international situations within current and previous global processes is a key factor within the contemporary Islamic resurgence. It is this frame of reference that is used not only to criticize the current global position but also to provide alternative solutions, at individual and social levels, based upon, and legitimized by, preceding Islamic successes. Under the emphasis upon both belief and action, periods of decline and the history of problems associated with secularization can be explained by the lack of practice of Islam as a way of life. As Kidwai (1959: 8) commented with respect to the global reduction in Muslim influence, 'the decline of Muslims is not due to any shortcomings in Islam but to their failure to live up to it.' Thus it was not the decay of Islam that was responsible for the end of global dominance, but the 'decay and bankruptcy of the hearts of the Muslims too lazy to respond to the Divine call'. These sentiments are supported by empirical research (Vertigans 2003: 127) into the beliefs of praxisitioners who, when asked about the reasons for the decline, responded that the main reasons were: 'Muslim people ignored their way of life', 'not due to West being good but as Muslims became bad Muslims' and 'problems are from copying West and forgetting Islamic ways'. Interestingly, Hassan's (2002: 78) research found that while levels of religiosity had grown, many respondents agreed that 'all over the Muslim world Muslims of today are devoid of Islamic character and morals, ideas and ideology, and have lost the Islamic spirit.' Such views are not entirely new. After studying bureaucracy within the Ottoman Empire, Lewis (2002: 23) notes a common theme within memoranda in the seventeenth century, namely that 'the basic fault ... was falling away from the good old ways, Islamic and Ottoman; the basic remedy was a return to them.'

Mandaville (2001) has argued that the *ummah* only re-emerged as a central concept during the nineteenth century and was applied to modern globalizing processes by Mawdudi and Qutb in the twentieth century. The challenge imposed by colonialism affected most Muslims and helped to generate a greater sense of univeralism and the revitalization of pan-Islamism that became prominent through the activities of Jamal al-Din al-Afghani (1838–97) as he sought to address the lack of Muslim unity and weak religious consciousness. Today, periods of local and global success are accounted for by the widespread practice and leading influence of Islamic interpretations; conversely, periods of decline in both support and power are explained by the reduction in religious behaviour. However, this does not explain the contemporary nature of the challenge to globalization, because clearly this conflicting ideological and contextual dichotomy has existed within interpretations since the demise of empire. But nor is the widespread penetration of globalization solely responsible, although the processes and mechanisms embedded within the system have been instrumental in the broad Islamic resurgence. This is because they have not only legitimized Islamic perceptions of the causes of global problems but have helped provide the means of highlighting both these examples and the Islamic alternative. In other words, globalization has helped, as part of what Waters refers to as the globalized cultural regime, unintentionally to raise awareness both of global problems and a global alternative that cross-cuts barriers and promotes a communal identity to help solve those problems whether at an individual, community, nation-state or international level. Support for solutions will depend on the subjective level at which people are experiencing or witnessing problems or events that lead to an intensification of their faith, how these interact with their religious interpretations and ultimately the extent to which the problems are considered rectifiable at the individual level through personal piety and/or structural change at a local or international level. Therefore the significance of the past depends on the perceptions both of present problems and possible future solutions.

In order to understand why levels of awareness have recently grown, attention needs to focus on the relative influence of socializing agents that have undergone considerable change in Muslim societies. Particular attention is placed upon the expanding role of the media and education and their interlinked relationship that have not led to a weakening of faith as many secularists have argued. Arjomand (1986: 88) observed,

> The spread of literacy and expansion of higher education . . . have been accompanied by an increase, rather than a lowering of religious propensity on the part of the majority of the population. In other words, with the development of media of communication, urbanization and the spread of literacy and higher education, religion has flourished: it has not declined.

The tremendous impact of education within Muslim societies and the Islamic resurgence is interwoven with shifts in the balance of relations of power (to be explored in chapter 6). In the remaining sections of this chapter, we wish to focus upon one of the central aspects within globalization that has contributed to the Islamic resurgence: the socializing role of mass communications.

Communicating with Muslims

Across Muslim nations, socialization processes have changed quite rapidly with the huge expansion of mass communications, including many religious journals and radio and television channels. Changes in production and distribution have meant that books and newspapers are easily available on a wider scale to better-educated populations, providing sources of information about developments, expanding people's knowledge, awareness and interests, and used to try to create a greater national or religious cohesion. McLuhan (1967) and Meyrowitz (1985) have both observed how particular types of media are able to portray images of events and people about whom the viewers have no other knowledge; unknown spaces become known and the viewer becomes familiar with alternative ideologies. This depends, to varying degrees, upon the extent to which the media are state or privately owned, and if national, international and global problems associated with secularism and the West are reported. Haynes (1994: 148) observes when discussing the global religious resurgence that 'one reason for the contemporary explosion of religio-political ideas and movements is that ideologues and activists read in newspapers, magazines and journals, see on television screens and video-cassettes, and hear from radios and audio-cassettes the proclamations and stated aspirations, as well as the practical successes and failures of politicized religious groups and movements around the world.'

Since the 1990s, satellite technology and the expansion of the Internet has brought about significant change which Keane (1995: 1) has labelled the 'restructuring of communicative space.' Huff (2001: 440) has also observed how, 'the advent of fax, E-mail, and other forms of electronic communication have captured the imagination because such communication can now be accomplished within seconds anywhere around the world for a tiny fraction of a worker's daily wages. Such possibilities were hardly imaginable just a few decades ago.' It should be pointed out, however, that the majority of people living in Muslim nation-states lack the necessary resources for software and hardware to access ICT technology and are usually reliant on relatively expensive Internet cafés. Restructuring has enabled some media providers, most notably al-Jazeera, to circumvent state censorship, although it has been banned from news-gathering in some countries, including Egypt, Iraq, Jordan, Morocco and Kuwait. International governance has been subsequently tightened and countries like Tunisia sought to ban the installation of satellite dishes and when that failed introduced a strict licensing policy (Sakr 2001). The new television stations have been transmitting information and images about events like protests, riots, terrorist attacks, war and genocide that would not previously have been broadcast to local populations and national citizens living abroad. And in countries where levels of illiteracy remain high, as in North African and Middle Eastern societies where it has been estimated that 38.7 per cent cannot read (UNDP 2001), television and radio have had a huge impact on socializing processes. These are 'people who, whether for reasons of sex, illiteracy, remoteness from newspaper distribution circuits, or disinterest in overt government propaganda, were previously left out of the media loop' (Sakr 2001: 25). The penetration of the media continues to pervade new territories, and satellite technology has also enabled transmission to citizens living abroad, including migrants to the West. Television stations like al-Jazeera, al-Arabiyya and Abu

Dhabi have also encouraged debate about sensitive issues like human rights, democracy, corruption and the conflict between Israel and the Palestinians that have raised levels of awareness and highlighted Western atrocities and problems within Muslims societies. Satellite channels are also involved in the transmission of Islamic programmes at a range of targeted audiences, including schedules for children, which in the Palestinian territories have featured cartoons, songs and music videos that promote the symbolism of childhood martyrdom and glorify bombers like Wafa Idris, the first female bomber of the second *intifada* (Victor 2004).

It is not only satellite channels that have contributed to raising levels of familiarity with local and international issues. State television has also been aided by improvements in technology, transport, communications and education resulting in more people becoming increasingly aware of problems within Muslim societies and Western involvement in recent conflicts. In chapter 1, we outlined how many media providers in Muslim societies, including television, Internet and newspapers and both state-owned and private media are providing extremely critical and partial analysis of Western actions that is contributing to anti-Westernism generally and anti-Americanism specifically (Darwish 2003; Sakr 2001). The same medium is also being used to transmit religious programmes and events as governments have sought to establish their religious credentials in the face of rising Islamic opposition. Muslim regimes, including Iran and Saudi Arabia, are, however, being challenged through satellite television and the Internet, particularly among younger users, by disparate groups whose views range from criticism of the weak application of Islamic laws to the imposition of too much religious jurisprudence and insufficient Westernization (Rahimi 2003). The media explosion can be seen to be contributing to the propagating of ideas, the rise of internal dissent and international affiliations that blur previous local and national identities and empower individuals to obtain and interpret readily available information. Eickelman (2003) argues that this is contributing to a greater critical awareness of Islam. This awareness has accelerated the undermining of the *ulema*'s monopoly of religious knowledge, which began with the widespread availability of Islamic texts and higher literacy rates (Mandaville 2001). Interestingly, as part of the media explosion, a number of *ulema* have become media figures, debating theological and social issues with members of the public and highlighting the potential for a much broader audience (Sa'ad al-Faqih interviewed in Mandaville 2001).

For many Muslims there is a 'restratification of audiences into imagined communities beyond national boundaries' (Sinclair et al. 1996: 24), and this can be witnessed in the international support for the Palestinians and, previously, the Bosnians. Images of Palestinian children being killed by the Israeli military during the *intifada*s have helped galvanise support for the Palestinians while highlighting the weakness of Muslim nation-states to resolve the conflict. These changes have also contributed to a greater sense of universalism with international news transmitting similar topics and the same Islamic texts (in various languages) now becoming available across the world. Overall therefore, the media have become a socializing agent that is being used across Muslim societies both to support and challenge secularization. The globalization of the mass media contributes to many individuals having shifting perceptions of themselves and a growing allegiance to Islamic internationalism.

Jihadi Salafist groups such as *al-Qa'ida* have proved extremely effective in using the media to relay their messages, gaining previously inconceivable exposure for their cause. Of course news and views have been spread for thousands of years, but the significant changes relate to the range, timeliness and depth of the 'information' being transmitted, the vividness of the images and the improved ability of the audience to interpret events. This growing awareness of local and global issues and events is occurring at a time when expectations had been raised and various ideologies, concepts and systems, including socialism, liberalism and democracy, have been tried and subsequently discredited in many Muslim nations. The perceived legacies of colonialism, the hypocrisy and inconsistencies of Western policies and actions towards countries considered allies – Israel, Jordan, Saudi Arabia, Iraq during the war with Iran and post-2003 American invasion – and those who are not – Iran, Iraq, after the invasion of Kuwait and Syria – the Cold War and the impact of its ending on international relations have all contributed to an undermining of the dominant ideologies of capitalism and socialism. In some senses, Islam as an alternative has gained credibility by *not* being involved in recent international and national problems.

Different media sources are being used to obtain information, which has legitimized and strengthened Muslims' beliefs rather than diluted them. Waters correctly highlights the importance of culture within globalization; however, for praxisitioners, culture is used as a means to an end; it is not the end. In this instance, culture is simply the conduit that helps many Muslims with access to multiple sources of information justify their beliefs and/or become more aware of the need to follow a Muslim way of life. Consequently, it can be argued that a major contributor to the radical Islamic resurgence has been the increase in, and awareness of, economic, socio-cultural and political problems within global processes and, crucially, an awareness of the alternative Islamic solutions. Developing this point, we can conclude that changes in the wider global context beyond nation-state boundaries have created greater and more highly visible disparities which people are able to witness, analyse and understand through improvements in education and communication systems. These people are able to respond through the internalization of opposing values at an individual level, often formulated, as Ahmed (1992) notes, in terms of the dominant secular discourse. Individuals are forming identities during socialization processes that revolve around Islamic tenets transmitted by local and global agents. These processes are leading to praxisitioners internalizing a frame of reference that provides a base on which to interpret personal experiences and witnessed international events and activities and ultimately contributes to the belief that intentional action can bring about local and global change. Moderate Muslims are similarly having their religious views strengthened. For them, increased awareness gained through the media of local and international problems and issues is enhancing their religiosity, but this is restricted to a local level. After centuries of assumptions that Islam was based around uniformity and thus consensus, international cultural variations have, through contemporary forms of globalization, become more noticeable. This challenges both the universalism of the praxisitioners, who have responded by stressing the construction of normative behaviour based around 'real' Islam, usually rooted in the 'authenticity' of Arabian interpretations, and the *ulema* whose guidance can now be seen as culturally specific.

Conversely, greater familiarity with Muslims in other countries can help to illuminate the diversity and richness within Islam and help promote feelings of greater unity around a hybrid form of Islam (Hassan 2002) while providing further distinction between moderates and praxisitioners. Mandaville's analysis (2001) of the diaspora complements these points, in particular his concept 'distanciated community' which, via information technology, communication systems and travel, enables people to engage in new forms of community, sharing experiences and discourses across vast distances. This relationship also impacts upon discourse within the original community while a hybrid culture emerges among migrants, but particularly the younger generations.

Another outcome of migration has been a greater acceptance of difference and fusion between migrant Muslim groups. The 'umma is affirmed and realised in diaspora while simultaneously fragmented, broken down into subunits which generate novel combinations' (Mandaville 2001: 151). As globalization continues to improve levels of knowledge and understanding about other Muslims, it seems that there will be even more opportunities for the sharing of ideas and behaviour, so we can anticipate that praxisitioners will become more fervent in their defence of homogeneity and a perceived pure type of Islam. Further strengthening of divides within Islam is in part a consequence of the media's portrayal of the actions and rhetoric of local and international praxisitioners. The images and discourse communicated by militants do not fit within moderate Muslims' life worlds or help to explain their situations and experiences. Consequently, it is likely that media messages and images will help to strengthen the moderates' moderation, as it were. Radical Islamic ideology has not been legitimized by their experiences and media exposure, the universalism of praxisitioners is not internalized and their messages and behaviour reaffirm the moderates' opposition.

Unlike most accounts of globalization which emphasize the unintended nature and consequences of this process, the religious basis of praxisitioners' ideological position seems to give them a strong sense that globalization can be directed. Groups associated with *al-Qa'ida* have tended to attract the most attention due to the violent methods they have adopted to bring about change, but less radical groups like the *Jamaat-I-Islami* and Muslim Brotherhood are also heavily involved within international settings. These groups are aiming to strengthen individual morality, discipline and piety, while working to mobilize support and replace overly Westernized Muslim governments (Hassan 2002). A key aim of these groups is to reinstate the *ummah* as the basis for collective identity and the primary loyalty, thus overcoming nationalist divisions at a time when modernization, industrialization and globalization are having a huge impact on Muslim lives. Hassan's research (2002) shows that a significant proportion of respondents share an *ummah* consciousness but increasingly this unity now has to acknowledge difference.

At a practical level the advent of global communications has been instrumental both in the broad Islamic resurgence and in the globalization of Islamic radicalism, exemplified by single issues like the reaction across Iran, Britain and the Indian sub-continent to the publication of *The Satanic Verses* in 1989 and the formation of international groups like *al-Qa'ida*. 'The possibility of achieving global religious systems has been facilitated by the emergence of modern forms of transport, communication and integration' (Turner 1994: 83). Turner (ibid.: 86) points out, 'while Islam had always claimed a universalistic status, it was, prior to the emergence of contemporary communication systems, actually unable to impose this type ['fundamentalist'] of uniformity and univeralism.' Although it is the case that intensified globalization has enabled global Islamic movements to emerge, it remains a mistake to refer to 'global uniformity'. Both moderate and radical Islamic groups still lack the central authority required to instil such conformity. It is clear though that a range of international groups across the world use modern technology and global communications to keep informed about global events, relay messages, raise finances and mobilize support. In addition, militant groups are also able to coordinate anonymous cells, undertake attacks and maintain contact within virtual movements that share ideology, strategies and resources (Vertigans 2004a; Vertigans and Sutton 2002a). It is very difficult, for instance, to imagine that the 11 September 2001 attacks on America could have been undertaken prior to contemporary levels of globalization and the use of modern transport, cellular phones and emails that enabled the well-planned and precisely timed operations to be carried out. The organization of groups such as *al-Qa'ida* and bin Laden's decision to name the terrorist coalition the 'World Islamic Front for the Jihad against the Jews and the Crusaders' have highlighted the internationalism of their campaign with sites and symbols attacked around the world and a cross-section of Western and Muslim nation-state actions and policies denounced.

Conclusion

To understand the contemporary nature of the Islamic resurgence, based upon a globalizing ideology that has been available for centuries, attention has to be paid to the changing roles and variety of socializing agents allied to an evolving global cultural context. Globalization processes are indeed instrumental in the Islamic resurgence and the production of increasing numbers of Islamic praxisitioners, as other studies have outlined. Moderate Muslims and Islamic praxisitioners clearly demonstrate an awareness of the kinds of global processes identified by Wallerstein, Robertson, Waters and others, as well as their long-term consequences for the Islamic faith. The theories we examined at the start of this chapter are therefore important in highlighting some of the features and consequences of economic globalization, cultural glocalization and increasing connectedness between and beyond nation-states. But it is not economic globalization, an awareness of globalization, postmodern culture or any other single cause that has brought about resurgent Islam or radical Islamic political groups aiming at fundamental change. Rather, socialization processes are being transformed in the present period, primarily due to developments in global communications and increasing transnational connections that are enabling greater circulation of information and ideas and economic, political, cultural, social and legal transformations in national societies that are placed differently in the international states system (examined in detail in chapter 6). As a consequence, the identity formation of Muslims now is significantly different from that of previous generations, resulting in enhanced religiosity within individual, community, national and international relations and activities.

The combination of these features is facilitating a more keenly felt comparison between contemporary Western and capitalist forms of globalization and their associated problems and an earlier period of Islamic expansion that is now perceived by praxisitioners and many moderates as successful globalization. Such a reading is a vital explanatory factor in explaining the contemporary legitimacy of Islam. Globalization has also contributed to greater comparisons within Islam. The *ummah* has been transformed, with globalization contributing to different peoples being brought together, information being more readily available and considerable cultural variations being highlighted. The realization that there are such significant vicissitudes is leading to further divisions within Islam. Moderates of different nationalities are sharing ideas and practices while praxisitioners are vehemently opposed to the lack of uniformity, defending what they consider to be 'pure' Islam. Both moderates and praxisitioners are finding evidence within global relations and communications to support their own discourses and thus strengthening the divisions between them.

5

Clash of Civilizations and Civilizing Processes

Introduction

Globalization theories suggest that international social processes are producing a significant movement towards closer integration and stronger bonds of interdependence between human societies. If they are right, then some form of global governance (Turner 2004) may eventually be required if solutions are to be found to global environmental problems, nuclear proliferation and a widening wealth gap between rich and poor nations. However, from the perspective of civilizational analysis, globalization processes can look very different. Rather than a centripetal trend towards closer ties and integration, some civilizationists perceive that centrifugal social forces are gaining the upper hand, leading to diversity, separation and possibly conflict. For these theorists, globalization is not spreading outwards from the West across the entire globe. Instead, Western culture and civilization is under threat and may well be in retreat over the very long term. If it is to survive in anything like its current form(s), then Westerners will have to take defensive action to preserve its distinctive features. At least, such is the logic of one strand of recent civilizational conflict analysis.

The question of how such opposing viewpoints can both be taken seriously is the subject of this chapter, which concentrates on the influential civilizational conflict thesis of Samuel Huntington (Huntington 1993a, 1998, 2000, 2004) and the critical reception of his work in the social sciences. The focus on Huntington's work is necessary as it has things to say about Islam and radical Islamic movements which chime with the concerns and fears of many

Western national governments and policy-makers, and possibly large sections of the public in these societies too. Such fears are of the unmaking of Western civilization and the destruction of civilized modes of conduct, less tolerance towards others and an Islamist suspicion of modernist movements towards equality, citizenship, multiculturalism and human rights. In a sense, these views echo the attitudes of cultural superiority held by many Western people, described by Norbert Elias in 1939 as one product of a 'civilizing process' during which Western societies came to be seen as the pinnacle of civilization in contrast to the less civilized or even barbaric behaviour of some non-Western societies. This same contrast between civilization and barbarism stands behind or underpins much civilizational conflict theory. In order to better understand why Huntington's work has been influential, this chapter brings Elias's developmental sociological perspective on civilizing processes to bear on the civilizational conflict thesis in the expectation that this will facilitate a more balanced understanding of the present global situation.

Returning to the long term

The systematic scholarly study of long-term human development is over a century old. It is concerned with the dynamics of long-term, large-scale social change, with the rise and fall of identifiable historical cultures and with comparisons between past and present civilizations. The French *Annales* School, associated with the enormously productive work on the *longue durée* of Braudel (1972 [1949], 1981–4) reinvigorated academic interest in long-term historical research. World-systems theory and research, though a more recent development stemming from the original work of Wallerstein (1974, 1980, 1989), has produced, through the extensions and revisions of others (Chase-Dunn 1992; Frank 1990; Gills 1995; Gills and Frank 1992), much insightful work which now rivals that of civilizationists and the *Annales* School, at least in the sheer breadth and scope of its inquiries. If we add in the work of world historians such as McNeill (1979, 1980), the large-scale comparative studies of Skocpol (1979), Moore (1966) and many others and the burgeoning literature on globalization (see chapter 4), then it is clear that there is an expanding interest among groups of historians and social scientists in human history and social change over very long periods of time.

Civilizationists disagree about their central concept of 'civilization'. For some, a civilization can be distinguished by the existence of several features that make up its 'essence'. These usually include language, religion, pattern of life, spatial dimension, ecological relationship (to the natural environment) and perhaps ethnic grouping. As defined by such multi-dimensional features, it is possible to identify a number of civilizations, some current, others long perished. Toynbee (1934–61) for example, classified between nineteen and 21 such civilizations (later revised downwards), whilst others estimate between eight and fifteen. One problem with this way of approaching human history is that civilizations may come to be seen as having lives of their own with 'identities' rather like individual personalities. This may then give rise to analyses that portray civilizations as self-contained, endogenously developing and coming into contact with each other or 'colliding'. This picture bears a remarkable similarity to the Western experience of self-contained individuals encased in their outer shells, also coming into contact with each other through 'inter-actions'. Elias describes this as a *'homo clausus'* experience that fails to recognize the social structural production (or 'sociogenesis') of such an individualized form of human experience which is not a human universal (Westen 1985).

More recently, however, Wilkinson (1995) has taken a somewhat different approach, defining civilizations as socio-political urban entities rather than cultural groupings (Sanderson 1995: 21–2). Wilkinson's definition is based on the criteria of 'connectedness'. This means that 'cities whose people are interacting intensely, significantly, and continuously thereby belong to the same civilization, even if their cultures are very dissimilar and their interactions mostly hostile.' On this definition, there is today only one 'Central Civilization', which contains many cultures and states, some of which are connected together in conflictual relationships. Nevertheless, despite the alternative definition and conclusions, Wilkinson's argument retains the language of mainstream civilization analysis. He suggests for instance that 'The single global civilization is . . . the current manifestation of a civilization that emerged about 1500 BC in the Near East, when Egyptian and Mesopotamian civilizations collided and fused. This new fusional entity has since then expanded over the entire planet and absorbed, on unequal terms, all other previously independent civilizations' (Wilkinson 1995: 46). Again, whether this is the most effective way of studying long-term human development is open to question as the reification of 'civilizations' may close off many other fruitful research avenues, an issue we return to later in the chapter. Nonetheless, since the 1980s there has been a resurgence of interest in civilizational studies with the ideas of key early civilizationists such as Toynbee and Sorokin being reassessed. Also, current debates between civilizationists and those working with or revising Wallerstein's world-systems theory (Sanderson 1995; Frank 1998) could lead to a greater measure of agreement on definitional questions, though the differences between the two research programmes are probably as significant as areas of agreement.

It was into this climate of a growing scholarly interest in very long-term social change, the emergence and development of world-systems and comparative civilizational analysis that Huntington's controversial thesis intervened. This thesis can be stated in deceptively simple terms. It predicts that the twenty-first century may well witness conflicts involving not just ethnic groups or nation-states, as witnessed throughout the twentieth century, but entire 'civilizations'. The new century will not conform to the patterns of conflict that characterized the old. If conflicts do escalate to clashes between civilizations, then Huntington's argument is that cultural distinctions, including religious beliefs and symbols, will be the most important motivating factors amongst peoples as well as key sources of identification and conflict. In his own words, 'Culture is to Die for' (1993b: 190). Inverting the focus on the political sphere within mainstream international relations (IR) theory, Huntington's emphasis on the significance of culture could usefully have expanded the remit of IR research. However, his argument instead tends to reduce political processes to cultural conflicts, with cultures elevated to relatively static thing-like entities (Harrison and Huntington 2001). This has generally been seen as unhelpful (Chiozza 2002; Wedeen 2003).

The basic thesis of increasingly central cultural conflicts has been influential in Western foreign policy circles as well as in academic discourse. The invasion of Iraq by a 'coalition of the willing' under American leadership has led to international Muslim protests, thus fuelling an increasing mistrust, resentment and widely reported hatred towards the West, though particularly towards the USA. Equally, American and European suspicion of and anger towards Muslims, many of whom reside in the West, has been exacerbated since the 11 September 2001 attack on the World Trade Center in New York as part of what Halliday (2002) refers to as 'anti-Muslimism'. Similarly, the emphasis upon the distinct cultural clash leading to conflicts between Western and Islamic 'civilizations' can be found across Muslim societies where 'the West' is increasingly seen as an enemy. Such mutual suspicion and resentment appears to reinforce Huntington's view that the greatest danger to the West comes from Muslims and the greatest danger to Muslims comes from the

West. Yet this kind of analysis only provides a partial, selective and incomplete picture of what is really happening (Turner 2002), and a first step towards building a more empirically valid picture is to demonstrate why and where Huntington's civilizational analysis goes awry. In doing so the focus will be on Huntington's application of his general thesis to understanding the specific challenge of what he calls 'the Muslim World'.

In his analysis of world civilizations, Huntington undertakes a comparative analysis, exploring what factors link people together and conversely what separates them. In this respect he challenges sociologists, anthropologists and historians who have tended to avoid using the concept of 'civilization', relying instead on the wider concept of 'culture' (Schäfer 2001). As Williams (1985: 59) argues, this is because civilization must be 'contrasted with *savagery* or barbarism', and yet Western 'civilization' has itself generated appalling acts of destruction, brutality and senseless killings as two world wars and the history of colonialism demonstrate. An implicit belief in the superiority of Western 'civilization' underlies much of Huntington's account and he is at pains to stress that 'identity at any level – personal, tribal, racial, civilizational – can only be defined in relation to an "other", a different person, tribe, race or civilization' (Huntington 1998: 129). Huntington often uses 'culture' and 'civilization' interchangeably, noting that these concepts share many common elements including religion, language, history and customs, though he is aware that the two terms are also relatively distinct, civilization being 'the highest cultural grouping of people and the broadest level of cultural identity people have' (ibid.: 43). Civilizations are therefore cultures 'writ large', as it were.

We should remember though, that usage of the term 'civilization' in this way, to describe a fairly homogeneous, though dynamic cultural entity, only took off after 1756 (Mazlish 2001). For Elias (2000 [1939]), the concept of civilization initially arose as a self-description of eighteenth-century modernizing European societies, enabling a normative contrast between their own civilization and non-modern societies. Civilization and civilized norms of behaviour came to be seen as the pinnacle of humanity, the farthest point yet reached in human progress. The discovery of older civilizations could then be interpreted from the standpoint of the present. Comparisons could be made between Egyptian, Greco-Roman, Chinese or Indian civilizations and Western modernity, with the latter as benchmark providing the criteria to facilitate comparison. In this way, the idea of large-scale human civilizations is rooted in reflexive attempts to understand Western modernity's distinctive features or perhaps its perceived decline.

Islam in civilizational conflict theory

Using a broadly culturalist classification system, Huntington divides the current 'world of civilizations' into seven, possibly eight, distinct groups: Western; Latin American; Islamic; Sinic; Hindu; Orthodox; Japanese; with the African considered to be a potential eighth civilization. This is not particularly original, but his main hypothesis is that 'culture and cultural identities, which at the broadest level are civilizational identities, are shaping patterns of cohesion, disintegration, and conflict in the post-Cold War world' (Huntington 1998: 20). He adds that 'in this new world order the most pervasive, important and dangerous conflicts will not be between social classes, rich and poor, or other economically defined groups, but between people belonging to different cultural entities' (ibid.: 28). As identifications based on political ideology and association with superpower relations are replaced by wider cultural identifications, 'Peoples and countries with similar cultures are coming together. Peoples and countries with different cultures are coming apart' (ibid.: 125). The possibility therefore exists that conflicts will occur at the 'fault-lines' between civilizations.

Huntington's analysis commences at the beginning of the modern era (around 1500 AD) and he argues that the Western nation-states 'constituted a multi-polar international system within Western civilization . . . and at the same time . . . also expanded, conquered, colonized, or decisively influenced every other civilization' (Huntington 1998: 21). This is to a large extent correct, but crucially he omits the impact of the 'Muslim' Ottoman Empire, which, as identified in chapter 4, was the dominant power within the international system until the eighteenth century. Huntington does later acknowledge that the Ottomans had considerable control within what was than thought of as Europe, but he does not address what this means for his thesis. He also qualifies Ottoman influence by adding that it 'was not considered a member of the European international system' (ibid.). This overlooks the huge impact of the Ottomans within the European 'international system' as the developing and more systematic international relationships generated higher levels of interaction.

With considerable stress on more recent historical developments, Huntington focuses predominantly on the Cold War and the post-Cold War period, speculating on what may happen in future. To this extent, his work is in part a modern version of 1960s and 1970s futurology (the extrapolation of present trends into the future, itself now ironically out of fashion). The tensions of the Cold War were based around ideological differences and economic development which cut across other distinctions, such as those between the First, Second and Third World categories of nation-states as well as other types of specifically cultural and national distinctions relating to language, religion, dress and so on. However, following the Iranian Revolution of 1979, Huntington argues that an inter-civilizational quasi-war has developed between Islam and the West. Throughout the 1980s therefore, inter-civilizational conflicts increasingly replaced the politically oriented Cold War conflicts between Communist and capitalist states. But as Huntington notes, these groups and states belong to different ethnicities and nationalities that are often in conflict over political power and economic resources. Many of the escalations into wars are arguably rooted in perceived threats to national identities, nation-states as 'survival units' and resource distribution rather than large-scale civilizational identities. It is therefore difficult to understand how these conflicts differ from many of those that existed both before and during the Cold War.

It is also unclear in Huntington's account how the ending of the Cold War actually produced the inter-civilizational conflict between Islam and the West. To take his own example, the Iranian Revolution of 1979, and subsequent conflict with America, occurred prior to the ending of the Cold War international state system which, as he points out, was brought to an end during the late 1980s (ibid.: 21). Consequently, the revolutionary conflict cannot be neatly attributed to a conflict between civilizations, nor can it be seen as a consequence of the ending of the Cold War. Indeed, something of the reverse may be the case, with American support for the Shah, given Iran's strategic Middle East location, forming a significant factor leading towards the revolution, in so far as this support was born out of the specific figuration of Cold War forces and its *realpolitik*. The Iranian Revolution was principally the outcome of an uprising by a wide cross-section of the population in reaction to enormous social, political and economic problems. Disparate social groups eventually united to overcome the Shah's regime, widely perceived as tyrannical and corrupt. It is the case that religious groups were significant elements during this process. Nevertheless, it can be argued that so were nationalists, Marxists, liberal reformers and feminists. It was only after the Shah had fled and the pre-revolutionary alliance fractured that the revolution became identifiably 'Islamic' in character (Bayat 1987; Keddie 1983). Similarly, Huntington's wider claims regarding the post-Cold War rise of religious fundamentalism, particularly Islamic 'fundamentalism', also lack strong empirical support. The available evidence suggests that this was not an inevitable consequence of the end of the Cold War. In another part of the thesis, Huntington contradicts his argument, stating that 'the most obvious, most salient, and most powerful cause of the global religious resurgence is precisely what was supposed to cause the death of religion: the processes of social, economic and cultural modernization that swept across the world in the second half of the twentieth century' (1998: 97). Huntington does not explain how this explanation and time period fits into the civilizational paradigm and his 'end of the Cold War' argument.

After emphasizing the dangers present to the world order, Huntington states that 'the components of order in today's more complex and heterogeneous world are found within and between civilizations. The world will be ordered on the basis of civilizations, or not at all' (ibid.: 156). The nation-state will remain the principal entity within international relations but will have its identity and interests shaped by its civilizational heritage. Identity plays a central role in the relations between states, defining their wider associations and in particular their friends and enemies. The stress on state identities leads Huntington (ibid.: 125) to proclaim what he considers to be a transformation in the fundamental geo-political question. Instead of asking, 'Which side are you on?' – a political identification – the post-Cold War question becomes 'Who are you?' – a cultural or civilizational identification. In some ways this is a return to a past period, specifically the pre-Cold War period. As Huntington says, 'wars between clans, tribes, ethnic groups, religious communities and nations have been prevalent in every era and in every civilization because they are rooted in the identities of people' (ibid.: 252). Throughout the period of the Cold War this pattern changed as political ideological allegiance overrode civilizational factors, though the specific reasons for this are not spelled out. This lack of clarity becomes more confusing when Huntington claims that the Soviet Union, amongst others, 'came apart' 'because it was united by ideology or historical circumstance but divided by civilization' (ibid.: 28). What this argument overlooks is that the Soviet Union imposed a regime on peoples, the majority of whom belonged to the same 'civilization'; there was no ideological unity. Of course, ultimately independence from the Communist regime was achieved. It is more consonant with the evidence to suggest that politics, economics and nationalism were the main drivers for both the formation and the break-up of the Soviet Union, rather than a reassertion of civilizational identification. Such a position would also be a more realistic way of considering the demands for independence within Europe, for example in Scotland, Northern Ireland or the Basque region.

Huntington argues that, during times of identity crisis, 'what counts for people are blood and belief, faith and family. People rally to those with similar ancestry, religion, language, values, and institutions and distance themselves from those with different ones' (ibid.: 126). So, for instance, Austria, Finland and Sweden are culturally part of the West (used here interchangeably with Europe), but during the Cold War these states remained unaligned. Since the end of the Cold War these nations have once again been able to join 'their cultural kin' within the European Union. This apparent rallying of different civilizations around cultural bonds overlooks the considerable number of examples where nations within the same category, according to Huntington's classification, develop relations with nations belonging to other 'cultural kinships'. An obvious recent example here is the 2003 invasion of Iraq by American-led forces. If studied in isolation, the involvement of Western nations in the coalition, together with widespread Muslim protests against the invasion, could be seen as solid evidence in support of Huntington's argument. In a similar manner, Huntington's discussion of the reaction to America's bombing of Iraq in 1993 identifies responses that seemed to legitimize his civilizational thesis because 'Israel and Western European governments strongly supported the raid; Russia accepted it as "justified" self-defense; China expressed "deep concern"; Saudi Arabia and the Gulf emirates said nothing; other Muslim governments, including that of Egypt, denounced it as another example of Western double standards' (ibid.: 251). However, this is only a partial description of events and a more detailed examination reveals something quite different. Closer attention identifies that it was not possible to categorize Muslim reactions as a generic civilizational response as these varied considerably, from endorsement to silence and deep hostility and outright resentment. If the reactions of individuals were taken into consideration within the Western nation-states, then opinion ranged from support to outright opposition, irrespective of 'cultural kinship'. The 'coalition of the willing' assembled by the USA in 2003 included states from across Huntington's civilizational categories. Huntington does acknowledge that cross-civilization alliances are possible, and he draws attention to numerous examples that he adopts in support of the thesis. For example, 'the call by Iran's president for alliances with China and India so that "we can have the last word on international events"' (ibid.: 39), is used as evidence in support of the civilization paradigm, despite seemingly demonstrating the opposite. This alliance was more likely an example of a typically pragmatic approach to global politics.

Over time, the cross-civilizational alliances are expected to become weaker and increasingly less meaningful. However, such a thesis gains little support from recognition of the wide-ranging opposition, particularly within Western nations, to the invasion of Iraq. In short, during the most recent case of armed conflict within global relations, cross-civilizational alliances do not seem to have become significantly weaker or less meaningful. This conclusion is clearly at odds with Huntington's position, which is that, despite multiple sources of identification which may compete with or reinforce each other, 'in the contemporary world, cultural identification is dramatically increasing in importance compared to other dimensions of identity' (ibid.: 128). Individual identifications rooted in culture and ultimately civilizations mean that people are becoming enmeshed within and drawn into the civilizational clashes that Huntington argues will become the central feature of global politics. In a comment that could just as easily apply to the Cold War period, he states, 'people use politics not just to advance their interests but also to define their identity' (ibid.: 21). Again, if we apply this notion to the recent example of the invasion of Iraq, it can be noted that not only did nations act 'against' (what should have been) their 'own kinship' but so did millions of individuals campaigning against the invasion as part of a global opposition, even in nations such as Britain and Spain, whose governments provided military support.

Huntington's analysis is clearly influenced by recent scholarship on globalization. He argues that the significance of 'the tribe' is increasing at the expense of the nation-state, which he believes to be experiencing problems of legitimacy (see Habermas 1976). This situation is, he argues, 'reflected in the fact that whilst numerous conflicts occurred between Muslim *groups* during the years after World War II, major wars between Muslim *states* were rare' (Huntington 1998: 175). On a broader level, attempts to foster Muslim civilizational unity through international conferences, congresses and leagues ultimately failed in the task of generating Islamic cohesion. Huntington attributes this to two paradoxes. First, the competition between different Muslim states to take the leading role worked to thwart any emerging unity. Second, the *ummah* that in theory would be the ultimate aim of any international movement is a concept rooted in a unified community that, in its purest form, de-legitimizes the existence of the nation-state. Consequently, any nation-states seeking to achieve the *ummah* would in the process destroy their own structure, institutions and territorial boundaries. These points are both valid but need to be developed to include the crucial pragmatic reasons that have prevented any deep-rooted unity emerging and which are linked to differences in language, culture, religious interpretations, ethnicity, tribal allegiances and strategic location. In short, such distinctions and divisions demonstrate that it is empirically inadequate to base social scientific analysis on the notion of an assumed generic 'Muslim civilization' (Turner 2003).

What unity exists seems to be related more to pragmatic political decisions rather than deep feelings of civilizational kinship. The despotic, nominally 'Sunni', regime of Saddam Hussein in Iraq (despite the majority of the population being Shi'a Muslims) invaded its 'Sunni' neighbour Kuwait and was involved in a long and brutal war with the majority 'Shi'a Muslim' Iran (1980–8). Huntington acknowledges that Iraq was involved in conflict, though he fails to explain why this occurred and overlooks other relevant conflicts such as that between the Jordanian military and the PLO in 1970, sectarian violence (with external support) between Sunnis and Shi'ites during the Lebanese civil war and disputes and protests across and within Muslim nation-states in reaction to the Iraqi invasion of Kuwait. The significance of support provided by some Muslim states to non-Muslims is also ignored. Thus, Iran supported 'Christian' Armenia against 'Shi'ite' Azerbaijan and does not support Pakistan or Muslim Kashmiris in their clashes with India (Halliday 2002). Turkey increasingly sought to trade with the Gulf and Turkic republics, largely for economic reasons and partly to offset difficulties during accession negotiations with the European Union (EU), which Huntington describes as 'its frustrating and humiliating role as a beggar pleading for membership in the West' (1998: 178). Today, support for the EU includes the Turkish government of the mildly religious Justice and Development Party, whilst the secular military is increasingly becoming opposed to closer ties. Turkey has also, to the consternation of many of its neighbours, strengthened its relations with Israel, again for pragmatic reasons. Further, Muslim nations did not support the Turkish invasion of Cyprus. American support for Bosnia (an 'anomaly' according to Huntington) demonstrates that it is also possible for the West to support the opposing 'civilization' for instrumental reasons. Such is the tenor of Huntington's line of reasoning that anomalies to the central thrust of his argument are perceived as pragmatically based and therefore not fundamental, whilst actions that may support his main argument are viewed as unconditional acts of civilizational kinship. The lack of balance is, at times, quite striking.

Underlying Huntington's civilizational conflict thesis are assumptions about human nature. Specifically, he believes that conflict is ubiquitous because 'it is human to hate. For self-definition and motivation people need enemies: business competitors, rivals in achievement or political opponents. They naturally distrust and see as threats those who are different and have the capability to harm them' (ibid.: 130). With no sense of irony just a few pages earlier, Huntington notes that 'sweeping generalizations are always dangerous and often wrong' (ibid.: 111). Nonetheless, his view of human nature could find support from the millions of Muslims and Westerners who do mistrust each other. Many Muslims consider America, in particular, to be a threat to their interests, particularly given its military capability, whilst many Westerners perceive Islam to be a violent religion that breeds terrorism. However, it is difficult to see this as the simple result of a biologically driven propensity shaped by civilizational pressures for identification. The inter- and intra-civilizational protests against the invasion of Iraq highlight that the situation is much more complex and multi-faceted than civilizational conflict theory allows for. Mistrust clearly does exist, but this is shared to varying degrees across the world and cannot be isolated to particular civilizations. However, concerning relations between Islam and the West, Huntington notes that 'some Westerners, including President Bill Clinton, have argued that the West does not have problems with Islam but only violent Islamist extremists. Fourteen hundred years of history demonstrate otherwise' (ibid.: 209), and that 'the underlying problem for the West is not Islamic fundamentalism. It is Islam, a different civilization whose people are convinced of the superiority of their culture and are obsessed with the inferiority of their power. The problem for Islam is not the CIA or the U.S. Department of Defense. It is the West' (ibid.: 217). At this point it seems even Huntington is confused about his own argument. Civilizational conflict between Islam and the West is 'fourteen hundred years old', yet in a response to Russett et al. (2000) he argued that 'throughout much of history most wars have been intracivilizational' (Huntington 2000: 610). These two arguments are clearly contradictory. Huntington dismisses Russett et al.'s critique by pointing out that the 'Huntington thesis' is only meant to apply to the post-Cold War world: 'That is what the book is about' (2000: 609). But Huntington himself has already strayed far beyond this strictly self-limiting time-frame. There is a persistent temptation to overstretch the post-Cold War analysis and to merge this with a contemporary normative position (Toprak 1996). That is, Huntington's work, particularly since publication of the original thesis, displays a strong tendency to impose his own political position into the 'clash of civilizations' argument.

For militant Muslims the problem of Islam and the West is crystallized in the division of the world into two categories: the world of Islam, *Dar al-Islam*, and the enemy world or world at war, the *Dar al-Harb*. It is not only Western commentators who have made use of the term 'civilization'. For example, in the letter left behind by the 11 September 2001 terrorists, reference was made to the [Western] 'civilization of the disbelievers' (reported in Paz, 2001b). However, as Halliday (2002: 204) remarks, this division has not been the case since the eighth century, whilst today, 'few Muslims . . . look at the world in such generalized and starkly divisive terms.' This conclusion is borne out in an empirical study amongst Middle Eastern Arab populations of the reasoning for the 11 September attacks on America. Sidanius et al.'s survey of Lebanese students at the University of Beirut (2004: 403) compared their responses to two positions. The first explained the attacks as the result of a 'clash of civilizations' or 'inherent conflict between Muslim and Western values'. The second drew attention to an alternative explanation, stressing an 'antidominance reaction to perceived American and Israeli oppression of Arabs in general and Palestinians in particular'. Although a small-scale survey, the conclusion is that 'Rather than regarding the present conflict between East and West as intractably framed in cultural and millennium terms, our results suggest that, at least among certain Middle East subelites, this conflict is actually framed in political and policy terms' (Sidanius et al. 2004: 414). We can say that Muslim opinion is much more diverse than simply the views of a relatively small group of radical praxisitioners.

As representative of his argument, Huntington selects some well-known examples of conflict between Muslims and the West. Starting with the Crusades and the battles that took place as the Ottoman Empire developed, he uses data to argue that 50 per cent of wars involving pairs of states of different religions between 1820 and 1929, were wars between Muslims and Christians (Huntington 1998:

211). Clearly there have been many conflicts between Muslim and Christian states, but if we examine the fourteen-hundred-year period in which the two religions have co-existed, then serious conflicts are actually few in number. In short, for the overwhelming majority of this time, Muslims and Christians have lived peaceably together and, as Chirot (2001: 349) points out, have formed many alliances that cut across religion and culture. In several empirical studies of the civilizational conflict thesis, only a very small percentage of conflicts are recognized as potentially 'civilizational' (Chiozza 2002; Fox 2001; Russett et al. 2000). In relation to the predicted increase in civilizational conflict following the end of the Cold War, no trend in this direction is discernible. Indeed, intra-civilizational conflict seems more likely, and just because conflict takes place between nations defined in religious terms, it by no means follows that the conflict is really *about* or is *defined by* religious adherence. If we subtract the number of conflicts which have been land disputes, related to claims for resources, colonialism and nationalism, then the number of wars that revolved around religion, culture and civilization would be very small. In Huntington's new era, territory is viewed as particularly important, although it is unclear how this is different from previous causes of conflict, leading to what he refers to as 'fault-line conflicts' between neighbours belonging to different civilizations. In line with his general thesis this means conflict between kin groups, including nation-states. Islam, he argues, has bloody frontiers. However, as Halliday (2002: 79) observes, Huntington does not provide 'an accurate account of where the responsibility for this bloodiness may lie – in some cases prime responsibility lies with Muslims, in others not. In Bosnia, Kosovo, Palestine, Kashmir, to take but four examples, it does not.'

Huntington (1998) also argues that following the Iranian Revolution, an intercivilizational quasi war developed between Islam and the West. He acknowledges that not all of 'the Islamic world' has been fighting all of 'the West' and simply names two fundamentalist states (Iran and Sudan), three non-fundamentalist states (Iraq, Libya and Syria), plus a wide range of Islamist organizations gaining financial support from other Muslim countries that have been fighting against the United States, Britain, France, other Western states and Israel. These Islamic states and groups represent a small minority of Muslims globally and, whilst acknowledging this to be the case, Huntington still feels justified in describing this 'quasi-war' as a general one between Islam and the West. The claim becomes even more difficult to sustain when examining motivations for involvement of the named states, three of which Huntington recognizes as secular and therefore not Islamically oriented. For example, Syria's activities have been predominantly directed at Israel, with the return of the Golan Heights its key strategic objective. Iraq's warlike actions during Saddam Hussein's reign were largely concentrated upon other Muslim groups and states, ranging from Iraqi Kurds and Shi'ites to Iran and Kuwait. The 'fundamentalist' Iran has also undertaken and supported attacks against other nation-states but these are connected to geo-politics of the area and to counter Saudi influence in the region. All three of these states are linked through their support for the Palestinians and some of their actions can be interpreted as helping towards this aim. Whilst there is sympathy for the Palestinians, as there is elsewhere in the world, these actions need to be placed in a broader context that takes in what that support means to the nation-states in terms of popular perceptions and wider influences. In the case of Syria, for example, the creation of an independent Palestinian state would ease its long-standing refugee problem.

The 'nature' of Islamic civilization?

Notwithstanding these significant criticisms, Huntington concludes that the Islamic civilization has a propensity for violence. This is, of course, not an original argument which as Esposito (1999) and Halliday (2002) have noted, can be traced back to images formed during the Crusades. Huntington says that Islam is a 'religion of the sword' that glorifies military virtues. The spread of Islam across Asia, Africa and Europe led to Muslims living in close proximity with people of other religions with whom they came into conflict. Muslims in Muslim nation-states have problems with non-Muslims. The latter have less difficulty in adapting to and living with each other than in adapting to and living with Muslims (Huntington 1998). Muslims are 'indigestible' to non-Muslims. Such overly simple arguments can be dismissed in turn. First, Islam's origins did include a militaristic element, but territorial expansion was also achieved through commerce, cooperation and alliances with non-Muslims. As Turner argues, Max Weber appears to have misunderstood ancient Islam as being carried forward by a 'warrior stratum'. More recent scholarship has conclusively demonstrated that

Islam was primarily urban, commercial and literate. Mecca was strategically placed on the trade routes between the Mediterranean and the Indian

Ocean; Muhammed's own tribe, the Quraysh, had achieved a dominant political position based on their commercial strength in the region. The Prophet himself had been employed on the caravans which brought Byzantine commodities to the Meccan market. The Qur'an itself is steeped in a commercial terminology. (Turner 1993: 51)

Islam was not and is not a 'religion of the sword', and, unlike Weber, Huntington does have access to recent historical sociological research in this area. Islamic theology clearly can be used in support of violent actions, but so of course can references and specific examples from the Bible, Torah and other defining religious texts.

Second, as the development of the Ottoman Empire shows, Muslim rulers were generally much more restrained, civilized and considerate in their treatment of colonized peoples than, for example, Europeans of the period, including peaceful relations with those who did not convert. As Huntington himself notes, in places like the Balkans, the Serbs were able to retain their own beliefs rather than being forced to convert to Islam. It is not a sufficient explanation simply to state that people of different 'civilizations' living in close proximity is a *cause* of conflict. This proximity may enable conflicts to spread more easily of course, but this does not explain the causes of conflicts that require detailed historical and empirical analysis. Finally, Huntington provides an example of the assimilation problems of the ethnic Chinese in South East Asian Muslim nation-states to support his argument. However, the focus upon civilizational analysis neglects the underlying social, economic and political causes of such assimilation problems. For instance, the 1969 riots in Malaysia were predominantly fuelled by the economic dominance of the ethnic Chinese and the resentment this caused to the relatively marginalized Muslim Malays, who were also the largest ethnic group. The historical legacy of Muslim treatment of other religions means that the argument regarding 'indigestibility' of Muslims is wildly inaccurate. There is some evidence that mistrust between Muslims and Westerners may currently be heightened, but this does not lend support to Huntington's thesis of an inevitable civilizational antagonism.

The civilizational conflict thesis tends to simplify and overgeneralize. This serves to highlight its empirical and historical failings and subsequent misunderstandings regarding the character of 'Islamic civilization'. For example, Huntington seems unaware that Islam can take on the role of an ideology for many believers (Vertigans 2003). It is incorrect therefore to state that 'no other civilization [beyond Western] has generated a significant political ideology' (Huntington 1998: 53–4). Islam can provide an ideological framework for life conduct, but for the overwhelming majority of Muslims, Islam is one element amongst other loyalties, such as ethnic or national identification, which may take precedence. This can be seen in Arab nationalism that united people across Egypt, Syria, Jordan and Iraq prior to defeat in the 1967 war with Israel. Huntington acknowledges this point, but fails to realize the extent of differences in ideology, beliefs, practices, goals and approach and, as explained below, the extent to which secularization has penetrated Muslim societies and the conflict this causes between secularists and praxisitioners. Examples of the tremendous variations to be found within Muslim nation-states and communities disqualify his generalizations, particularly the concept of 'Islamic civilization' or a 'Muslim World' as reifications of cultural processes.

The emphasis placed upon 'the Muslim world' in all forms of Western and praxist communication is telling and often gives the impression of a unified, homogenous threat that simply does not exist. This characterization can also be found in the work of other influential American scholars such as Daniel Pipes, who, with Mimi Stillman (2002), brackets together American Islamic organizations, politicized Islam and violent Islamic terrorism in arguing for US action against Muslims. By equal measure, there is rarely any mention in the West about the 'Christian world'. Similar attempts to present Islam as homogeneous can be noted in the political rhetoric of radical Muslims such as Osama bin Laden, who seek to overcome diverse interpretations of doctrine and the many social and theological divisions in order to expand their levels of support. Even in the neighbouring countries of Iran and Iraq, there have been very different forms of Islam. In Iraq, considerable differences can be identified within national boundaries, perhaps too simplistically along Sunni Kurd, Sunni Arab and Shi'a Arab lines. Equally therefore, Huntington's notion of a generic 'Islamic culture' which is largely used to explain the failure of democracy to emerge in much of the Muslim world and 'the inhospitable nature of Islamic culture and society to Western liberal concepts' (Huntington 1998: 114) are largely mythical. Finally in this section, many peoples who live within states that are predominantly Muslim, who are agnostic or belong to other religions, but who still share some loyalties with Muslims, again cannot fit easily within Huntington's thesis.

The civilizational conflict thesis fails to explain, first, why, if Islamic culture is largely anti-democratic, democracy *has* developed within nations with predominantly Muslim populations, such as Turkey, Bangladesh and Malaysia. Islamists have secured power through democratic elections within professional associations across the Middle East. Second, the argument cannot explain why increasing numbers of Muslims in diverse national contexts across the Middle East and North Africa are demanding democracy. Lastly, the cancellation of democracy in Algeria by secularists supported by Western states fearing the election of the Muslim coalition, the Islamic Salvation Front (FIS), shows that support for democratic ideals does not reside within particular civilizations but often depends on political decisions, in this instance, the need to prevent an Islamic party from taking power democratically.

In seeking to explain what he refers to as a 'global religious resurgence', Huntington argues it is 'both a product of and effort to come to grips with modernization' (ibid.: 116). Setting aside the problems this generalization causes, in the case of resurgent Islam there is some substance in the factors he identifies. As a consequence of modernization, 'long-standing sources of identity and systems of authority are disrupted. People move from the countryside into the city, become separated from their roots, and take new jobs or no job. They need new sources of identity, new forms of stable community, and new sets of moral precepts to provide them with a sense of meaning and purpose' (ibid.: 97). There are, however a number of important points that need to be raised about this. Many migrants already possess a religious identity and moral precepts prior to their move to urban areas; the main difference is that they are no longer quite so invisible. It is also not necessarily true that 'recent migrants to the cities generally need emotional, social and material support and guidance, which religious groups provide more than any other source' (ibid.: 101). The resurgence is not just a consequence of migrant behaviour. Long-standing urban dwellers also play prominent roles, which usually include leadership.

In addition to modernization and its corollaries – urbanization, social mobilization, literacy, education and improved communications – Huntington argues that the resurgence of Islam has been driven by tremendous rates of population growth (ibid.: 116). This is important because 'for years to come Muslim populations will be disproportionately young populations, with a notable demographic bulge of teenagers and people in their twenties'; it is particularly significant as, for Huntington, young people are 'the protagonists of protest, instability, reform and revolution' (ibid.: 117). The role of young people can be overstated though; to use both of his own examples, whilst young people were important in the Iranian Revolution they were just one group amongst many and certainly did not play the leading role, and in the Algerian postponed elections, there is no data available to support Huntington's view that 'it is not perhaps entirely coincidental' that the proportion of youth amongst the population reached 20 per cent. Certainly the FIS was not, at that point, a party that would generally appeal to protagonists of 'instability and revolution', nor would a significant proportion of the young have been able to vote because they would have been below the minimum age of eighteen. The growth in population is however a crucial issue for other reasons which Huntington fails to develop, namely the massive pressures it places on the infrastructure of a society in terms of employment opportunities, health services, utilities, transport, welfare and education. There are also demographic changes to take into account. Kepel (2004) has pointed out that during the 1990s the birth rate dropped dramatically in many Muslim societies as people grappled with accommodation shortages and lifestyle choices.

In the short term, Huntington clearly believes that the Islamic resurgence is a major problem for the West but

> at some point the Islamic resurgence will subside and fade into history. That is most likely to happen when the demographic impulse powering it weakens in the second and third decades of the twenty-first century. At that time, the ranks of militants, warriors and migrants will diminish, and the high levels of conflict within Islam and between Muslims and others are likely to decline. (ibid.: 120–1)

The demographic 'impulse' is an important influence and will continue to be so because, whilst the sharp increases in population may not continue, the former baby boomers are likely to reproduce, with further implications for the state infrastructure. It is also interesting to note that whilst Huntington earlier refers to 'fundamentalism' being only one component of a wider resurgence, he reverts to the more general depiction of Muslims as violent extremists and migrants who are invariably considered to be the excluded and disoriented, or more implicitly part of life's losers. It seems, however, that the resurgence will continue until the grounds for it are undermined and people are no longer socialized into Islamic norms and values, legitimized by local and global interactions and activities. Equally, the de-legitimization of Islam as an ideology, for example through more involvement in established political systems, could have a similar outcome. At present, the latter seems more likely, though ironically the considerable activities undertaken by the West to prevent Islamic movements taking power is contributing further to the legitimization of Islam and limiting the chances that it will become de-legitimized.

In summary, Huntington's extremely influential thesis is inherently flawed and is based on selective readings of historical and contemporary events and statistical materials. Huntington has, in many instances, simply expressed the common-sense views of many people and given them an academic gloss. The extreme views on both sides readily accept the inevitability of confrontation, that cultural distinctions are the basis for conflict and hold that the other is inherently threatening its own existence. In many ways these views are developing into a self-fulfilling prophecy. Sociologists have a responsibility to provide a more balanced understanding of Islam that is able to explain why conflicts have sometimes arisen as well as putting such conflicts into the long-term historical context. Hopefully, this book as a whole brings together the importance of globalization, international transfers of people, technology, capital, ideas and ways of behaviour, as well as changing socialization processes that are linking together such seemingly disparate groups of people and altering our perceptions of 'civilizations'. One way towards this goal is to consider an alternative study of 'civilization' stemming from the work of Norbert Elias.

Up against the limits of civilizationism and world-systems theory

Since the 1980s, a debate has continued between those working within a civilizationist perspective and others pursuing a research programme established by Wallerstein and rooted in his world-systems theory. Whilst civilizationists and world-systems theorists both take account of the *longue durée*, or very long-term development of human societies, they differ on what constitutes the appropriate 'unit of analysis' (Sanderson 1995). For civilizationists, whole civilizations are the most effective conceptual units, though there is no single and accepted definition of 'civilization'. As described above, civilizations have been seen by some writers as cultural entities and as socio-political forms of connectedness by others (Tiryakian 2001). Huntington's work clearly constitutes a strong interpretation of the former, which points up some of the problems with such an approach.

For world-systems theorists, the focus on culturally categorized civilizations tends to reify dynamic social processes and is not a realistic conceptualization. Instead, world-systems theory concentrates on the spreading capitalist division of labour established within expanding spatial boundaries (Wallerstein 1974). In this sense we may speak of several previous 'world-systems' but also perhaps, of a single world-system based on the process of 'ceaseless capital accumulation' over the last 5,000 years (Frank 1998; Frank and Gills 1993). Such a perspective avoids the tendency to reification of cultural civilizationist theories but has ironically been forced to reintroduce the concept of culture in *ad hoc* ways to counterbalance the world-systems emphasis on economic processes and modes of production (Robertson and Lechner 1985). The idea of 'ceaseless' accumulation is just one example of the introduction of a cultural value – ceaselessness – as a causal concept, from outside the world-systems perspective. This move may well be necessary, but it can also be seen as ultimately theoretically unsatisfactory (Roudometof and Robertson 1995: 275).

Given the problems of one-sidedness in these various accounts, in recent years several scholars have either made use of Elias's theory of civilizing processes or suggested that his 'process' or 'figurational' sociology might offer some advantages over other approaches (Roudometof and Robertson 1995: 279–92; Tiryakian 2001: 286–7; see also several contributions to the special issue of *International Sociology*, 'Rethinking Civilizational Analysis', 2001, 16(3)). Such usage and recognition marks an appreciation of the potential of Elias's sociology for understanding and explaining globalization processes and long-term social development, but it needs to be extended and revised in order to bring the contemporary interest in relations between 'Islam and the West' within its purview. In the next section, Elias's theoretical perspective is outlined as potentially useful in studying relations between 'Islam and the West'. Although such a detailed analysis lies outside the scope of this book, chapter 6 makes an initial attempt to explore some of the contours of a 'figurational' analysis of the contemporary Islamic resurgence, pointing towards ways of better understanding the present global situation. What we can usefully do here is outline the main elements of such an approach.

The process of civilization

As is now quite well known, Elias (2000 [1939]) described the main finding of his theoretical-empirical study into changing behavioural patterns and codes of manners and etiquette as the 'civilizing process'. Over several centuries, individual people gradually came to experience a heightened sense of their unique individuality, developed a more complex and even control of emotional outbursts and in consequence, a perception of the superiority of their own (Western) behavioural codes and manners over those other 'non-civilized' societies that did not seem to share them. Elias illustrates these changes with a series of 'micro-level' examples concerned with self and emotional controls over natural bodily functions such as spitting, urination and defecation and recourse to interpersonal violence and aggression. However, such changes were set within the context of the gradual elimination of competing feudal and regional power centres (an 'elimination contest') during the often violent process of state formation. What Elias describes in detail are the consequences of a particular dynamic figuration of human group relationships and their transformation. In this way Elias's study attempts to bridge the obstructive dualisms of micro- and macro-level processes, social structure and human agency, sociogenetic and psychogenetic processes and to draw attention to the uses of and transformations in attitudes towards violence.

The figurational sociological research tradition Elias founded has continued to pursue such an inclusive and social developmental approach to the study of human life, producing much insightful work in relation to violence, sociologies of the body and human emotions and many other fields. One of the main challenges for figurational sociologists today, however, has been said to be 'The extension of Elias's figurational perspective outside Europe' (Roudometof and Robertson 1995: 281). In principle, there are no convincing reasons why this task should not be possible. In fact, there have already been some significant applications of Elias's ideas in this direction (Brandstadter 2003; Goudsblom 1992; Ikegami 1995; Spier 1994; Stauth 1997), though such studies are not numerous when compared to civilizational research and world-systems analysis. Figurational sociology is also not hidebound by a Eurocentric globalization thesis, but sees globalization as a very long-term process through which human groups gradually come into regular contact and become more interdependent with each other (de Swaan 2001a; Goudsblom 1996; Kilminster 1998; Mennell 1990). Goudsblom (1996: 29) argues that

There never was a time when the history of any people could evolve for generations without its being affected by its neighbors – who were affected by *their* neighbors, and so on. Therefore, the history of humanity forms the all-encompassing framework in which all the events have taken place that form the subject matter of more particular histories.

Of course, such a starting point is not a serious criticism of those current globalization theories which perceive a *speeding up* of the pace at which wider interdependencies are being formed, but it does significantly expand the scope of sociology, bringing sociological studies closer to civilizationism and world-systems research. It is also somewhat at odds with civilizationism's general focus on the independent development of identifiable civilizations and the way that these 'come into contact', 'collide', 'fuse together' and so on. Whilst civilizational analysis tends to concentrate on the internal growth and eventual decay of cultural wholes, figurational sociology investigates the underlying social processes of the intertwining of human beings and the phases or stages of human development within these processes.

In a similar way, investigating the relationship between sociogenetic and psychogenetic changes (social and individual 'habitus') should be applicable across all human groups. Elias's original investigation of European state-formation processes also provides another useful starting point for the study of societies outside that context (Mennell 1996, 2001; Arnason 1996, 2002; Szakolczai 2001), though such research is still at a formative stage and needs more historical and empirical work. A useful illustration here is Mennell's recent work, which begins to take Elias's ideas outside the European context in studying civilizing processes in America (2001) and Asia, particularly Japan and China (1996). Mennell (1996: 117) argues that in pursuing Elias's civilizing process perspective, five areas can be identified as significant:

• State formation and allied processes
• Taming of warriors and courtization
• Changes in manners and forms of cultural expression
• Psychogenetic changes or changes in habitus
• Science and knowledge

The suggestion here is that the theory of civilizing processes can be used as a means of orientation in studying *the structure of underlying social processes* (ibid.: 119). This means that rather than concentrating on the unique features of different civilizational 'entities' or world-systems based on trade and economic exchange, figurational sociology shifts the emphasis towards dynamic social processes. The significant advantage of such a reorientation is that it avoids the temptation for reification that exists within other approaches to long-term human development.

In relation to Huntington's civilizational conflict thesis, a figurational investigation of the present situation needs to explore the dynamics of established–outsider relationships at the international or increasingly global level. The relations between intrastate and interstate processes can be seen as an important area for further study as it also brings into focus changes to codes of manners, uses of and attitudes towards violence and changes in social habitus. A social process perspective therefore opens up an alternative way of thinking through how and why some radical Islamic groups are prepared to use violence, why some Western states similarly have used violence and military force and why fears and mutual suspicion appear increasingly to characterize many people's perception of relations between 'Islam and the West'.

Before the World Trade Center attacks, Muslims had been considered to be a threat within Western Europe and the United States in combination with what Halliday (2002) refers to as 'anti-Muslimism' based on ethnic prejudice. But this was principally connected to perceived challenges from migrant workers to both national culture and employment prospects, making them subject to some public resentment and violent assaults. Today anti-Muslimism has been extended to incorporate images of violence, extremism and terrorism that are at odds with Westerners' perceptions of their own civilized behaviour. Such images neglect the intentionally constructed political programmes designed to 'civilize', secularize and modernize Muslim societies. These programmes have been implemented to varying degrees across Muslim societies and with differing levels of success. At the level of everyday life, a number of reforms were introduced, including the prescription of wearing the fez to show equality amongst all religions within the Ottoman Empire during the nineteenth century. Following the formation of the Turkish Republic in 1923, Atatürk initiated a reform process that included banning the fez and replacing it with Western-style rimmed hats, arguably to prevent male Muslims from touching the ground with their foreheads during prayer. Secularization was also aimed at more substantive sociogenetic and psychogenetic processes delivered through state institutions such as education systems, mass media and the control of religion. In other words, various processes initiated across Muslim societies to modernize the populace have led to the distinct development of Western-style civilizing offensives. However, while many Muslims have adopted secular ways, the forced and relatively short-term nature of these processes has contributed to the emergence of significant opposition. This is often clearly signified through physical appearance, with secularists identified by their Western-style appearance whilst praxisitioners are associated with more traditional attire, including the veil.

In chapter 1 it was argued that Western perceptions of Islam have been disproportionately influenced by violent and unrepresentative imagery, expansively spread through the mass media. The work of academics such as Huntington, Kramer, Lewis and Pipes tends to contribute to the stereotyping of Muslims as 'strange, backward-looking figures from another age' (Esposito 1999: 221) within the West. In some respects, there is disturbing evidence that the rhetoric of supporters of the 'Clash of Civilizations' argument within the West and praxisitioners using similar language are contributing to a self-fulfilling prophecy.

The sociological phenomenon of the unintended consequences of intentional actions has been discussed by Merton (1957) and more systematically by Elias (1978, 1987). Elias (1978: 22) describes the emergence of 'double-bind' social processes in which mutual loathing and mistrust can quite quickly escalate into violence. These are doubly binding because the emotional commitments to the 'in-group' on both sides of the emerging conflict tend to militate against the production of more reality-congruent knowledge of the situation. In turn, this leads to a continuing lack of control over the social processes that have been set in train. The circularity of double-bind processes acts rather like the maelstrom dragging down the fishermen in Elias's recounting of an Edgar Allan Poe tale (1987: part II). Caught up in a whirlpool at sea and thrown overboard, one fisherman, immobilized by fear, is unable to gain a synoptic picture of events and thus cannot work out how to improve his chances of survival. His brother manages to achieve a relative emotional detachment from the dire situation he is in and observes that the floating barrels remain buoyant even in the mouth of the maelstrom. Clinging onto one, he manages to survive whilst his brother drowns. Elias uses this tale to explore how, in many violent conflict situations, fears and heightened emotionality often prevent those involved from understanding the underlying social processes producing the conflict and hence any possibility of finding a resolution to the problem, thus feeding more stereotypical understandings of the other party in the conflict, reducing them to a 'less than human' status. In this respect Fletcher (1997: 58) argues that 'A lessening or lack of human control over any set of events will increase the tendency for people's thinking about such events to involve a higher emotional and fantasy content; and the more emotional their thinking becomes, the less able they are to formulate more realistic or adequate models of these events.'

This is quite an accurate description of the current 'Islam and the West' discursive frame of reference which is reinforced at a higher 'civilizational' level of understanding in the work of Huntington and those using a 'civilizational conflict' perspective. Such work does not simply obscure the production of more reality-congruent knowledge of the present situation, but actually contributes to the continuation of the double-bind process in which relations between Muslims and Western people seem to be increasingly caught. It is precisely to avoid falling into this emotion-laden trap that a relatively detached socio-logical analysis becomes an urgent necessity in the quest to understand and explain how and why such a double-bind process has been generated and, in doing so, help to reduce tensions and open up a space for the creation of possible solutions. An initial exploration of the explanatory potential of such a social process perspective is the subject of the next chapter.

6

$\mathcal{S}$ecular Establishment and Islamic Outsiders

Introduction

As noted in previous chapters, explanations for the contemporary Islamic resurgence have been heavily influenced by the secularization paradigm. This paradigm has contributed to the widely held viewpoint that the Islamic resurgence is largely a reaction of 'outsiders', principally dislocated peasants and bazaaris, rural dwellers and unemployed graduates, to expanding globalization and interlinked forms of Western-centred social, political and economic change. There is some evidence partially to support the links between these 'outsider' groups and the wider Islamic resurgence. However, such generalizations are limited and cannot be applied to groups of people who are not excluded under secular criteria. In particular, the secularization paradigm cannot explain why intellectuals, the relatively wealthy, non-threatened, highly skilled and/or educationally successful social groups are becoming more religious. Also, the recent spate of sociological debate focusing on globalization (see chapter 4) has raised the question of whether new theoretical perspectives are required to understand and explain processes adequately at this level, rather than persevering with ideas such as 'international relations' which may fail to capture the way that social and political groups such as the Jihadi Salafist groups associated with *al-Qa'ida* actually operate in a globalizing world.

This chapter seeks to expand upon these perspectives by including groups who are seemingly ensconced successfully within nation-states but who can still be considered as 'outsiders' according to the oppositional nature of their beliefs and actions. Drawing on Elias and

Scotson's established–outsiders thesis, this is reworked using the changing globalizing context and consequent changing socialization processes. This helps to explain both why Islamic influence has increased and why praxisitioners are becoming a powerful contemporary force capable of challenging the established secular states. Using illustrative examples, the chapter focuses on attempts to establish secular states, new forms of global information exchange, the unintended consequences of certain state policies and the shifting balance of power between secular modernists ('the established') and praxisitioners ('the outsiders').

Established–outsider relations

The problem of conflictual insider–outsider relations between interdependent social groups has been seen as a human universal (Fletcher 1997: 71; Turner 1994: 101). While this may be a reasonable research assumption, what we also need is a conceptual framework for the investigation of the dynamic social processes through which social groups *become* established and in the process *create* 'outsiders'. In addition, we need ways of analysing the way that the power balance between these groups shifts over time. Arguably, the merit of Elias and Scotson's original community relations study (1965) is that it attempts to do just this. The study provides a conceptual toolkit with which to approach established–outsider relationships of various kinds and at different levels of analysis. However, in order to analyse established–outsider relations at levels above communities and small groups, such as those between states or between social groups across state boundaries, this conceptual framework needs to be re-examined and re-considered in relation to specific empirical cases. A useful example here is Jáuregui's study (2000) of British and Spanish attitudes to closer European union, which revolve around their perceived place within the figuration of nation-states, using the concepts of 'group charisma' and 'group disgrace'. Simplifying somewhat, for many British, particularly English people, entry to the EU represents the failure of British colonial expansion and thus marks a stigma for their group: a form of sometimes keenly felt 'group disgrace'. Hence, there exists in Britain a relatively strong strand of 'Euro-scepticism' that resists further integration and pooling of national sovereignty. However, for many Spanish people, EU entry symbolizes a new confidence and inclusion that enhances their 'group charisma'; thus closer union with Europe tends to be seen as enhancing a positive form of identification.

In the original study of 'Winston Parva' in the East Midlands of England, Elias and Scotson's attempt to understand local conflictual group relations led them to create a set of interrelated concepts that have proved to be extremely productive. 'Group charisma', 'group disgrace', 'praise and blame gossip', 'minority of the best', 'minority of the worst', 'status ideology' all allow for a more processual study of established–outsider relations. Although the area contained two working-class and one relatively wealthier middle-class estate, it was relations between the two working-class groups, whose social characteristics and behaviour were broadly similar, that formed the basis of the original research. One group saw themselves as the 'established' group and perceived the other as 'outsiders'. The 'established' lived in a settlement dating back around 80 years known as 'the village', though its employment was industrial not agricultural. The 'outsiders' lived on a much more recently built 'estate'. 'Villagers' often described the estate in unflattering terms as 'less civilised', 'dirty' and dishonest. Elias and Scotson argued that there was no objective basis for this characterization, but the perceptions of the established were not based on an objective state of affairs but were generated through the conflictual process of group dynamics operating at the local level. As W. I. Thomas's famous dictum (1928) states, if people believe a situation to be true then it is true, in its consequences, because people will act on the basis of their perception of that situation. And of course, if such perceptions continue to exist then it matters little if the original conflict has long passed. To later participants their perceptions may be just as real as those generated at that time and with similar consequences.

The paired concepts of 'group stigma' and 'group charisma' are fundamental to Elias and Scotson's understanding of established–outsider relations. Established groups tend to generate group charisma, a sense of their own superiority as a group, based on a 'minority of the best', as part of their social and self-identity. That is, their self-image tends to be based on evelution rooted in the best aspects of the group, ignoring other elements that might contaminate such an image. This forms one important aspect of the group's internal solidarity and sense of community. However, this also tends to produce a stigmatizing of non-established outsider groups, with this basic social group process as fundamental to an understanding of group dynamics. It means that social life is inherently conflictual, as group conflicts are part and parcel of the way social identities are formed and sustained. When outsider groups are seen as threats to the identity and social status of the established, the latter respond by exaggerating their own positive aspects as well as the outsiders' negative ones. Group disgrace and group charisma are sustained through the vital mechanisms of communal 'gossip' and everyday conversation. Established groups produce 'praise-gossip' when discussing their own group, but use 'blame-gossip' to describe outsiders. Praise-gossip means that the best elements perceived by the established group form the basis for discussion and evaluation whilst negative elements are not openly discussed. Blame-gossip is exactly the reverse, as outsider groups are discussed and assessed in terms of what are considered to be their worst elements. Villagers' comments about the estate tended to concentrate on the small minority of relatively large families who were seen as 'problem families', for example. For the established villagers, such families came to be seen as representative of the estate in general. Clearly this kind of evaluation generates feelings of mistrust, antagonism and even hatred towards outsiders, which can continue to be reproduced over generations. This is because blame-gossip becomes part of the routines of everyday life and is passed on orally, embedded in the group habitus over successive generations and continues to exert influence even when the outsider group has achieved some measure of territorial 'establishment' themselves.

Elias and Scotson's account provides a detailed and balanced description of the creation of social stereotypes. Within this work negative stereotypes of outsiders are one side of a coin and the established group's own positive self-stereotype can be found on the other. The implication of this argument is of tremendous significance, because it is unlikely that negative stereotyping can be simply eliminated without some movement on the part of the established group's view of themselves. The focus upon the role of the dominant group's self-perceptions helps to balance accounts of social change in normative, political accounts which have tended to centre on the creative agency of social movement actors. Established–outsider relations are underpinned by unequal power relations, without which stigmatizing labels could not be made to stick. The established group's communal feelings of belonging and ownership, membership of important community roles, integration into informal (and formal) local networks and local knowledge, all of these power resources give established groups the upper hand in the 'relations of definition' between themselves and newer groups, enabling the established to make their evaluations stick.

For outsiders, their relative lack of power resources leaves them vulnerable to the gossip and stigmatization of the more powerful group, and, over time, members of the outsiders can come to accept and take on the stigmatized form of identity created for them by the established. They come to see their own group as inferior and often see themselves as inferior people, idealizing and imitating the established's behavioural codes, manners and so on in order to raise their valuation of themselves. At least in the short term, this reduces their power chances even further by reinforcing the claims to superiority of the established. Thus, the generational transmission of stereotypes ensures that outsiders are continually reminded of their inferior status. This does not mean that outsiders have no power resources at all, merely that in the situation in which they find themselves, they cannot initially prevent established groups from imposing their definitions and labels. Over time, outsiders may narrow the gap between their own and the established's power chances. For example, outsiders may fill a niche in local labour markets or become important sources of assistance, though in the original study Elias and Scotson found that social stigma was still powerfully in evidence long after the estate was built.

Nevertheless, it is possible to identify instances where formerly outsider groups have begun to challenge negative stereotypes and create their own positive evaluations in the process. One instructive example of this is in the field of 'race relations', which Elias and Scotson (1994: xxx–xxxi) see as one type of established–outsiders relationship. Dunning (2004) makes use of the established–outsiders framework to study the shifting balance of power between white and black groups in America, from a highly asymmetrical pattern during the 'plantation slavery' period, through a 'colour caste' phase beginning with the 1890 segregation Acts, moving towards an 'urban ghetto' phase from the 1950s (ibid.: 84–93). Particularly during the latter period, slogans such as 'black is beautiful' (and later, the appropriation of pejorative terms such as 'nigger' in popular black music) symbolize the growing confidence in a specifically black group self-image. In Elias's terms, this marks a strengthening of the group's 'We' identity, which allows the previously negative stereotypical imagery to be challenged more effectively in the process of altering the subordinate position of the group itself. Hence we can see that 'consciousness-raising' groups, changes in language use and the promotion of positive images of black people, as well as higher levels of self-organization, are not epiphenomena of more central class-based struggles, but are fundamental elements in the transformation of power relations. A similar underlying social process could perhaps be traced in relation to other social movement activities such as those found in women's movements, disabled people's movements and gay and lesbian movements. In so far as such shifts in power balances can be empirically demonstrated, a pessimistic attitude towards the possibility of altering existing power relations may seem misplaced. However, it should be remembered that, in all likelihood, changes in the position of excluded outsider groups such as women, ethnic minorities and disabled people form part of a long-term process of social change over many generations. These long-term processes are subject to reversals of present trends, rather than being simply linear pathways which once embarked upon become somehow inevitable. Established–outsider relations rarely seem to change their fundamental structure rapidly, and perhaps the increasingly significant protests against immigration and Faludi's identification (1991) of an American 'backlash' against the movement towards gender equality can be seen as evidence of this.

One final factor identified by Elias and Scotson is the established group's shared common history or, at least, their perception of a common history. This helps to sustain their own sense of superiority and creates an 'us and them', insider–outsider attitude. In this way, 'tradition' or the 'longevity' of sharing a common fate becomes a significant marker of social status, and part of the self-understanding of relatively powerful groups about their own position, their 'status ideology'. The generational transmission of such a shared history and experience keeps alive the social constructions of 'established' and 'outsiders' long after the original constructors of this view have passed on: 'An old group of people need not be a group of old people' (Elias and Scotson 1965: 150). This recognition goes some way towards explaining why, in the current situation of mutual mistrust and suspicion between groups of Muslims and Western people, the imagery of the Crusades and of earlier periods of successful Islamic expansion can still appeal to younger generations, many centuries after the events themselves. This is why it is possible even for successive generations to continue to see outsider groups negatively, despite the increasing longevity of their settlement. So although originally length of residence was a key factor in the processes of exclusion, once stereotypical views of outsiders are in play, it matters little whether length of residence is real or simply perceived. Group identity comes to be based on ideals transmitted from the past which continue to have a resonance in the present. This does not mean that relations between particular individuals are inevitably hostile. It is quite possible for people to be on friendly, speaking terms with others from across the divide, but individually they are unable to alter the social figuration of which they form a part. This figuration produces compelling forces of territorial, psychological and social kinds, which generate distrust, negative comparisons and conflict. Once set in train, this dynamic can become increasingly hard to change and is effectively out of the control of all the people bound up in it. In short, social forces, figurational forces, act, according to one of Elias's well-used phrases, 'behind the backs' of all the people involved. Elias and Scotson do suggest however, that attempts to understand these figurational forces may in time lead to practical measures to control them (ibid.: 173).

Established–outsiders beyond the community level

Whilst the established–outsiders framework provides an effective way of describing and accounting for conflictual dynamics, two potential problems can be identified which are outlined here and traced through in our analysis of praxisitioners, including 'Islamic' terrorists.

First, the heavy emphasis on the role of blame- and praise-gossip in perpetuating conflictual group relations tends to focus on the level of everyday life. Gossip works both to reinforce the in-group's positive sense of identity and continually to reinforce negative images and beliefs about outsiders. At the local or community level it is easy to see how the role of gossip is vitally important in this process. However, it is more difficult to see this process operating so effectively where there is less or no face-to-face contact between the established and outsider groups, particularly at the national, international and global levels. Instead of focusing only on gossip therefore, analysis at these levels needs also to concentrate upon aspects of communication that can be seen to make a contribution within the wider relations similar to that of gossip at the local level. Ideologies and ideological beliefs can be seen to perform similar functions, especially those ideologies which present dominant national cultures as 'civilized' and others as 'barbaric', or in relation to our subject in this book, as 'progressive' (secular/modernist) or 'backward-looking' (religious). This is of more value when trying to work out why it is that some outsider groups face more discrimination than others, perhaps in turn drawing on ideological beliefs about inferior and superior 'races' or 'national characters', which provide the basis for 'blame-ideology' and 'praise-ideology'. Political and racist ideologies can perform a similar function at the national and international levels to gossip at the community level. In all likelihood, ideologies and everyday gossip are interrelated, with political ideologies lending 'official' support to the valuations of established groups, while everyday gossip keeps political ideologies alive and pertinent.

Second, the role of a common history can be seen to be somewhat more complex when moving to higher levels. Elias and Scotson showed how the common stock of historical memories transmitted across generations provided a strong sense of a shared fate uniting the established against the perceived threat felt at the influx of outsiders. This sense of sharing a common fate helps to bolster an established group's identity as a coherent group and inevitably leads to dismissive attitudes towards social groups who are not part of it. In essence, the process of 'disestablishment' goes hand in hand with the process of establishment. With many Muslim countries adopting secular political systems and Western forms of dress and culture, formerly insider groups that do not share the newly established identity have been labelled as 'traditional' or 'backward-looking' and the outsiders may come to see themselves as such. However, the process of institutionalizing secularism, which involved attacks on Islamic culture and traditions, has proved to be conflict-ridden and difficult to sustain. Islam remained an influential cultural and practical resource within these societies and increasingly radical Muslim groups have built upon the existing cultural sources that have led them to consider themselves to be outsiders. The praxisitioners' activities are fundamentally different from those witnessed at 'Winston Parva', not least because they have not passively accepted the negative self-image and stigmatized identity. Instead, praxisitioners can be seen as embracing their excluded status, often using the criteria that secularists associate with stigma as the source of their in-group charisma. In a further development, praxisitioners then reverse the process, actively stigmatizing the established as 'insincere', 'unprincipled', 'decadent' and not true to their own 'civilized' standards.

There are considerable disputes amongst Muslims about the historical development of Islam, but there are some central tenets that are agreed upon, such as the role and significance of Muhammed and the period of early Islamic expansion. A shared Islamic history exists that has been denigrated throughout the existence of the majority of modern Muslim nation-states and demeaned by secular established forces as part of the attempt to implement secularism as the basis for state structures and societal ways of life. Cultural histories have been portrayed as sources of shame and embarrassment, even guilt, rather than national pride, and social processes of stigmatization were set in train that denigrated Islam. Islamists' beliefs and identities were attacked and diminished in status within society as part of the processes by which the secular state sought to impose its own definitions. Across Muslim states, such policies were based around neglect (Islam not included in the educational curriculum), indifference (no support for Islam from official bodies) or outright hostility (the banning of religious sects, groups and parties and imprisoning Muslims considered to be a threat to the secular state). These policies did not lead to the intended outcome of isolating Islam within the private sphere. Governments have also tried to control and manipulate religion directly, partly to reduce the popularity of radical groups when it became apparent that the generic 'blame ideology' was not having the desired effect. These regimes have inadvertently contributed to the growth in the phenomena that the policies were designed to prevent, namely the expansion in numbers of the Islamist outsiders.

International established and outsiders

In applying this framework to the study of the global resurgence of Islam and the emergence of the extreme groups associated with *al-Qa'ida*, we need to focus on processes of establishment and the ways in which 'the established' and dominant forces are able to shape perceptions and conversely why outsiders are increasingly resisting these processes. Our argument in this regard is that, whilst secularization *has* been formally established within the institutions, polities and state systems throughout Muslim nations, secularism never became *culturally* established and the process of establishment was only partially concretized. Islamic culture continued to be practised and many Muslims retained their belief in Islam as a way of life beyond the private sphere. Thus the efforts of states to portray Islam as a backward, reactionary trend, using a form of 'blame-gossip' or 'blame ideology', was really only ever partially successful. Certainly considerable numbers of people were made to feel inferior as part of the wider implementation of secular modernization but such processes were unable to penetrate the self-perceptions of many Muslims who continued to see their own beliefs and culture as valued, if not always superior.

By breaking down the process of establishment into political, economic and cultural processes across global spheres in chapter 4 we were able to explain why Muslims do not always adopt secular beliefs, attitudes, cultural codes and lifestyles, and indeed are increasingly challenging them. In the case of *al-Qa'ida* and praxisitioners more generally, the challenge is emphasized in their adaptation of the classical concepts of *Dar al-Islam*, 'the world of Islam', and *Dar al-Harb*, 'the enemy world'. Similarly crude distinctions can be noted in George W. Bush's insistence that, 'you are either with us or you are with the terrorists' (Bush 2001a) with reference to the support of people and nations for recent American military action. This simple division between 'Good' and 'Evil' and references to 'civilization' are prominent features of much 'Islam and the West' discourse on both sides (Halliday 2002). Such dichotomies could again be noted in George Bush's comment that 'This is a regime [Iraq] that has something to hide from the civilized world. States like these [at that time Iraq, Iran and North Korea], and their terrorist allies, constitute an axis of evil, arming to threaten the peace of the world' (Bush 2002). Elements within both Islamic and Western groups use their own 'historical memory' to justify these views. For example, the Christian Crusades and Islamic control of parts of Europe are used to help explain contemporary relations. To reiterate the salient points from the previous chapter, these examples do *not* provide support for the view popularized recently, that Islam and the West are *inherently* oppositional (Huntington 1998). That significant elements within the different groups *do* believe that conflict between Islam and Christianity, or Muslim nation-states and the West, is inevitable is not in dispute, but such simplistic dichotomies fail to take into account the centuries of cohabitation and 'cross-civilizational' alliances. This type of analysis also neglects to note that the 'other's' rhetoric and actions, whether they are individuals, political parties, social movements, terrorists or nation-states, are not uniquely oppositional, and could easily have been made by alternative groups, continents or even intra-ethnic or religious factions.

Across Muslim societies, the power relationships between religious authorities and the populace changed with the growing influence and colonial presence of Western nation-states and organizations. Moderates and praxisitioners hold different common histories and interpretations of Islamic control and subsequent experiences within nation-states. Today the relationship between religion and power has become the site of debates and disputes about the reasons for the decline of Muslim empires, the suitability of secularism and democracy within Muslim societies and the inability of Muslim nation-states to gain greater global prominence. The relationship is one significant element in the changing power relations and interrelated socio-dynamics of stigmatization in the current period.

Reciprocal stigmatization: secularization and Islamification

Identifying secularists and praxisitioners is generally relatively easy, except when members of one group want to penetrate the 'other' for their own purposes, such as terrorists wanting to destroy elements within the societies they have penetrated. Ideological beliefs and practices' and often appearance, are used both to identify and reinforce collective identities. Within these groups, ideology is used in a similar manner to praise-gossip and strengthens their beliefs and group self-identity whilst reinforcing, often deepening, negative other-images. The socio-dynamics of stigmatization between the established and outsiders are interwoven in a reciprocal relationship and indeed are an integral part of the respective dogmatic ideological positions.

Secularizing states stress the inherent superiority of secularism and use their ideological frameworks both as sources of 'group charisma' and to propagate 'group stigma' about praxisitioners based upon their religious actions and historical role. This kind of approach can be found in many speeches by leading political figures, particularly Atatürk, probably the most prominent secular figure in Middle Eastern history, who stated in 1925 that 'the Turkish Republic cannot be a country of sheikhs, dervishes, devotees, and lunatics . . . we derive our strength from civilization and science' (cited in Sakallıoğlu 1996: 236). As part of this secularizing offensive, praxisitioners were reduced to stereotyped images replicated in the media, based on violent extremism, fundamentalism and ignorance.

Western states and population groups also stigmatize Islam and Muslim nation-states and people. There has been a history of ignorance about Muslims and Islam within the West that has tended to reinforce stereotypes about Muslims being dirty, shifty, untrustworthy, uncivilized and heathen. Clearly these are terms that can be located directly within Elias and Scotson's study (1965). Western perceptions have, however, become more extreme, less gossip-based and more blame-ideological. These views can be linked into the growing profile of Muslims through a variety of events such as the conflict in the Middle East, the Iranian Revolution, terrorism in the 1970s, the 11 September 2001 attacks on America and the subsequent 'war on terror'. Perceptions have become exaggerated since both the attacks of 11 September and reactions to it within the Middle East and other Muslim nation-states. Criticism of the terrorists' actions has adopted a broad-brush approach that fails to distinguish between the majority of peace-loving Muslims and a small minority whose radical approach includes killing civilians. The gross generalizations and inaccurate, simplistic reporting and commentary are exemplified by Italian Prime Minister Silvio Berlusconi's remark (2001) about both Western 'group charisma' and Islamic 'group disgrace' when he claimed that '[Western civilisation] has guaranteed well-being, respect for human rights and – in contrast with Islamic countries – respect for religious and political rights.' He hoped that the West will 'continue to conquer [Muslim] peoples, like it conquered communism.' Such statements are perhaps instances of growing Western sentiments, stimulated by heightened fears, which have contributed to the amplification and politicization of existing stereotypes and processes of stigmatization. For example, the involvement of fifteen terrorists of Saudi origin in the attacks on America led to sustained and widespread criticism of Saudi Arabia, including commentary on its support for terrorism and on other aspects of Saudi society, including its lack of democracy, its authoritarianism and its failure to promote the rights of women. Simultaneously the American government has been targeting perceived Muslims for rigorous assessment, surveillance and frequently detention, whilst individuals and businesses thought to be or actually belonging to Muslims have been attacked by American citizens.

However, the stigmatization of Islam by the West and secular Muslim nation-states has not had the impact upon the stigmatized that might be expected. After generations of secularism within Muslim states, it remains the case that religious texts are still widely used, the activist potential of Islam was never lost and contemporary praxisitioners and many moderates have not adopted a negative self-image. On the contrary, they have developed their own 'group charisma' around shared ideological beliefs based upon the perceived superiority of a version of Islam. In a similar process of reciprocal stigmatization they have stigmatized the established both within Muslim nation-states and the West according to their interpretation of Islam. As part of this trend, anti-Americanism continues to increase within Muslim societies and has accelerated since the invasion and occupation of Iraq (Abdallah 2003; Haddad and Khashan 2002; Pollack 2003). Sentiments used as part of Muslim ideological processes of stigmatizing others are well represented by Dr Tareq

Hilmi, an Egyptian Islamist, who recently declared in an article entitled 'America we hate' that

> This is the America that declared war against Islam and the Muslims under the title of world terrorism. This is the America that gives unlimited and unconditional support for the Zionist entity. This is the America that wants the Muslims to surrender and submit to the forces of occupation, otherwise they are considered terrorists. This is the America that is issuing weapons that are internationally prohibited to crush the Muslims of Iraq and Afghanistan, and is using its planes and missiles to attack the Muslims in Palestine. This is the America that protects the agent governments in the Islamic world, which act against the will of the Muslim peoples . . . The history of America is full of evilness against humanity . . . This is the America that occupies the world with the culture of sex and deviation . . . This is the American civilization whose object is the body and its means is materialism. (Hilmi 2003)

Hilmi emphasizes a number of themes that can be found within Islamic discourses and are used to stigmatize rival ideologies. This stigmatization encompasses both narrow and broad issues ranging from attacks on Islam, nation-states and Muslims within countries, through support for Israel and corrupt Muslim governments, to American culture and its leniency towards criminal behaviour. Praxisitioners' emphasis upon ethics and morality is located within many attempts to stigmatize Western and Muslim leaders and their 'moral bankruptcy'. There are other noticeable themes within stigmatization processes as some praxist groups extend the focus of their rhetorical or violent attacks to incorporate anyone who does not hold radical views. For example, *al-Qa'ida* has sought to stigmatize not only the West and many Muslim regimes, but also non-praxisitioners and members of the *ulema* who are considered to be using religion for the benefit of corrupt anti-Islamic rulers.

It is interesting in light of the general perception of praxisitioners as 'traditionalists' to note that such groups are partly opposed to the *ulema* for their traditionalist views. The divorce of the *ulema* from radical groups is highlighted when examining the leading and influential figures (al-Banna, Sayyid Qutb (probably the first influential radical Muslim to stigmatize Western civilization and the United States in particular), Mawdudi, Khomeini, and bin Laden) within Islamic movements. These figures, with the exception of Khomeini, have not been members of the *ulema*; although Mawdudi was trained he never acknowledged this. As part of socialization processes, individuals are learning that Islam can offer explanations for much of contemporary life; that can lead to religiosity increasing at a personal or wider level as the controlling relations and systems are delegitimized. Interpretations of Islam as a way of life (as argued in Chapter 4) are legitimized by history and contemporary experiences and communal consciousness based around the *ummah* are the sources of 'group charisma'. The outcome is that the established's definitions and resultant negative self-image fail to transform identities in a secular direction.

Disputing common history

Analysis of the different perspectives within Muslim nations highlights the significance of history both for the established secularists and for outsiders, the praxisitioners. There have been numerous historical events that remain central to understanding contemporary relations between secularists and praxisitioners. Events include the success of Muhammed and subsequent expansions and decline of Muslim empires, the Christian Crusades, colonialism, the Cold War and the impact of secularism. For example, it is within the historical context that the Muslim reaction to George W. Bush's warning after the 11 September attacks that 'this crusade, this war on terrorism is going to take a while' (2001b) needs to be considered. The atrocities committed by Christians during the Crusades, and ultimately the Muslims' success, have become ingrained within contemporary Islamic imagery which radicals frequently use in seeking to generate anti-Western attitudes and Muslim 'group charisma'. This could be noted, for example, when bin Laden named his coalition the 'World Islamic Front for the Jihad against the Jews and the Crusaders'. Not surprisingly, this common history, going back generations in some instances, is highly contested. One of the main differences lies in the reasons given and accepted for the decline of Islam as a global power and the subsequent implementation of secularism. When comparing the decline of Islam and rise of the West in global relations, Hiro (2002: 44) notes in respect to Ottoman reformers' attempts to understand the empire's changing fortunes, that there are two obvious broad possibilities: (1) Islam is inferior to Western social systems, or (2) Muslims have deviated from the true path of Islam.

Secularists have tended to agree with the first possibility and have sought to identify factors within Muslim societies that they consider responsible for the decline, using Western criteria as the benchmark for success. The established ideologies that stemmed from influential secularists like Atatürk, Nasser and Bourguiba consider 'common history' to be one of success for the Western secular forces over the irrational forces of religion and superstition that had caused the demise of Muslim empires. For the established, the integral involvement of Islam in the defeated Ottoman Empire and the absence of religion in the victorious nations' power relations provided a double legitimacy for secularization as the basis for modernization and the subsequent exclusion of Islam. By comparison, the radical outsiders' 'common history' shows Islam was the basis for the expansion of the empire to include significant parts of the West, with the empire only declining when Islam stopped being correctly practised.

More recent 'common history' is also disputed, in particular the effectiveness of secularism within Muslim societies. Praxisitioners argue vehemently that secular states and capitalism generally are facing a legitimation crisis, confronted by problems that they find insurmountable. Examples provided by Muslims highlight the inequalities and injustices experienced within these arrangements, for example poverty, corruption, alienation, immorality and unemployment (Vertigans 2003). Secularism, whether cloaked in nationalism, socialism or capitalism, is considered a foreign, inappropriate imposition that has failed to meet its promises and fulfil expectations. Ultimately, secularism is considered to be unsuitable for Muslim nations, not least as it is fundamentally opposed to radical Islamic ideologies. Following the argument developed in chapter 2, the existence and growing popularity of Islam highlights the extent to which secularization and associated ideologies can be seen to have failed. Secularists, whilst often acknowledging problems with secular states, believe that secularism is the only real possibility for nation-states to progress, 'copying American ways. If we do not we cannot survive' because 'Islam is too old. It cannot help . . . today' and it 'slows down secularism' (ibid.: 127).

Contemporary global and local events and experiences are also interpreted according to ideology and used to support and legitimize views and practices. Obvious examples of 'global common history' include the 11 September attacks and the invasion of Iraq. People who experience this international history also have their own 'local common history' and the interaction between individuals' local circumstances and wider events seems to reinforce their ideological beliefs. For instance, the disgust of Muhammed Atta (one of the key figures in the 11 September attacks) about what he witnessed in Egypt, bin Laden's dismay at Saudi Arabia's decision to allow

American forces to establish bases in the country and Sayyid Qutb's anti-American views, which followed two years living in America, demonstrate that the local and the global can come together in the production of meanings. These perceptions have had a significant impact upon interpretations of common history and contemporary life and highlight that exposure to Western ways or residence in the West does not inevitably lead to accommodation with Western beliefs and values.

There is also evidence to challenge popular Western perceptions about the universal appeal of the rationalist philosophy and cultural mores dating back to the European Enlightenment period. People in the West may believe in the inherent superiority of the values of equality, justice and fraternity, but they are values that do not easily export elsewhere in the world, particularly when associated with the 'dark side' of the Enlightenment, such as the legacies of slavery, imperialism, colonialism, Western *realpolitik* and American military dominance. Exposure to Western culture, its freedom of opportunity and basic principles can have the opposite effect from that anticipated and can strengthen or help to contribute to the formation of Islamic identities. For example, Muslim students in the UK have commented upon seeing 'behaviour of English daily, [which] reinforces belief that they have no moral belief and, see much poor peoples . . . Also other many things are bad. For example, drugs, unmarried mothers, crime and much alcohol' (Vertigans 2003: 148). It is within this context that the decision, in a long-standing dispute, by the French government to stop Muslim girls from wearing headscarves in schools as part of a general ban on visible religious symbols needs to be considered.

Popular Western perceptions consider the veil to be a symbol of female oppression as part of a traditional Muslim approach to control women. There are countless examples to support this perception, including harrowing images of women being harassed for being inadequately covered up in Afghanistan and Iran. But these generalizations fail to acknowledge that wearing the veil is context-specific and not necessarily 'Islamic'. For instance, it was worn in the Arabian area before the birth of Muhammed. There are considerable variations in veil-wearing between and within more egalitarian South East Asian societies like Indonesia and Middle Eastern countries like Saudi Arabia where the *ulema* have gradually interpreted the religious doctrines to undermine improvements in females' position and status that are also apparent within the *Qu'ran* (Mernissi 1989). These differences have evolved historically, linked to the ways that gender rela-

tions developed within political, social and cultural settings and communities' economic requirements. For example, women in rural areas
have participated more in the local economy and so experienced less
exclusion than some of their urban counterparts (Hassan 2002).

If we examine why women are wearing the veil a more complex
picture emerges. Göle (1997) has observed increasingly politically
active, educated women are consciously choosing to wear the headscarf as a source of their Islamic identity. Waxman (1998) has argued
that secular opposition to religion is not based upon the requirement
to 'look Western' or reflect secular values but upon the politicization
of the veil that has led to it becoming a 'symbol of resistance' to secularism (Ahmed 1992: 235). In essence, parallels can be drawn to symbolic actions undertaken by Western feminism, black civil rights
movements in the USA or disabled people's movements. Zubaida
comments upon the seemingly paradoxical relationship between the
veil and female freedom. Improved educational systems and developing economies within Muslim societies have created more opportunities for women. For many of these women, 'the veil has facilitated
rather than inhibited this much wider social and economic participation . . . in bestowing respectability and modesty on female public
appearance' (2000: 76) and is facilitating the emergence of Muslim
feminists. In Iran, which is widely considered the most patriarchal of
societies, families refused to send girls to school when the Shah
banned the *chador*. Following the revolution, women have become
more emancipated, making up 50 per cent of students, entering the
labour market in large numbers and becoming much more politically
active (Hassan 2002). Similar reasoning can also be found in the
protest over the French banning of the veil that is also notable for
the way in which protesters have turned the republic's ideals on itself,
arguing they are being denied human rights, freedom of expression
and belief (Kepel 2004). This usage of the veil does of course raise
questions about why the veil bestows respectability and modesty
upon women within everyday life. In this respect women can still be
seen as outsiders against the patriarchal established. Zubaida's point
shows that relations are changing in some contexts but these relations are far from Western perceptions of egalitarianism. As relations
in nation-states like the Arab states and Macey's study (1999)
of Muslim relations in Bradford, England show, men continue to
exclude women from economic and social spheres. Indeed it could be
argued that greater levels of religiosity in many households are
increasing the extent of female exclusion. The exclusion of women is
justified by a variety of reasons that include perceptions of family

honour, religious interpretations, moral rules and threats to male-dominated employment sectors. Consequently the meaning of the veil, like so many other symbols associated with Islam, is subject to different interpretations according to context.

The challenge to central tenets and values within secularization can also be found within Muslim converts from Christianity. These Muslims have remarked upon a variety of different factors that have contributed to their conversion, which challenge the fundamentals upon which Western ideologies have been based. For example, some converts found life in Britain to be too secularized, materialistic and sexually permissive and part of the appeal of Islam was the stability, behavioural framework and clarity offered by strong values and greater spirituality (Köse 1999). Sultàn's study (1999) of conversion in Sweden discovered that women who became Muslims were attracted, rather than repulsed (as is the popular Western perception) by the role for women associated within popular interpretations of Islam, the security and regulation it offered and the lack of oppression and exploitation through the forbidding of pornography and other demeaning aspects of Western gender relations. Unity amongst Muslims was another important experience in the process of confirming their conversion. In Wohlrab-Sahr's analysis (1999) of American and German converts she discovered a 'double frame' which relates to the indigenous religious, social and cultural factors that converts turn away from and the religious and cultural attractions that they turn to. Converts highlight the disillusionment people can feel from their experiences within the contemporary West and the perception that Islam can provide a better alternative. Clearly these people are very much in a minority, but their experiences highlight how people belonging to the same religion can begin to hold fundamentally different views based on their interpretation of reality and common history. These interpretations are intertwined with very different levels of group charisma and group stigma.

The shifting power balance

The established–outsiders thesis sheds invaluable light on the dynamics involved in the changing relations between secularists, praxisitioners and other Islamic interpretations within nation-states. After a long period during which the previously established Muslims gradually became 'outsiders', as secularization was implemented through a series of intentional state reforms, popular revolutions and upheavals beginning in the eighteenth century and clearly demarcated across many Muslim nations in the twentieth century, the balance of power between secular powers and Islamic outsider groups is now in flux. This has also affected gendered power relations, with women experiencing greater exclusion within private praxist settings whilst at a public level national reforms have sought to undermine patriarchy and remove some of the obstacles to greater participation. The reforms have had variable impact. At one level, many women have benefited, as discussed above, with more learning and employment opportunities. But the reforms have also caused considerable consternation among Islamic traditionalists, including many members of the *ulema*, who have argued that the changes violate religious law and have sought to reinforce gender divisions. Men who 'have experienced greater status loss relative to women . . . have compensated . . . by developing more conservative attitudes towards women, including support for veiling, seclusion and patriarchy' (Hassan 2002: 204). Many of these men become part of social protest groups that promote such behaviour. Overall, it can be seen that at societal levels, the power balance is changing but within praxist and traditional households patriarchy remains firmly rooted.

The economic marginalization of Muslims, Westernization of cultures, urban migration, dislocation and alienation that are often put forward as explanations for the rise in Islamic consciousness have been part of many Muslim societies prior to the contemporary resurgence. Conversely, there are examples where smaller-scale resurgences took place prior to the recent rapid globalization, for example in Iran during the Tobacco Revolution, Egypt and the formation of the Muslim Brotherhood and during the fight for Algerian independence (1954–62). These elements are interwoven in the process of 'Islamification', but the focus needs to be expanded to look at why the broader and deeper resurgence is happening now. Attention also needs to be paid to why groups who may not face these factors are also becoming radical 'outsiders', when in many instances they could become part of the 'established'.

Clearly there have been significant changes in processes of identity formation, and these ultimately confirm the extent to which secularization and Westernization have stalled across many Muslim countries. These changes can be linked to socialization processes that were deliberately changed by secular states as a means to socialize the population into new norms and values. As part of such modernizing attempts, nation-states sought to train and educate. Some responsibility was consequently taken away from the institution of the family and to some extent from the *ulema*, both of which generally tended to follow or preach traditional practices. However, the *ulema* retained a role in support of the state and have been used by their respective governments to maintain social control and to attack praxisitioners. As a consequence, the potential of the *ulema* as a source of political opposition has been seriously undermined by their role in attempting to legitimize nation-states while seeking to de-legitimize radical groups. This has resulted in the *ulema* being increasingly considered to be part of the establishment. All of this has led to a breach between considerable numbers of the *ulema* and the more radical groups and weakened the potential for broader Muslim challenges to nation-states. This has also contributed to an increase in popular Islam, especially Sufi orders, within the broader resurgence. Followers of popular Islam are attracted by emotional worship and spirituality that cannot usually be found within state and praxist Islam; indeed, both these interpretations tend to be opposed to popular Islam (Roy 2004). It should be stressed however that this does not apply to all *ulema*. In Egypt, the secular regime's frequent reliance upon the *ulema* to provide theological legitimacy for its policies has enabled some members to promote more radical interpretations than would be otherwise anticipated within secular patronage.

The movement towards secularization also led to state institutions increasing rapidly. These institutions have employed increasingly well-qualified professionals, taught as a consequence of the expansion of education across Muslim societies. Many professionals have been exposed to a religious curriculum taught by radical teachers who gained a foothold when governments increasingly tried to use religion for their own purposes. This has contributed to many thousands of well-educated praxisitioners who, partly through periods of patronage, are subsequently employed in influential positions where they are able to transmit Islamic messages, gain resources and knowledge and establish networks. As some commentators (discussed in chapter 2, for example: Ayubi 1991; Cederroth 1996; Euben 1999; Fischer 1980; Hiro 2002; Huband 1998; Mehmet 1990; Munson 1988; Roy 1994; Williamson 1987) have noted – although ignoring the significant number of radical graduates who do find appropriate employment – many countries are providing people with education but not sufficient jobs, leading to further disillusionment as expectations are not met.

Political opportunities to challenge the established have been unintentionally created by the established themselves as they tried to manage the religious threat. For example, during generations of secularization, crucial concessions have been made that include the tremendous increase in religious teaching within state and private schools across a broad range of Muslim societies from Senegal to Malaysia to attract political support and/or to counter Communism or hostile nationalists which at that time were considered to be a greater threat. Interestingly, following praxisitioners' criticism in a number of Muslim-majority nation-states about the archaic systems of learning, religious teaching in *madrasas*, *Imam-Hatip* schools and within 'secular' schools has led to the inclusion of more modern subjects within curricula (Ahmad 1994; Akşit 1991; Loimeier 1996). The extent of the criticism highlights the way that many praxisitioners interpret contemporary Islamic ideology as a framework that integrates modern and theological ways. Outside of state control, there has been a tremendous increase in privately funded Islamic schools, often sponsored by wealthy individuals, charitable organizations or other governments, in particular from the Gulf. The rise of such institutions became noticeable when it was discovered that many members of the Taliban had been educated at private *madrasas* within Pakistan that lacked modern curricula. Stern (2003) points out that the lack of state supervision has resulted in the curriculum being determined by the *madrasas*, and students often leave holding radical Islamic views but few practical skills. Despite this, these subsidized schools are popular across Muslim societies because they offer children the chance of an education that would otherwise be unaffordable.

Government concessions were not intended to reverse processes of secularization but they have contributed both to intended greater individual piety and unintentionally growing feelings of anti-secularism. As Byman and Green report, 'in the 1960s and 1970s, the [Saudi] regime encouraged religious radicals to organize, correctly anticipating that this would reduce the influence of the then-dominant school of Arab nationalism, which was often anti-monar-chist. In so doing, however, the regime strengthened groups that would later challenge it (1999: 7).' Other perceived threats have led to greater support for Islam. When Sadat came to power in Egypt in 1970, following the death of Nasser, he sought to counterbalance the perceived threat from Nasserists and leftists by releasing jailed members of the Muslim Brotherhood, permitting their publications to be issued and covertly encouraging greater religiosity; this contributed to the Islamic groups quickly becoming very influential. The 1969 riots in Malaysia led to a process of 'Islamification' as the government sought to appease ethnic Muslims. This process was accelerated during the 1980s when Islamic courses became compulsory and schools employed graduates from religious institutions (Kepel 2004). Governments have also made arrangements for state departments to provide for prayers during working hours, made provisions for employees in both the public and private sector to attend Friday noon prayers and emphasized their leaders' piety and austerity. In Pakistan, President Zia-ul-Haq (ruled 1977–88) not only enhanced the prominence of Islam within education and state ideology, but also encouraged state officials to be more Islamic in appearance; when not dressed in military uniform he himself wore traditional attire of *kurta* tunic and baggy *shalwar* trousers. Mortimer argues that the President was aspiring 'to be a kind of Atatürk in reverse'(1982: 227). From the late 1970s even Tunisia, one of the most ardent supporters of secularization, began to weaken its opposition to Islam and its symbols, encouraging the population to fulfil their religious obligations, building more mosques and revitalizing religious teaching in schools (Enhali and Adda 2003). By the time modern states realized that they were helping to mobilize the opposition that their policies had been designed to prevent, the number and influence of both moderate Muslims and praxisitioners had grown considerably. Radical groups were now visibly challenging nations-states. In Egypt, the threat was realized belatedly by Sadat, who clamped down on dissent and opponents' activities. However, this contributed to opponents being forced underground, where their actions were harder to monitor. Groups such as *al-Jihad* were mobilized to take more radical action against the state, culminating in the assassination of Sadat in 1981.

The earlier concessions have meant that secularists have conceded ground to the outsider groups that it is proving very difficult to reclaim. Praxist Islam has penetrated social institutions, and radical norms, values and practices are embedded within processes of socialization. The moderate Saudi author Abdallah Thabit (2003: 1) has claimed in the aftermath of a legal case involving the author Ibrahim Shahbi being unsuccessfully sued for 'secularism' that

> don't you know that I, like millions of others, have learned since childhood that anyone who is not with me is the enemy of Allah and His messenger . . . ? After all, you are the product of [the same system of] education that advocates that whoever shaves his beard, changes the [style of] his clothes, and thins his moustache is a secular [person] who wants to control me, my family, my society, and my country with his Western ideas.

Governments across Muslim societies have adopted similar approaches that have conversely led to many Muslims viewing gov-

ernment policies as opportunistic, lacking legitimacy when set alongside their broader secular direction. As Pollack (2003: 34) notes, 'the
attempts of the [Saudi] ruling family to counteract the opposition by
burnishing its own Islamic credentials yielded the terms of the argument to the extremists, and ultimately served to increase their
freedom of action and access to resources.' The Saudi government
increased spending on Islamic aid, charitable organizations abroad as
well as on Islamic education, which, 'proved, at best, counterpro-
ductive; subsequent revelations strongly suggest that *al-Qa'ida* was
among the beneficiaries' (ibid.). Governments have therefore found it
difficult to reclaim the political use of religion, particularly after
radical movements had emerged into the space left vacant by previous irreligious policies, and are having to develop other strategies that
connect with the increased moderate Muslim religiosity while isolating the praxisitioners.

The unintended consequences of government actions are not restricted to internal attempts at controlling religion and other ideologies. There have been a series of decisions made by nation-states that
have contributed to the Islamic resurgence and radicalization, in particular within other countries. Examples include a mixture of American, Pakistani and Saudi training, military equipment, financial and
logistical support and, in the latter two cases, recruits for the Afghan
mujahideen during their war against the Soviet Union. Saudi Arabia
and the other Gulf nations generally have also used some of their
petro-dollars to provide considerable funding to Islamic groups and
schools in many countries. These policies have provided praxisitioners with more resources, military and technological knowledge,
finance, freedom to operate and recruit new members, long-lasting
ties and loyalties, and to establish long-term plans ultimately to challenge some of the states that have provided them with support. The
implications of support for the Afghan *mujahideen* did not become
apparent until long after the Soviet Union had been defeated. In a
different manner, the American-led invasion of Iraq in support of
'freedom' and 'democracy' and the subsequent military control have
led to the reported humiliation and degradation of Iraqi prisoners
and the deaths of several thousand civilians. This has strengthened
anti-American feeling, fed the appeal of praxist Islam and provided
groups associated with *al-Qa'ida* with contemporary 'evidence'
which can be used to justify their violent terrorist campaign against
the West.

Muslim societies, and more recently Western governments, have
become increasingly aware of the threat that radical Islam is posing.

Nation-states have taken different approaches to suppress the religious opposition but this has tended to be 'dual track', aimed at repressing radicals while promoting Islam as a means of social control designed to appeal to moderates. This is a very difficult balancing act. For example, North African and Gulf states have frequently sought to repress radical Islam through mass imprisonment while cultivating what they consider to be more moderate Islam which they have relied upon to legitimize state policies and institutions and focus attention upon individual piety. Few Muslim states have been willing to permit the existence of a political Islamic party, and in cases where this has been allowed, such as Turkey and Morocco, religious parties have been closely regulated. This dual-track approach has a number of effects. It gives the radicals' ideology greater significance and a higher profile than they might otherwise achieve and drives them underground where they use clandestine tactics. As such they are harder to detect and monitor. With limited democratic means of protest such groups frequently seem to turn towards violent resistance. Conversely, the policy of using Islam as a mechanism for social control contributes to undermining the *ulema* and provides people with awareness of an opposing ideology that has a 'double legitimacy', by being involved in historical successes but not associated with contemporary problems. Legitimacy is also gained within the social, political and cultural networks that religious groups have established within Muslim communities. These groups are able to utilize the space left vacant by nation-states' limited social welfare provisions to gain support for their pragmatic approach, which then legitimizes more radical interpretations than the grassroots organizations actually hold. As Paz (2003: 58) argues, this, 'Islamic atmosphere' provides a greenhouse effect 'for violent groups as well as the preservation of worldviews where hostility towards the West or Western culture dominates'. Finally, the increasing influence of radical Islam within wider Muslim cultures has, over time, resulted in conflicting concepts and challenging ideologies being immersed and frequently adapted or accepted, within those cultures (Paz 2001a).

Different approaches have been adopted to make use of, control and repress Islam that have contributed to the broad Islamic resurgence and radical Muslim movements. The repression, weak civil societies and restricted levels of political participation within many Muslim societies have resulted in very limited opportunities for societal debate, discussion and disagreement, which in turn is resulting in groups feeling that existing Islamic networks and radical approaches are the only viable methods for mobilizing opposition.

When these circumstances are allied with widespread problems, frustration and anger, Halliday's observation (2000: 83) on the behaviour of the most extreme praxisitioners is most apt. Acts of terrorism are the 'politics born of desperation, not in the sense that people are necessarily destitute, although some of them certainly are, but in the sense that all other means of change are apparently exhausted' or perhaps seen as discredited.

Other pragmatic factors must also be taken into account when explaining the growth of praxisitioners, including the increase in organizational, financial, intellectual and technical resources allied to technological and weaponry advancements, which have provided radical outsiders with the means, skills, experience and capability to build support and oppose the established at nation-state and global levels. All of these factors have combined to provide radical outsiders with growing support, legitimacy and opportunities to challenge the established. Many of the influential figures within Jihadi Salafist groups like *al-Qa'ida* are well educated, often at *madrasa*s or religious schools, particularly in Pakistan and Saudi Arabia, from relatively prosperous families, possessing technical and technological skills, conversant with different cultures and ideologies. As the attackers on 11 September 2001 showed, they are able to integrate within Western societies.

Recent attacks across the world have all played a part in reinforcing the role of 'common history' within the radicals' 'group charisma'; even though it is different groups that are committing the attacks (Burke 2003) they are contributing to a generic praxist charisma. More particularly, these show, as did the victory in Afghanistan over the Soviet Union, what 'Islam' is capable of. As bin Laden (1997) said, 'the glory and myth of the superpower was destroyed not only in my mind, but also in [the minds] of all Muslims.' Reported Muslim responses to the 2001 attacks in America indicate that the terrorists seem to have achieved this objective. For example, Brown (2001) reports on Muslim reactions within the Middle East, quoting a Palestinian respondent who stated, 'I feel like I am in a dream. I never believed that one day the United States would come to pay a price for its support to Israel.' A Lebanese resident remarked that 'we're ecstatic. Let America have a taste of what we've tasted.' Much newspaper coverage adopted a similar interpretation of events, exemplified by the Iraqi al-Iraq claiming that 'the myth of America was destroyed with the World Trade Center.' And as earlier examples showed, praxist Muslims have attributed stigma to the West, based upon common history, commencing with the Crusaders. Crucially however for most moderate Muslims, whose religiosity has either remained constant or has grown in part due to governments' policies but remains focused at an individual or community level, these attacks have reinforced their beliefs in moderation and the stigmatization they associate with the terrorists. In other words, rather than being motivated to overthrow governments by the terrorists' actions, the attacks are repulsing moderate Muslims and confirming the appropriateness of Islam as a private and not radically political practice.

The above analysis suggests that the radical Islamic approach to conflict is now globalized. Certainly some groups remain loyal to local and national concerns; for example, *Hamas* and *Hizbollah* are predominantly linked to Palestinian and Lebanese issues respectively. However, there is an increasing perception of a global challenge by groups associated with *al-Qa'ida* that cross-cuts international barriers, as witnessed by attacks on Western targets by people of other nationalities. Western nation-states readily promote this perception when seeking to justify their increasingly repressive actions and restrictions of individual liberties. There are questions over the extent that government concerns about coordinated international terrorism are well founded or even exaggerated. But such concerns provide further strengthening of the stigma attributed to radical groups, which reciprocally strengthens the praxisitioners' group charisma within elements of Muslim societies. In short, challenging and being denounced by the West appears to be strengthening their profile and appeal. The acts of terrorism associated with *al-Qa'ida* are also contributing to growing divisions within Muslim communities. The majority of Muslims are repulsed by terrorism carried out in the name of Islam, and these attacks are reinforcing their moderate beliefs and values. This is not to say that their repulsion will lead to an inevitable increase in pro-Westernism. On the contrary, there are signs that Western, especially American, policies and actions are contributing to growing feelings of anti-Americanism amongst moderate Muslims. Attempts to bifurcate Muslim societies and communities into militant and pro-Western secularist groups are contributing to the importance of groups within the resurgence, who support neither, being neglected.

Conclusion

The established–outsiders framework gives us a useful way of analysing the Islamic resurgence around the world, and praxisitioners in particular, and takes us beyond the dominant secularization theories by focusing attention on the social relations and activities involved in shifting power relations. However, the theory of intensified globalization adds an additional element, the rapidly changing context, through which these changes become explicable. Although the balance of power continues to weigh against radical Muslims, the latter do not accept the former's definitions and labels as part of an imposed 'group stigma'. On the contrary, groups like *al-Qa'ida* have internalised a positive self-image based upon an ideology that is legitimized by success interpreted within 'common history' and recent events, that provides explanations for the contemporary situation and offers solutions. These outsiders generate 'group charisma' around their beliefs and practices and attribute 'group stigma' to the established as part of the reciprocal nature of the diametrically opposed positions between state secularists and praxisitioners. This process applies for praxisitioners who have internalized these beliefs during socialization, irrespective of socio-economic classifications. It can therefore explain why radical Islam can appeal to members of the established and outsiders, the educated and uneducated, employed and unemployed and urban and rural inhabitants.

Both the established and outsiders are entrenched within their opposed positions. The outcome of this relationship will depend to a large extent upon how the causes of stigma and charisma are approached. In many ways *al-Qa'ida* and related groups can be seen as a reaction to, and consequence of, Western and secular actions. Without widespread structural changes that address economic inequalities, cultural concerns, political injustices and conflicts such as that between Israel and the Palestinians, the praxist challenge to the established, in all likelihood, will continue. Islamic symbols and actions are increasingly visible and prominent within Muslim societies, becoming widely accepted and embedded, with social relations and activities leading to a new generation being socialized, internalizing more radical views. The destruction of high-profile groups like *al-Qa'ida* will have only limited impact, both within the contemporary context and on longer-term support. The challenge will continue as praxisitioners identify and oppose the secular forces that they have identified as 'operating behind their backs' and proactively campaign both to raise the awareness about national and international events and experiences and moderate Muslims' levels of Islamic consciousness. Indeed, unless the approach being adopted by Western nation-states becomes multi-layered and able to incorporate the political, economic, cultural and social factors behind the more widespread

Islamic resurgence, then the ongoing 'war on terror' will continue both to reinforce and reinvigorate the radicals' group charisma and their own group disgrace. In this context, the invasion of Iraq may well strengthen the group charisma of many in the West, but for many Muslims (and it should be said, for many other non-Muslims in the West) it has helped to stigmatize Western nations, especially America and Britain.

7

$\mathcal{R}$esurgent Islam and Sociology

Introduction

Can sociology adequately deal with the resurgence of Islam and the emergence of international and global Islamic social movements? Is sociological research inevitably prejudiced in this task by its Western or European origins? What, if anything, can a sociological analysis add to current understandings of the contemporary global situation regarding relations between 'Islam and the West'? Can sociologists identify the social processes that are contributing towards the Islamic resurgence? It is questions such as these that have stimulated the production of this book. The issue of sociology's response to dramatic events such as Islamic terrorism was recently thrown into stark relief and stated quite bluntly in Steve Fuller's provocative and ultimately productive contribution (2001) to a special 'Rapid Response' section of the British journal *Sociological Research Online*, in the immediate aftermath of *al-Qa'ida's* destructive 11 September attacks on America. Fuller (ibid.: 1.1) argued that many of the initial contributions to this debate tended to 'reduce events to instances of already recognisable tendencies', rather than viewing unpredicted events such as violent acts of terrorism and the mass murder of civilians in the name of religion as demanding further conceptual development. The implication of this critique is that there is an inherent conservatism within the sociological establishment, which fails to allow empirical evidence to drive the discipline forward, but instead shoehorns evidence into ready-made, familiar and comfortable theoretical frameworks. Such a description is not altogether inaccurate, though may be somewhat overstated.

In response it can be argued that although real world events should always be reality checks on our often firmly held assumptions and theories about social life, the special contribution of sociology, as compared to political analysis, journalism and other forms of writing, is the creative combination of sociologists' inevitable involvement in social life and its events with a systematic attempt to achieve a measure of relative detachment from such events in order to locate the latter in a wider and longer-term perspective (Vertigans and Sutton 2001). This book has consistently tried to demonstrate the benefits for understanding underlying social processes of such a sociological perspective, though, of course, much more empirical work needs to be done to substantiate some of the explanations developed here. This kind of sociological focus is badly needed amidst the dominant, politically inspired attempts to understand Islam, particularly Islamic movements, and the relationship between Islam and the West, which hold sway in recent social scientific studies.

Sociology in the 'new world order'

Not surprisingly, the *al-Qa'ida* attacks on 11 September 2001 and later Islamically oriented terrorism continue to attract widespread interest within the academic world as it seeks to understand and explain such acts and to speculate about the future course of events. This volume has drawn on existing resources from within the broad sociological tradition to show what these may be able to contribute to current debates, and it is for readers to make up their minds on whether the attempt has been successful. In taking a lead from sociological theories and research, we have been mindful of Zygmunt Bauman's argument (1982) regarding the temptation for sociologists to frame their analyses of contemporary events in terms of previous social structures and sociological habits. Bauman sees this as potentially a source of error. In relation to 1980s sociological discussions of changes in the social class structure of the industrialized capitalist societies, Bauman observed that many of these remained based on empirically outdated and therefore ultimately misleading 'historical memories' of cohesive class-based cultures. Such historical memories prevented sociologists from accurately observing recent trends in the class structure. In the same way, many contemporary discussions of relations between Islam and the West are informed by the idea of a 'new Cold War' and are thus framed by the historical figuration known as the 'Cold War', now defunct. This similarly restricts and misleads more than it provides any real insights. The example of a 'new Cold War' analysis highlights the need to distinguish between concepts very much designed for specific cases (the post-1945 'Cold War'), which are therefore time- and space-limited in application, and those general sociological concepts that are applicable across many differing cases. The more general problem of sociology adopting a 'reactive' mode to contemporary events relates to the introduction of new concepts without the evaluation of existing theories and concepts, which may still have useful contributions to make in understanding and explaining such events.

Reactions to, and attempts to explain events can be particularly problematic in the study of violent terrorist attacks, which Laqueur (2001: 3) notes, when committed in and against Western nations, 'attract inordinate attention because of [their] dramatic character and . . . sudden, often wholly unexpected, occurrence.' In part, this is because of the diverse and wide-ranging mass media in Western nations, which are able to reach an overwhelming majority of the population, creating a common framing of events, often simplifying reasons and underlying causes. Violent terrorism also, of course, punctures people's sense of social stability and safety in the pacified social spaces of the self-defined 'civilized countries'. In this way it is not unusual that acts of terrorism committed in the West are seen not only as 'barbaric', but often also as special and even unique events. This collapsing of memory was clearly evident in some of the immediate responses and commentary, suggesting that 11 September 2001 marked the shift to 'a new world order', that 'the world has changed forever' and so on. Nevertheless, in spite of, and perhaps precisely because of, this type of widespread feeling, sociological analysis needs to strive towards some measure of relative detachment (Elias 1987), to achieve some measure of distantiation from current events, however unpalatable this may be to those with prior political commitments, if the discipline is not to be reduced to journalism by other means. This is not, of course, an easy or perhaps even widely accepted task and one that is even more difficult to argue for at the present time. Hence, whilst concept formation has long been a familiar part of sociological work, this should not simply be event-led but has to be tied to ongoing research programmes, as it is these which enable us to make that critical step of detachment that marks out systematic sociological work from that of our 'intellectual cousins'. Such a conclusion is not an injunction to 'reduce events to instances of already recognisable tendencies' as described by Fuller, but is rather to suggest that in a very real sense, *all events* are 'reality checks' on sociological theories and concepts if sociology is a discipline that is, or should be, inherently theoretical-empirical, with theories developing in continuous interplay with empirical evidence of many kinds.

It may well be, as Fuller suggests, that recent terrorism will lead to the development of new concepts, but this cannot occur in a theoretical vacuum and should be considered within ongoing research programmes. The import of this argument is that we should be careful about adding to the often criticized (sometimes unfairly) sociological lexicon unless existing concepts are demonstrably shown to be inadequate for the purpose. Much of the analysis of 11 September 2001 has been journalistic in approach, providing snapshot analysis of the terrorist actions, their impact and possible underlying causes. Perhaps this was inevitable so soon after the events, but attempts to identify and explain the underlying reasons have tended to be limited, possibly tempered by the penetration of the 'for us or against us' perspective that often arises when national identities are seen to be under threat. Such reasoning is vividly illustrated in Potter's argument (2001) that 'the depraved, the mad and the disenchanted will sign up for *jihad*.' As argued in chapters 2 and 3 here, this line of argument does not add anything to our understanding of the complex reasoning of Islamic radicals in particular social and historical contexts and fails to explore significant social and political change. The expansion of the role of the mass media and education in Muslim and formerly Islamic nations, geographically expansive communication networks, new developments in information technologies, the unintentional opening up of political opportunities by measures at statecraft and the effects of radical Islamic terrorists' 'successes' on interpretations of the Islamic faith, all of these need to be built into explanations of Islamic resurgence and terrorism. Similarly, recommendations for Western states to take military action and to use violence against those whose views and actions are seen as 'irrational' and not amenable to rational discourse and argument tend to reproduce the mutual antagonisms they claim to have discovered and analysed, as in Huntington's thesis of civilizational conflict (see chapter 5). The interpretation of committed religious argument and behaviour as 'irrational' demonstrates that the intellectual roots of many contemporary explanations for different forms of Islam lie within the secularization perspective derived from the early twentieth-century sociology of religion, though this secularization analysis is ultimately grounded in theories of economic and cultural modernization.

If sociology is to have distinctive things to say about Islam in the increasingly global context of interdependent social relations, then it has to work hard to avoid taking the side of the relatively powerful or that of the relatively powerless. In their distinctively sociological work, it is only by taking a 'detour via detachment' (Elias 1987: 105) that sociologists are able to gain a better view of the web of social relations and its underlying social processes. Hopefully, this book will stimulate debate on this significant matter, particularly amongst those who might disagree with the analysis outlined here. In the final sections therefore, it may be helpful to summarize and bring together the explanatory 'yield' of the book.

Secularization, globalization, socialization

1 Secularization

One particular sociological explanatory model does not come out of this analysis with much support, namely the mainstream sociological theory of secularization. The growth of Islam across the world highlights the inadequacies, Eurocentrism and Christian-centredness of the secularization thesis. In so far as Western, majority-Christian nations *have* experienced a secularization of social life, belief systems and state power, the thesis continues to hold up pretty well, though even here the demise of Communist systems in Eastern Europe has enabled traditional religions to make headway once again (Martin 1991). Outside Europe of course, the American case raises some serious questions about the secularization thesis as applied in the West (Warner 1993). In relation to Islam, the secularization thesis tends to mislead and take on a more ideological cast rather than being a testable social scientific hypothesis. Whilst, as forecast by the thesis, people *have* developed secular beliefs and ideologies and nation-states *are* formally in control of religion, the growth of practising Muslims, the establishment of Islamic states and the emergence of radical Islamic social movements forces sociologists of religion to reassess the validity of the claim that secularization is a dominant social process across the world. Secularization now seems *not* to be an irreversible or unstoppable social process, nor is it *inevitably* accepted within non-Western countries. Instead, it appears that even traditional religions may flourish within the context of (post)modern consumer societies, even with their focus on choice in the context of a 'pick and mix' approach to religious belief and practice. Although such a social context may be leading in some instances to less uniform religious adherence, it may well be that 'This is consumerism, perhaps, but of a deeply serious kind' (Aldridge 2000: 215).

A more optional religious adherence may not imply a lessening of religious *experience*, which simply takes new forms and applies even to interpretations that preach a universalism based upon the past but adapted for the present. In this respect, we can remind ourselves that it is a basic tenet of functionalism that, in order to survive, social institutions have to change with the changing social context. Thus it would be a sign of ossification and irrelevance if religions failed to change in relation to wider social processes. In relation to Islam, the process of diversification can be seen in the varied Islamic interpretations discussed throughout the book which build upon the multifarious practices throughout the religion's history. Such variety may be seen not as the failure of Islam in face of the forces of secular modernity, but, on the contrary, of the creative modification of the religion by groups of Muslims adapting their faith in differing social contexts.

Despite flaws that make the straightforward application of the secularization thesis to the Islamic resurgence inappropriate, the thesis remains extremely influential. The majority of attempts to understand and explain why Muslims are becoming more religious or turning towards terrorism can be traced to the pervasive influence of secularization arguments. This is because such arguments continue to rely on the merits of the thesis, using it as a benchmark by which to compare what *is* happening with what the thesis suggests *should* be happening. Thus we are regularly informed that the resurgence is a reaction to modernization and urbanization, that people are becoming more religious as a consequence of exclusion from employment and material wealth, isolation from previously strong social bonds or as a result of feeling threatened by pervasive Western culture or, at least for Muslims in the West, that racism and discrimination are causing a turn towards Islamic extremism. Such factors have indeed been significant, but as generalizations they can mislead, as the multilayered appeal of Islam across socio-economic groups, rural–urban divides, communities, nations and across continents shows. In short, the factors above tend to be viewed through the lens of the secularization tradition, which then leads to increasing levels of religiosity being seen as the consequence of an inadequate or incomplete implementation of secularization and modernization. By continuing to anticipate that secularization will win out eventually, that values associated with Western modernity will prove universally popular, that once economic and political modernization programmes bring onboard excluded and isolated groups then religious challenges will be reduced or eliminated, analyses of the Islamic resurgence are not able to explain its longer-term development or produce a programme which might genuinely tackle terrorism.

We may conclude that the secularization thesis is now too blunt an instrument to capture the diversity of resurgent Islam, and although we cannot ignore the impact of secularizing forces and the intentional secularizing offensives adopted by governments over the twentieth century, the deeply embedded assumptions of inevitability and irreversibility underpinning the strong secularization thesis are now increasingly open to empirical challenges. The latter will hopefully lead to a more reality-congruent understanding of the position of and prospects for religions in an increasingly globalized world.

2 Globalization and civilizations

Sociological theories of globalization capture some important dynamics which are helping to shape the contemporary world; these include the spread of trade and economic connections across larger areas of the planet, challenges to indigenous cultures posed by the expansion of Western patterns of consumer culture and the interplay between pressures for globalizing uniformity and the preservation of local diversity. Globalization theories therefore alert us to some of the changing contexts within which religious groups, including Islamic movements, operate. However, we should avoid reading globalization as simply a recent, late twentieth- and early twenty-first-century process that might then explain a multitude of social developments, not least the rise of religious 'fundamentalist' movements opposed to globalization in its secular 'Westernizing' form. Globalization can instead be theorized as a very long-term social process that involves the gradual spread of interdependent social relationships across larger geographical regions, though this expansion involves violent conflict, inequalities and asymmetrical power relations as well as peaceable cooperation. As Georg Simmel reminds us, conflict is not simply the breakdown of a relationship; sociologically, conflicts are themselves specific *types of* social relationship that force people to take cognisance of each other's existence in very direct ways. Simmel (1966 [1955]: 14) explains this aspect by comparing conflict with indifference: 'Whether it implies the rejection or the termination of sociation, indifference is purely negative. In contrast to such pure negativity, conflict contains something positive. Its positive and negative aspects, however, are integrated; they can be separated conceptually, but not empirically.' As de Swaan (2001a: 140) argues, 'States come into existence through violent competition. The relations formed in such struggles also constitute a system of mutual dependence but not one of mutual co-ordination.' Though perhaps difficult to align with modern values and diplomatic forms of conflict resolution, over the long term, globalization processes have very often been driven through conflictual and violent group relations, sometimes involving the annihilation of 'enemies'.

Adopting such a long-term approach to globalization puts current debates into perspective and shows why, in the deteriorating climate of rising antagonism and mutual suspicion, radical praxisitioners and American Presidents make highly significant references to the European Crusades which took place more than 850 years ago. Nonetheless, for many, such a historical reference point remains a meaningful way of framing global politics for twenty-first-century people. As explored in chapters 1 and 4, Islam *was* the first globalized religious empire, expanding rapidly between the sixth and eighth centuries AD (Held et al. 1999: 415). The long-term process of globalization can be interpreted by Islamic radicals as developing in phases, from an expansive Islamic form of globalization, through a gradual decline leading to an extended period of European and Western-dominated globalization. Such a reading tends to accentuate the feelings of group disgrace that are a motivating factor for praxisitioners, who argue that the Islamic globalizing phase failed because of a lack of commitment to practice on the part of Muslims. In order to grasp the currently antagonistic relations between militant Islamic groups and Western governments, it becomes important to examine the way that historical development is reconstructed and reinterpreted as a way of making sense of the present. Chapters 2 and 4 began to unravel some of this process in relation to Islamic radicals, though of course, some Western interpretations continue to view their own historical cultural origins as dynamic and creative whilst imputing backwardness and a lack of economic dynamism to others.

3 Socialization

Technological advancements in communications associated with globalization have also had a major impact on socialization processes across the world. These technological developments, allied to shifting social relationships, have been particularly significant within

Muslim societies. This is because these societies have been undergoing more rapid periods of change than Western societies. Following independence and/or attempts to undergo rapid modernization, most majority-Muslim nation-states have implemented far-reaching reforms. Ultimately these were designed to modernize nations and economies in order to provide resources for increasing security and defending national sovereignty, to develop an economic base on which enhance their power chances and international status and allow for internal wealth distribution to confer legitimacy on governments and weaken opposition. A range of approaches has been adopted, ranging from vigorous secularization in Turkey and Tunisia to theologically cloaked Saudi reforms. All have shared the belief that modernization is only possible by reforming state structures and political ideologies and generating more individualistic personalities, though some governments have tended to concentrate their efforts on what are considered to be the key strategic regions, invariably urban areas. With the exception of Saudi Arabia, which has sought to emphasize its traditionalism, one common feature of reform programmes has been an intention to undermine the role of traditional sources of authority, including the *ulema* and the family, whose values were considered an impediment to progress. Conversely, governments have simultaneously used the *ulema* to provide theological legitimacy for national state policies.

Education systems have been rapidly developed both to provide well-qualified and competent workers and to socialize them into the nation-states' secular ideology. However, education has also been used to attract support from religious groups and individuals seeking more Islamic influence, to provide solace for those undoubtedly suffering from rapid social changes and also as a means of countering rival ideologies such as Arab nationalism and socialism. It was felt that these different objectives could be achieved by enhancing the religious component within curricula, and this required a dramatic increase in the numbers of Islamic teachers, together with the establishment of more religious schools. The common outcome has been that while both socialism and Arab nationalism have been undermined, partly due to their own internal problems, levels of individual religiosity have increased within broad resurgences. Secular states have also inadvertently contributed to the radicalization of many Muslims. Opportunities have been provided for praxisitioners in education systems, and radical Muslims have been able to develop into well-educated professionals, able to obtain influential positions within government departments or the private sector and use their newly created skills to recruit new praxisitioners and provide important leadership roles for militant groups and movements. The problem has been compounded by the expansion of communication systems, increasing accessibility of the mass media, the emergence of satellite television and the development of electronic communications. As a consequence, better-educated audiences are finding information and seeing images that were previously denied them by a weak electricity infrastructure, patchy and slow communications and repressive governments. The latter seem to be much less adept at censoring the newer methods of communication. Such changes have therefore provided Muslims with more information both about radical forms of Islam and about experiences and events that can be explained by the radicals' ideological position, feeding into levels of support for them. Moderate Muslims whose religiosity has increased at a personal level are also having their beliefs strengthened by their perceptions of local, national and international problems and increased familiarity with Muslims from different cultures, which is helping to revitalize the *ummah* into a vibrant, heterogeneous source of unity. Conversely, improved levels of information exchange have contributed to greater awareness about the discourse and actions associated with more radical groups and this is solidifying the opposition many moderate Muslims feel towards such groups.

The way forward: resurgent Islam and sociology

The current Islamic resurgence is associated with a 'triple legitimacy' that Islamic doctrines have received from three main sources: historical events and their interpretation; provision of social services and community networks; and social and international problems associated with secular ways of life. The directions in which the different resurgences will continue to develop depend largely on the levels of legitimacy allocated to Islamic doctrines and practice, together with the emerging combinations of tradition and modernity. Interpretations of Islamic history seem set to continue as a source of legitimacy for the resurgence, as the formerly prosperous and expansionist Muslim empires have become a source of group charisma which is a key feature in the construction of modern Islamic identity formation and group solidarity. This may well be the case for both moderate and praxist Muslims. However, the continuing relevance of such reinterpretations will depend on their ability to provide a meaningful narrative and this, in part, depends on the changing contemporary context.

Moreover, there are continuing gains in legitimacy for Islamic religious movements and brotherhoods that provide practical support for poorer elements in local communities. This is likely to change only if such Muslim groups stop providing services or if governments were able to extend welfare provision considerably and introduce a more comprehensive social welfare system to address poverty, housing shortages, health and educational inequalities and unemployment. Clearly there are enormous cost implications which are beyond the budgets of the overwhelming number of majority-Muslim nation-states operating within the current global division of resources. When even the relatively rich nations in the global figuration of states have been cutting back on welfare spending, it appears unrealistic to think that relatively poorer states would buck this trend. Therefore without the contributions of religious groups, the lives of many Muslims would be considerably poorer and this helps to legitimize Islam as a religious support network in societies. In addition, the increased presence of religious beliefs and rhetoric, religious symbols and appearance as elements in what Paz (2003) describes as the 'Islamic atmosphere' has led to greater familiarity and acceptance of religion within civil societies. Both historical interpretation and religious support networks are therefore instrumental in generating higher levels of religiosity that feed into the broader Islamic resurgence.

Militant Islam has also been legitimized for some praxisitioners and potential supporters by the successful transformation by groups associated with *al-Qa'ida* of beliefs into actions against nation-states and international symbols. However there are signs that the weakening of *al-Qa'ida*'s 'hardcore' has had a detrimental impact upon the long-term strategic struggle, with associated groups' acts of terrorism lacking the popular symbolism of earlier attacks and increasingly de-legitimizing their cause (Burke 2004). The indiscriminate killing both of Spanish civilians in the 2004 Madrid bombing and of Muslims in attacks in Saudi Arabia (2004) and atrocities committed against Shi'a Muslims and aid workers in Iraq cannot be justified to the overwhelming majority of Muslims.

Islam as a radical ideological position has been legitimized, in part, because of what it has *not* been involved in. That is, the marginalization of Islam in the secular reform programmes of majority-Muslim states has not tarnished the religion at an individual level.

Radicals have used this exclusion to argue that a return to 'pure' forms of Islam would mark an end to economic mismanagement, autocratic elites, nepotism, political corruption and military and diplomatic weaknesses as well as providing the necessary social cohesion to solve a range of seemingly intractable social problems such as unemployment, failing businesses, anomie and alienation. In this way, secular ideologies such as nationalism and socialism have been significantly undermined by their perceived failures in the spheres of international relations and national development.

At the national level, societies are encountering rapid change as modernization processes, allied to globalization, continue. Millions of Muslims have experienced a mixture of consequences as their lifestyles and communities are being transformed, involving both positive and negative effects. Many Muslims have benefited from modernization, which has brought opportunities for relatively well-paid employment. Businesses have flourished as transport and communication systems have considerably expanded and improved. On the other hand, social inequalities have tended to widen, shifting employment patterns have led to some sectors experiencing higher levels of unemployment with negative consequences for local small businesses, the disruption of social networks and heightened feelings of insecurity. All these factors have made a contribution but explanatory frameworks which focus only on the negatives, seeing social exclusion as both the necessary and sufficient cause of the Islamic resurgence simply fail to take account of the variety of social groups which are integral to it and the religion's broad appeal. Such explanations can therefore only ever be partially successful and have tended to obscure the character of the resurgence today, not least the increasing religiosity and commitment of well-educated social groups with established or promising careers, which do not fit the stereotype of the 'fundamentalist'.

Fluctuating levels of support amongst educated groups for 'Western values' such as democracy, freedom, equality and justice are not due to any inherent 'Muslim' dislike or opposition from within the *Shari'ah*. Passages that support or oppose such values can both be found within the *Qu'ran* and *ahadith*. Opposition seems to be growing as 'Western' has increasingly come to be associated with 'American', an interpretation which has become stronger since the end of the Cold War. The development of anti-Americanism and greater exposure to 'Western values' has had a detrimental impact upon Muslim perceptions. For example, 'democracy' in Israel seems to many Muslims only applicable to Jews and Israeli Arabs as Palestinians are currently excluded with no political representation in the governing Knesset, which ultimately controls the occupied territories (of course, Palestinians are not requesting participation in Israeli politics as this would undermine their claims for independence). The cancellation of elections in Algeria when the FIS, the religious coalition, was set to win and American support for autocratic, nominally Muslim regimes have undermined Western claims to support democratization across the world. More recently, the latest American push for democracy in the Middle East is viewed cautiously. There is considerable popular support for greater political participation, but there is also much scepticism and concern over American intentions. The controversy surrounding the 2000 American elections has also drawn negative comments and tarnished America's self-image as guardian of democratic principles. Equally, the concepts of freedom and justice have been called into question, even in the West, following the deaths of thousands of civilians during the invasion and occupation of Iraq and the widespread shock at the abuses committed in the Abu Ghraib prison, presented graphically in mass media across the world. The incredulity expressed by many Americans, including some politicians, demonstrated the effect of these events on the national self-image. For many Muslims, these abuses provide new sources of the 'minority of the worst' from which to confirm their assessment of Western culture as a whole, as decadent and immoral. When the partisan role of America in the Israeli–Palestinian conflict and the repressive measures legitimized by the 'war on terror', which threatens to 'criminalize' Muslims in the West, are added into the picture, it becomes easier to understand why Muslim religiosity is growing and the ideology of radical Islamic movements is gaining credibility, especially amongst younger generations.

Where praxist movements have come to power in Iran, Sudan and Afghanistan, moderate Muslims have tended to become much more critical of the potential of radical forms of Islam to solve social problems. Hassan's research (2002) found that the influence of religious institutions is greatest when functioning independently, because the public loses trust when Islam becomes integrated with political structures. The failure of such regimes significantly to improve the lives of the majority has meant that no contemporary, attractive Islamic governmental models exist for others to strive for. This suggests that the appeal of radical Islamic movements would be adversely affected if they became established in the governments of other nation-states. At present this is unlikely. Within mainstream political participation, the exclusion of radical movements has meant that their programmes and policy positions are rarely subjected to critical scrutiny in the public arena and their inconsistencies and internal contradictions are thus not fully exploited by opponents. In this way, the lack of political representation in many majority-Muslim nations tends, unintentionally, to benefit praxisitioners.

The argument in favour of allowing greater democratic participation within the majority of Muslim nation-states is a strong one. It would probably lure some radical groups into mainstream political life; examples of this are the FIS in Algeria (prior to the cancellation of the 1992 elections), *Hezbollah* in Lebanese politics, *Jamaat-I-Islami* at various stages of the democratic process in Pakistan and the restricted involvement of the Muslim Brotherhood in Egypt. Such involvement has a propensity to weaken the mobilizing potential of radical Islamic ideologies. *Hamas's* participation in municipal elections in December 2004, in which it gained control of nine local councils, could be considered as part of this process. However, it is currently unclear if this marks a significant change in the group's strategy or whether democratic participation is a short-term policy or possibly part of a twin-track approach alongside continuing terrorist activities. Of course, such a strategy cannot be applied to all radical groups, many of which reject any involvement in democratic arrangements. In particular, the international terrorist networks would probably not change their violent approach, though their potential pool of support may be weakened. Alternatively, the more that moderate Islamic parties participate in organized politics, the more likely it is that they may themselves be tainted by being associated with social problems and corruption, thus losing credibility and lending support to radical activity. Introducing democracy into majority-Muslim societies, or indeed any society, will not inevitably produce a representative, secure, sovereign government. It has to be remembered that democracy in the West was implemented gradually, with the franchise rolled out to more social groups as the supporting legal, economic and humanitarian policies were developed, or as some might argue, until the electorate could be trusted to vote for the 'right' parties. In undemocratic Muslim nations, governments tend strictly to control the economy, judiciary and civil society. Such arrangements would have to change if democracy was to be successfully introduced. The power of states would have to be circumscribed, economics and legal systems given more autonomy, civil society encouraged and human rights and freedoms rigorously protected (Saikal 2003).

There is popular support for political liberalization in majority-Muslim societies, but the possibility that this will be introduced extensively remains unlikely in the short term. Secular governments and the Gulf monarchies feel they have much to lose and nothing to gain from doing so. Despite Western politicians' rhetoric regarding the need for political liberalization, this is often tempered by fears that democracy would provide the means for Islamic parties to gain ground that state repression currently seeks to deny them. Western fears may well be generally unfounded as the majority of Muslims are moderates, not praxisitioners. However, the widespread feelings of anti-Americanism across Muslim populations make it unlikely that political parties would be overtly pro-American. The opportunity to build upon the achievements of moderate Muslim parties in countries like Turkey and Malaysia still exists. It is for this reason that the impact of the governing Justice and Development Party (JDP) in Turkey is the focus of so much interest, especially in the Middle East. Since attaining power in November 2002, the JDP has managed the difficult balancing act of retaining, and indeed expanding, its broad popular support while not causing undue concern to the military who are the 'guardians' of the secular constitution and have banned a number of its predecessors over the last thirty years. The government has some difficult decisions to take but is widely seen to have made impressive progress thus far. What the example seems to show is that Islam and democracy are not inevitably incompatible. Although it is still too early to draw any firm conclusions, the long-term impact of the JDP's appeal partly stems from the charismatic Prime Minister, Recep Erdogan, whilst much will hinge on the progress of European Union accession talks which have finally been agreed to commence in October 2005, despite negative public opinion in several EU countries, especially Austria and France. Agreement to start the accession talks has been widely seen as vindication of the economic, political, legal and cultural changes that the JDP has implemented, but there is a realization that further reform is required before Turkey would be allowed to join the EU. If Turkey's application was ultimately rejected at this relatively late stage then, under present conditions, it would cause widespread annoyance and call into question the current balanced approach to relations with East and West. On the other hand, acceptance would facilitate a more rapid modernization and powerful competitive forces that would bring some considerable benefits and many problems, particularly in uncompetitive, labour-intensive areas like agriculture. The JDP currently provides legitimacy for moderate Islamic parties and strategies of democratic participation, which had been previously discredited through the combination of mismanagement by relatively weak governments and a series of military coups.

The Turkish example seems to demonstrate that a gradual increase in political liberalization and the opening up of more ideological competition could pave the way for compromises as participants move from excluded outsider status towards political inclusion and establishment. Without such political liberalization, there will be limited opportunities for opposition to be incorporated within legitimate political structures, and the prospects for violent activities by people restless for change will be enhanced.

What the analysis here has, hopefully, demonstrated is that the religious beliefs and practices of the vast majority of Muslims are not a threat to global peace and international stability. If Islam is approached in a relatively detached, sociological way, the religion is evidently providing multi-faceted functions to a diverse range of people within many different social contexts. Conflating moderate Islam with radical movements and Islamic terrorism lends weight to the impression that the threat to Western people is much more serious and widespread than the evidence suggests. The dangers of social stereotyping and the creation of 'outsiders' are thus increased.

One final question remains. What role, if any, is there for sociologists in coming to terms with the future direction of relations between 'Islam and the West'? It is a truism that many sociological texts end with a call for more research and this one is no exception. Nevertheless, our plea for originality in making this call stems from the clear lack of sociological research in this area (Ernest Gellner and Bryan Turner being perhaps the most obvious exceptions), which has become more apparent during the writing of the book. There is much scope for sociological research in this area. First, there is a need for much more empirical research in different national contexts which would help to throw some light on the localized conditions in which Muslim experiences are embedded. Second, we need to understand better why only some people become praxisitioners, particularly those who turn towards violent forms of terrorism, when many others with broadly similar experiences do not. Third, sociologists could provide a useful function by exploring how terrorists are able to produce techniques of justification that allow them to undertake such atrocities whilst continuing to adopt a recognizably 'Islamic' self-image. Some initial attempts to begin this process are contained in the chapters above, though our hope is that others will be encouraged to take further the arguments presented here or to pursue alternative lines of sociological inquiry. It is well known that Max Weber's magisterial study of the world religions was cut short before he completed his work on Islam. Surely the time is now long overdue for sociologists to bring Weber's project to fruition and take the study of Islam into the mainstream of twentieth-first-century sociology.

Glossary

Abbasids Dynasty of ruling Baghdad caliphs, 750–1258.

Ayatollah 'Sign or token of Allah'; highest religious title of Shi'a Islam.

Burqa A loose garment (usually with veiled holes for the eyes), worn by Muslim women, especially in India and Pakistan.

Caliph 'Successor'; originally referred to the *rashidun* who succeeded Muhammed.

Dar al-Harb 'House of war'; countries outside Muslim rule.

Dar al-Islam 'House of Islam'; usually refers to all of those areas under Muslim rule.

Dawa 'Call' or 'invitation'; today associated with the Dawa movement that seeks both to proselytize and increase Muslims' levels of religiosity.

Deobandi Conservative Islamic movement, named after town of Deobandi in India, the ideological inspiration for the Taliban.

Fatwa (plural, *fataawa*) Legal decision of religious scholar on a specific issue of Islamic law or formal legal opinion by the same.

Fiqh The study and application of Islamic law.

Hadith (plural, *ahadith*) Documented sayings and traditions of the Prophet Muhammad's teachings and actions, not in the *Qu'ran* but recorded by his family and close companions.

Hajj Pilgrimage to Mecca which Muslims are expected to make at least once in a lifetime if able to do so; fifth of the five pillars of Islam.

Hamas 'Harakat al-muqawama al-islamiyya', the Islamic Resistance Movement; Palestinian branch of the Muslim Brotherhood, founded 1987.

Hezbollah 'Party of God', revived in 1960s Yemen and then by Lebanese Shi'a militants in 1980s. In 2000, the latter group achieved its primary goal of removing Israeli and Israeli-backed forces from Lebanon.

Hijab 'Dressing modestly'; applies to all Muslims. Is also used to mean a headscarf and veil worn by Muslim women.

Hijrah 'Migration' or 'withdrawal' of the Prophet Muhammed and the first Muslims from Mecca to Medina in 622.

Hizb al-Tahrir 'Party of Liberation' which aims to restore the caliphate. Founded in Jordan in 1953; has a following in Britain and Western Europe, Arab and Central Asia.

Ijtihad Independent judgement or interpretation of religious text.

Imam 'Leader' (of the prayers) of the Muslim community. For Shi'a Muslims, refers to the Prophet's descendants, the true Muslim leaders, descended from his daughter Fatimah and her husband, Ali ibn Abi Talib.

Intifada 'Uprising', mostly (not exclusively) associated with Palestinian movements against Israeli occupation, 1987–92 and al-Aqsa *intifada* since 2000.

Islam 'Submission' to God or surrender to God's will. Faith of over 1.2 billion believers, majority Sunni, minority Shi'a Muslims.

Jayiliyyah 'Time (or Age) of Ignorance'; originally described pre-Islam Arabia, but today used by some to describe any society which refuses to submit to God's sovereignty.

Jihad 'Struggle' or 'effort'. Takes two main forms: (1) *Lesser jihad* – war to free Muslims from oppression or to take new lands for Islam, sometimes described as 'Holy War'. (2) *Greater jihad* – internal struggle with the self to reform bad habits.

Jihadist-Salafism New ideological hybrid that combines Salafist interpretations with absolute commitment to (lesser) *jihad* and associated most notably with *al-Qa'ida*.

Kabah Cube-shaped shrine in Mecca, dedicated to God by Muhammed. The most sacred place for Muslims and destination for pilgrims.

Kufr Atheism or ingratitude to Allah.

Madrasa 'School'. In traditional systems where there is no state education, refers to Islamic education for Muslims.

Mecca Ancient trading and pilgrimage city in western Saudi Arabia, site of the Kabah. Now has 30 km exclusion radius with access to Muslims only.

Middle East Coined by US Admiral Mahan (1902) as a geo-strategic term.

Mufti Muslim leader and interpreter/expounder of Islamic law, capable of issuing *fataawa*.

Muhammad ibn Abdallah (570–632) Prophet who brought the *Qu'ran* to Muslims and established the monotheistic faith and single polity in Arabia.

Mujahid (plural, *mujahideen*) Muslim fighter engaged in *jihad*.

Mullah 'Master, friend'; Islamic clergyman considered an expert on religious matters due to study of the *Qu'ran* and *ahadith*.

Muslim Literally, 'one who has surrendered'; a follower of Islam.

Ottomans Turkish dynasty (1299–1918) which took over the caliphate from the Abbasids.

Purda In Persian, 'curtain'; refers to the seclusion of women.

Ramadan Ninth month of Islamic calendar, time of fasting and abstinence from sexual activity from dawn to sunset.

Rashidun Four 'rightly guided' caliphs, the companions and immediate successors of Muhammed: Abu Bakr, Umar ibn al-Khattab, Uthman ibn Affan and Ali ibn Abi Talib.

Salafism Based upon the *salafiyya* movement that originated in the late nineteenth century, focusing upon the piety within early Islamic ancestors. Associated mostly with the Arabian peninsula.

Salah Five daily prayers offered to Allah; second of the five pillars of Islam.

Sawm Fasting during the month of Ramadan; third of the five pillars of Islam.

Shahadah The expression of faith, declaration of belief in the unity of God and the prophethood of Muhammed; first of the five pillars of Islam.

Shaheed 'Witness'; used to describe a martyr.

Shari'ah 'Path to the watering hole'; Islamic law mainly derived from the *Qu'ran* and *sunnah*.

Shi'a Islam Second largest branch of Islam (10–15 per cent); those Muslims belonging to the Shiah-I-Ali (Party of Ali). Shi'a Muslims believe that the Prophet's closest male relative, Ali ibn Abi Talib, should have ruled after Muhammed's death rather than the first *rashidun*. This disagreement led to the fracture of the early Islamic community into Shi'ites and Sunnis. Shi'a Muslims revere several imams directly descended from Ali and Fatimah.

Sufism Diverse range of mystic forms of Islam, not directly derived from Muhammed.

Sunnah 'Path' or 'a way' (of the Prophet); religious practice and habits of the Prophet Muhammed, regarded as the ideal Islamic norm.

The *sunnah* has been enshrined in Islamic law to guide Muslims to become closer to the Prophet's surrender to Allah.

Sunni Islam Largest branch of Islam (85–90 per cent). Sunnis or Sunnites make up the majority of Muslims who accept and revere the *rashidun* and validate the existing political order.

Talib (plural, *Taliban*) 'Religious student'; term used to describe recruits to the Taliban movement from the Pakistani Deobandi *madrasas* in 1994.

Tawhid 'Declaring God one'; affirmation of the unity of Allah, which demands correct knowledge, correct understanding and correct motivation.

Ulema (singular, *'alim*) 'Learned men'; guardians of the legal and religious traditions of Islam.

Ummah 'Community'; contemporary meaning: the global community of Muslims.

Wahhabism 'Fundamentalist' form of Sunni Islam and a major sect of Saudi Arabia. Founded by Muhammad Ibn Abd al-Wahhab (1703–87).

Zakat 'To grow or increase'; obligatory almsgiving of Muslims, being a fixed proportion of income and capital, normally 2.5 per cent; fourth of the five pillars of Islam.

[*Sources*: Distilled from numerous sources, but primarily: Armstrong 2002; Ayubi 1991; Burke 2004; Halliday 2002; Hiro 2002.]

Bibliography

Abdallah, A. M. (2003) 'Causes of Anti-Americanism in the Arab World: A Socio-Political Perspective', *Middle East Review of International Affairs*, 7(4): 62–73.

Abootalebi, A. R. (2003) 'Islam and Democracy' in B. Rubin (ed.) *Revolutionaries and Reformers: Contemporary Islamist Movements in the Middle East*. Albany, N.Y.: State University of New York Press.

Abu-Amr, Z. (1994) *Islamic Fundamentalism in the West Bank and Gaza*. Bloomington: Indiana University Press.

Afshar, H., (ed.) (1985) *Iran: A Revolution in Turmoil*. Basingstoke: Macmillan.

Ahmad, F. (1977) *The Turkish Experiment in Democracy 1950–1975*. London: C. Hurst & Co.

Ahmad, K. (1970) *Islam and the West*. Lahore: Islamic Publications.

Ahmad, K. (ed.) (1977) *Islam: Its Meaning and Message*. New Delhi: Ambika Publishers.

Ahmad, M. (1991) 'Islamic Fundamentalism in South Asia: The Jamaat-I-Islami and the Tablighi Jamaat of South Asia' in M. E. Marty and R. Scott Appleby (eds) *Fundamentalisms Observed*. Chicago: University of Chicago Press.

Ahmed, L. (1992) *Women and Gender in Islam: Historical Roots of a Modern Debate*. New Haven and London: Yale University Press.

Ahsan, M. (1991 [1997]) *Islam: Faith and Practice*. 2nd edn, Leicester: The Islamic Foundation.

Ahsan, M. and A. R. Kidwai (eds) (1991) *Sacrilege Versus Civility: Muslim Perspectives on The Satanic Verses*. Leicester: The Islamic Foundation.

Akhavi, S. (1980) *Religion and Politics in Contemporary Iran*. Albany, N.Y.: State University of New York Press.

Akşit, B. (1991) 'Islamic Education in Turkey' in R. Tapper (ed.) *Islam in Modern Turkey*. London: I. B. Tauris.

Al-Azmeh, A. (2001) 'Civilization, Culture and the New Barbarians', *International Sociology*, 16(1): 75–93.

Aldridge, A. (2000) *Religion in the Contemporary World: A Sociological Introduction*. Cambridge: Polity Press.

Al-Hunud, M. A. (2003) Transcript reported in MEMRI, http://www.memri. org/bin/opener_latest.cgi?ID=sr2403.

Alkan, T. (1984) 'The National Salvation Party in Turkey' in M. Heper and R. Israeli (eds) *Islam and Politics in the Modern Middle East*. Sydney: Croom Helm.

Al-Sayyid Said, M. (2001) reported in *Financial Times*, 13–14 October 2001.

Al-Zawahiri, A. (2001a) 'Knights under the Prophet's Banner'. Extracts available at http://www.fas.org/irp/world/para/ayman_bk.html.

Anderson, L. (1997) 'Fulfilling Prophecies: State Policies and Islamist Radicalism' in J. L. Esposito (ed.) *Political Islam: Revolution, Radicalism or Reform*. Boulder, Colo.: Lynne Rienner.

An-Na'im, A. A. (1999) 'Political Islam in National Politics and International Relations' in P. Berger (ed.) *The Desecularization of the World*. Washington and Grand Rapids, Michigan: Ethics and Public Policy Center and William B. Eerdmans Publishing Company.

Ansari, M. (1987) *The Qur'anic Foundations and Structure of Muslim Society*. Karachi: Inds Educational Foundation.

Antoun, R. (2001) *Understanding Fundamentalism: Christian, Islamic and Jewish Movements*. Walnut Creek, Calif: AltaMira Press.

Arjomand, S. A. (ed.) (1984) *From Nationalism to Revolutionary Islam*. London: Macmillan.

Arjomand, S. A. (1986) 'Social Change and Movements of Revitalization in Contemporary Islam' in J. Beckford (ed.) *New Religious Movements and Rapid Social Change*. London: SAGE Publications.

Arjomand, S. A. (1989) 'The Emergence of Islamic Political Ideologies' in J. Beckford and T. Luckmann (eds) *The Changing Face of Religion*. London: SAGE Publications.

Arjomand, S. A. and E. A. Tiryakian (eds) (2001) *Rethinking Civilizational Analysis: International Sociology*, 16(3).

Arkoun, M. (1988) 'The Concept of Authority in Islamic Thought' in K. Ferdinand and M. Mozaffari (eds) *Islam: State and Society*. London: Curzon Press.

Armstrong, K. (2001) *The Battle for God: Fundamentalism in Judaism, Christianity and Islam*. London: HarperCollins.

Armstrong, K. (2002) *Islam: A Short History*. London: Phoenix Press.

Arnason, J. P. (1996) 'State Formation in Japan and the West', *Theory, Culture and Society*, 13(3): 53–75.

Arnason, J. P. (2001) 'Civilizational Patterns and Civilizing Processes', *Rethinking Civilizational Analysis: International Sociology*, 16(3): 387–405.

Arnason, J. P. (2002) *The Peripheral Centre: Essays on Japanese History and Civilization*. Melbourne: Trans Pacific Press.

Arnason, J. P. and G. Stauth (2004) 'Civilization and State Formation in the Islamic Context: Re-reading Ibn Khaldūn', *Thesis Eleven*, 76(Feb.): 29–48.

Atacan, F. (2001) 'A Kurdish Islamist Group in Modern Turkey: Shifting Identities', *Middle Eastern Studies*, 37: 111–40.

Atkinson, J. M. (1978) *Discovering Suicide: Studies in the Social Organization of Sudden Death*. Pittsburgh: University of Pittsburgh Press.

Ayata, S. (1993) 'The Rise of Islamic Fundamentalism and its Institutional Framework' in A. Eralp, M. Tunay and B. Yeşilada (eds) *The Political and Socioeconomic Transformation of Turkey*. Westport, Conn.: Praeger Publishers.

Ayata, S. (1996) 'Patronage, Party and State: The Politicization of Islam in Turkey', *Middle East Journal*, 50: 40–56.

Aydın, Z. (1993) 'The World Bank and the Transformation of Turkish Agriculture,' in A. Eralp, M. Tunay and B. Yeçilada (eds) *The Political and Socioeconomic Transformation of Turkey*. Westport, Conn. Praeger Publishers.

Ayubi, N. (1991) *Political Islam*. New York: Routledge.

Azzam, A. (1977) 'Foreword' in K. Ahmad (ed.) *Islam: Its Meaning and Message*. New Delhi: Ambika Publishers.

Baier, G. (1984) 'Islam and Politics in Modern Middle Eastern History' in M. Heper and R. Israeli (eds) *Islam and Politics in the Modern Middle East*. Sydney: Croom Helm.

Bauman, Z. (1982) *Memories of Class: the Pre-history and After-life of Class*. London: Routledge & Kegan Paul.

Bauman, Z. (1998) *Globalization: The Human Consequences*. Cambridge: Polity Press.

Bayat, A. (1987) *Workers and Revolution in Iran*. London: Zed Books.

Beck, U. (2000) *What is Globalization?* Cambridge: Polity Press.

Beckford, J. (ed.) (1986) *New Religious Movements and Rapid Social Change*. London: SAGE Publications.

Beckford, J. (2001) 'The Construction and Analysis of Religion', *Social Compass*, 48(3): 439–41.

Beckford, J. and T. Luckmann (eds) (1989) *The Changing Face of Religion*. London: SAGE Publications.

Bendix, R. (1962) *Max Weber: An Intellectual Portrait*. New York: Doubleday.

Berberoglu, B. (ed.) (1989) *Power and Stability in the Middle East*. London: Zed Books.

Bergen, P. (2001) *Holy War Inc*. London: Weidenfeld & Nicolson.

Berger, P. L. (1969) *The Social Reality of Religion*. New York: Faber & Faber.

Berger, P. L. (1979) *Facing up to Modernity*. New York: Penguin Books.

Berger, P. L. (ed.) (1999) *The Desecularization of the World*. Washington and Grand Rapids, Michigan: Ethics and Public Policy Center and William B. Eerdmans Publishing Company.

Berger, P. L. and S. P. Huntington (eds) (2003) *Many Globalizations: Cultural Diversity in the Contemporary World*. New York: Oxford University Press.

Berger, P. L. and T. Luckmann (1966) 'Sociology of Religion and Sociology of Knowledge', *Sociology and Social Research*, 47: 416–27.

Bergesen, A. (1980) 'From Utilitarianism to Globology: The Shift from the Individual To the World as the Primordial Unit of Analysis' in A. Bergesen (ed.) *Studies of the Modern World System*. New York: Academic Press.

Berkes, N. (ed.) (1959) *Turkish Nationalism and Western Civilization: Selected Essays of Ziya Gökalp*. London: Allen & Unwin.

Berkes, N. (1964) *The Development of Secularism in Turkey*. Montreal: McGill University Press.

Berlusconi, S. (2001) cited in the *Guardian*, 27 September.

Bianchi, R. (1984) *Interest Groups and Political Development in Turkey*. Princeton, N.J.: Princeton University Press.

bin Laden, O. (1997) Interview with CNN, Afghanistan, aired May 10.

bin Laden, O. (1998) World Islamic Front Statement. 23 February. www.fas.org/irp/world/para/docs/980223-fatwa.htm

bin Laden, O. (2001a) Statements released by al-Jazeera satellite TV, aired 10 October.

bin Laden, O. (2001b) Statements released by al-Jazeera satellite TV, aired 2 November.

Bourdieu, P. (1984) *Distinction: A Social Critique of the Judgement of Taste*. London: Routledge & Kegan Paul.

Brandstadter, S. (2003) 'With Elias in China: Civilizing Process, Local Restorations and Power in Contemporary Rural China', *Anthropological Theory*, 3(1): 87–105.

Braudel, F. (1972 [1949]) *The Mediterranean and the Mediterranean World in the Age of Philip II*. London: Fontana Collins.

Braudel, F. (1981–4) *Civilization and Capitalism 15th–18th Century* (3 vols). London: Fontana Press.

Breault, K. D. (1986) 'Suicide in America: a Test of Durkheim's Theory of Religious and Family Integration, 1933–1980', *American Journal of Sociology*, 92(3): 628–56.

Brown, C. S. (2001) 'The Shot Seen Around the World: The Middle East Reacts to September 11th', *Middle East Review of International Affairs*, 5(4): 69–89.

Bruce, S. (2003) *Politics and Religion*. Cambridge: Polity Press.

Burke, J. (2004) *Al-Qaeda: The True Story of Radical Islam*. London: Penguin Books.

Burke, J., A. Asthana, M. Bright and T. Panja (2004) 'Hardline Youths Divide Muslims', *Observer*, 4 April: 8–9.

Bush, G. W. (2001a) cited in *Financial Times*, 22–3 September.

Bush, G. W. (2001b) cited in *Sunday Telegraph*, 23 September.

Bush, G. W. (2002) cited in http://www.whitehouse.gov/news/2002/01/20020129-11.

Byman, D. L. and J. D. Green (1999) 'The Enigma of Political Stability in the Persian Gulf Monarchies', *Middle East Review of International Affairs*, 3(3): 20–37.

Cederroth, S. (1996) 'Islamism in Multireligious Societies: The Experience of Malaysia and Indonesia' in D. Westerlund (ed.) *Questioning the Secular State: The Worldwide Resurgence of Religion in Politics*. London: Hurst & Co.

Champion, D. (1999) 'The Kingdom of Saudi Arabia: Elements of Instability within Stability', *Middle East Review of International Affairs*, 3(4): 49–73.

Chase-Dunn, C. (ed.) (1982) *Socialist States in the World System*, Beverly Hills, Calif.: SAGE Publications.

Chase-Dunn, C. (1992) 'The Changing Role of Cities in World Systems' in V. Bornschier and P. Lengyel (eds) *Waves, Formations and Values in the World System*. New Brunswick, N.J.: Transaction Publishers.

Chiozza, G. (2002) 'Is there a Clash of Civilizations? Evidence from Patterns of International Conflict Involvement, 1946–97', *Journal of Peace Research*, 39(6): 711–34.

Chirot, D. (2001) 'A Clash of Civilizations or of Paradigms: Theorizing Progress and Social Change', *International Sociology*, 16(3): 341–60.

Choueiri, Y. M. (1990) *Islamic Fundamentalism*. London: Pinters Publishers.

CIA (2004) *The World Factbook: Saudi Arabia*, www.cia.gov/cia/publications/factbook.

Constituent Assembly of Pakistan (1949) *Objectives Resolution*, 12 March.

Cornell, E. (2001) *Turkey in the 21st Century*. Richmond, Surrey: Curzon Press.

Crook, S., J. Pakulski and M. Waters (1995) *Postmodernization*. London: SAGE Publications.

Dabashi, H. (2001) 'For the Last Time: Civilizations', *International Sociology*, 16(3): 361–8.

Darwish, A. (2003) 'Anti-Americanism in the Arabic Language Media', *Middle East Review of International Affairs*, 7(4): 44–52.

Davies, C. and M. Neal (2000) 'Durkheim's Altruistic and Fatalistic Suicide' in W. S. F. Pickering and G. Walford (eds) *Durkheim's Suicide: A Century of Research and Debate*. London and New York: Routledge, in conjunction with the British Centre for Durkheimian Studies.

Davis, J. M. (2003) *Martyrs: Innocence, Vengeance and Despair in the Middle East*. New York: Palgrave Macmillan.

Davison, R. (1990) *Essays in Ottoman and Turkish History – The Impact of the West*. London: Saqi Books.

Dawisha, A. (ed.) (1983) *Islam in Foreign Policy*. Cambridge: Cambridge University Press.

Dawkins, R. (2001) *Guardian*. http://www.guardian.co.uk/Archive/Article/0,4257777,00.html.

Day, L. H. (1987) 'Durkheim on Religion and Suicide – a Demographic Critique', *Sociology*, 21(Aug.): 449–61.

Debray, R. (1994) 'God and the Political Planet', *New Perspectives Quarterly*, 11: 15.

Deeb, M.-J. (1997) 'Islam and National Identity in Algeria', *The Muslim World*, 87(2) (Apr.): 117–33.

Dekmejian, R. H. (1980) 'The Anatomy of Islamic Revival: Legitimacy Crisis, Ethnic Conflict and the Search for Islamic Alternatives', *Middle East Journal*, 34: 1–12.

Dekmejian, R. H. (1994) 'The Rise of Politicized Activism in Saudi Arabia', *Middle East Journal*, 48: 627–43.

Dessouki, A. (1982) *The Islamic Resurgence: Sources, Dynamics and Implications in the Islamic Resurgence in the Arab World*. New York: Praeger.

de Swaan, A. (2001a) *Human Societies: An Introduction*. Cambridge: Polity Press.

de Swaan, A. (2001b) *Words of the World: The Global Language System*. Cambridge: Polity Press.

de Tocqueville, A. (1956 [1835, 1840]) *Democracy in America*. New York: Mentor.

Dilipak, A. (1993) *Sorular, Sorunlar ve Cevaplar*, vol. 1. Istanbul: Beyan Yayınları.

Dodd, C. H. (1988) 'Political Modernization, the State, and Democracy: Approaches to the Study of Politics in Turkey' in M. Heper and A. Evin (eds) *State, Democracy and the Military – Turkey in the 1980s*. Berlin: Walter de Gruyter & Co.

Douglas, J. D. (1967) *The Social Meanings of Suicide*. Princeton: Princeton University Press.

Dunn, J. (1989) *Modern Revolutions*. Cambridge: Cambridge University Press.

Dunning, E. (2004) 'Aspects of the Figurational Dynamics of Racial Stratification: A Conceptual Discussion and Developmental Analysis of Black–White Relations in the United States' in S. Loyal and S. Quilley (eds) *The Sociology of Norbert Elias*. Cambridge: Cambridge University Press.

Du Pasquier, R. (1992) *Unveiling Islam*. Cambridge: Islamic Texts Society.

Durkheim, E. (1987 [1897]) *Suicide: A Study in Sociology*. London: Routledge & Kegan Paul.

Durkheim, E. (1938) *The Rules of Sociological Method*. New York: Free Press.

Durkheim, E. (1961) *The Elementary Forms of the Religious Life*. New York: Collier Books.

Durkheim, E. (1984) *The Division of Labour in Society*. London: Macmillan.

Eickelman, D. (2003) 'Inside the Islamic Reformation' in B. Rubin (ed.) *Revolutionaries and Reformers: Contemporary Islamist Movements in the Middle East*. Albany, N.Y.: State University of New York Press.

Eickelman, D. and J. Piscatori (1996) *Muslim Politics*. Princeton, N.J.: Princeton University Press.

Eisenstadt, S. N. (1968) *The Protestant Ethic and Modernization*. New York: Basic Books.

Elias, N. (1978) *What is Sociology?* New York: Columbia University Press.

Elias, N. (1987) *Involvement and Detachment.* Oxford: Blackwell.

Elias, N. (1991) *The Symbol Theory.* London: SAGE Publications.

Elias, N. (2000 [1939]) *The Civilizing Process: Sociogenetic and Psychogenetic Investigations.* Oxford: Blackwell Publishers.

Elias, N. and J. L. Scotson (1965) *The Established and the Outsiders: A Sociological Enquiry into Community Problems.* London: Frank Cass.

Elias, N. and J. L. Scotson (1994) *The Established and the Outsiders: A Sociological Enquiry into Community Problems.* London: SAGE Publications.

Enayat, H. (1982) *Modern Islamic Political Thought.* London: Macmillan.

Endress, G. (1988) *An Introduction to Islam.* Edinburgh: Edinburgh University Press.

Enhali, A. and O. Adda (2003) 'State and Islamism in the Maghreb', *Middle East Review of International Affairs*, 7(1): 66–76.

Entelis, J. (1996) 'Political Islam', *MESA Bulletin*, 30: 165–9.

Eralp, A., M. Tunay and B. Yeşilada (eds) (1993) *The Political and Socioeconomic Transformation of Turkey.* Westport, Conn.: Praeger Publishers.

Erikson, E. H. (1950) *Childhood and Society.* New York: Norton.

Erikson, E. H. (1968) *Identity: Youth and Crisis.* London: Faber & Faber.

Esposito, J. L. (ed.) (1980) *Islam and Development: Religion and Sociopolitical Change.* Syracuse, N.Y.: Syracuse University Press.

Esposito, J. L. (ed.) (1987) *Islam in Asia.* Oxford: Oxford University Press.

Esposito, J. L. (ed.) (1997) *Political Islam: Revolution, Radicalism or Reform.* Boulder, Colo.: Lynne Rienner.

Esposito, J. L. (1999) *The Islamic Threat: Myth or Reality?* New York: Oxford University Press.

Esposito, J. L. (2002) *Unholy War: Terror in the Name of God.* New York: Oxford University Press.

Euben, R. L. (1999) *Enemy in the Mirror: Islamic Fundamentalism and the Limits of Modern Rationalism.* Princeton, N.J.: Princeton University Press.

Faludi, S. (1991) *Backlash: The Undeclared War Against American Women.* New York: Crown.

Fischer, F. (1980) *Iran from Religious Dispute to Revolution.* London: Harvard University Press.

Fischoff, E. (1944) 'The Protestant Ethic and the Spirit of Capitalism: The History of A Controversy', *Social Research*, 11: 53–77.

Fletcher, J. (1997) *Violence and Civilization: An Introduction to the Work of Norbert Elias.* Cambridge: Polity Press.

Fox, J. (2001) 'Two Civilizations and Ethnic Conflict: Islam and the West', *Journal of Peace Research*, 38(4): 459–72.

Frank, A. G. (1990) 'A Theoretical Introduction to 5,000 Years of World System History', *Review*, 13: 155–248.

Frank, A. G. (1995) 'The Modern World System Revisited: Rereading Braudel and Wallerstein' in S. K. Sanderson (ed.) *Civilizations and World Systems: Studying World-Historical Change.* Walnut Creek, Calif.: AltaMira Press.

Frank, A. G. (1998) *ReORIENT: Global Economy in the Asian Age.* Berkeley: University of California Press.

Frank, A. G. and B. K. Gills (eds) (1993) *The World System: Five Hundred Years or Five Thousand?* London: Routledge.

Frisch, H. (2003) 'The Palestinian Media and Anti-Americanism: A Case Study', *Middle East Review of International Affairs,* 7(4): 74–82.

Fukuyama, F. (1989) 'The End of History', *The National Interest,* 16: 3–18.

Fukuyama, F. (2001) 'Turkey Can Play Leadership Role in Liberalising Islam', *Turkish Daily News* (7 Dec.).

Fuller, S. (2001) 'Looking for Sociology After 11 September', *Sociological Research Online,* 6(2).

Gellner, E. (1969) 'A Pendulum Swing Theory of Islam' in R. Robertson (ed.) *Sociology of Religion.* Harmondsworth: Penguin Education.

Gellner, E. (1981) *Muslim Society.* Cambridge: Cambridge University Press.

Gellner, E. (1992) *Postmodernism, Reason and Religion.* London: Routledge.

Gerth, H. H. and C. W. Mills (1964) *From Max Weber: Essays in Sociology.* London: Routledge & Kegan Paul.

Geyikdağı, N. (1984) *Political Parties in Turkey – The Role of Islam.* New York: Praeger Publishers.

Gibbs, J. P. (1994) 'Durkheim's Heavy Hand in the Sociological Study of Suicide' in D. Lester (ed.) *Emile Durkheim: Le Suicide 100 Years Later.* Philadelphia: The Charles Press.

Giddens, A. (1984) *The Constitution of Society.* Cambridge: Polity Press.

Giddens, A. (1991) *Modernity and Self-Identity.* Cambridge: Polity Press.

Giddens, A. (1999) *Runaway World.* London: Profile Books.

Gills, B. K. (1995) 'Capital and Power in the Processes of World History' in S. K. Sanderson (ed.) *Civilizations and World Systems: Studying World-Historical Change.* Walnut Creek, Calif.: AltaMira Press.

Gills, B. K. and A. G. Frank (1992) 'World System Cycles, Crises, and Hegemonial Shifts, 1700 BC–1700 AD', *Review,* 15: 621–87.

Gilsenan, M. (1992) *Recognizing Islam – Religion and Society in the Modern Middle East.* London: I. B. Tauris.

Goldman, H. (1991) *Max Weber and Thomas Mann: Calling and the Shaping of the Self.* Berkeley: University of California Press.

Göle, N. (1996) 'Authoritarian Secularism and Islamist Politics: The Case of Turkey' in A. R. Norton (ed.) *Civil Society in the Middle East.* Leiden: E. J. Brill.

Göle, N. (1997) 'Secularism and Islamism in Turkey: The Making of Elites and Counter-Elites', *Middle East Journal,* 51: 46–58.

Goudsblom, J. (1977) *Sociology in the Balance.* Oxford: Basil Blackwell.

Goudsblom, J. (1992) *Fire and Civilization.* London: Allen Lane, The Penguin Press.

Goudsblom, J. (1996) 'Human History and Long-Term Social Processes: Toward a Synthesis of *Chronology* and *Phaseology*' in J. Goudsblom,

E. Jones and S. Mennell, *The Course of Human History: Economic Growth, Social Process, and Civilization.* New York and London: M. E. Sharpe.

Gove, W. R. (1973) 'Sex, Marital Status and Mortality', *American Journal of Sociology,* 79: 45–67.

Green, M. (2002) 'Muslims at Odds with the US', reported in *Financial Times,* 26 February.

Guillaume, A. (1990) *Islam.* London: Penguin Books.

Gülalp, H. (1999) 'Political Islam in Turkey: The Rise and Fall of the Refah Party', *The Muslim World,* 89: 22–41.

Gülalp, H. (2001) 'Globalization and Political Islam: The Social Bases of Turkey's Welfare Party', *International Journal of Middle East Studies,* 33: 433–48.

Haddad, S. and H. Khashan (2002) 'Islam and Terrorism: Lebanese Muslim Views on September 11', *Journal of Conflict Resolution,* 46(6): 812–28.

Hadden, J. and A. Shupe (eds) (1989) *Secularization and Fundamentalism Reconsidered.* New York: Paragon House.

Haferkamp, H. (1987) 'From the Intra-State to the Inter-State Civilizing Process?', *Theory, Culture and Society,* 4(2–3): 545–57.

Haim, S. (1982) 'Sayyid Qutb', *Asian and African Studies,* March.

Halbwachs, M. (1978 [1930]) *The Causes of Suicide.* London and Henley: Routledge, Kegan Paul.

Hale, W. (1981) *The Political and Economic Development of Modern Turkey.* London: Croom Helm.

Haller, M. (2003) 'Europe and the Arab-Islamic World. A Sociological Perspective on the Socio-Cultural Differences and Mutual (Mis)Perceptions between Two Neighbouring Cultural Areas', *The European Journal of Social Science Research,* 16(3) (Sept.): 227–52.

Halliday, F. (1996) *Islam and the Myth of Confrontation.* London: I. B. Tauris.

Halliday, F. (2000) *Nation and Religion in the Middle East.* London: Saqi Books.

Halliday, F. (2002) *Two Hours that Shook the World.* London: Saqi Books.

Halliday, F. and H. Alavi (eds) (1988) *State and Ideology in the Middle East and Pakistan.* Basingstoke: Macmillan Education.

Hamzeh, A. N. (1997) 'Islamism in Lebanon: A Guide', *Middle East Review of International Affairs,* 1(3). http://meria.idc.ac.il/journal/1997/issue3/jvol1no3in.html.

Hardacre, H. (1993) 'The Impact of Fundamentalism on Women, the Family and Interpersonal Relations' in M. E. Marty and R. Scott Appleby (eds) *Fundamentalism and Society: Reclaiming the Sciences, the Family and Education.* Chicago: University of Chicago Press, vol 2.

Harris, G. (1986) 'Republic of Turkey' in D. Long and B. Reich (eds) *The Government and Politics of the Middle East and North Africa.* Boulder, Colo.: Westview Press.

Harrison, L. E. and S. P. Huntington (eds) (2001) *Culture Matters: How Values Shape Human Progress.* New York: Basic Books.

Harvey, D. (1991) *The Condition of Postmodernity: An Enquiry into the Origins of Cultural Change*. Oxford: Blackwell Publishing.

Hassan, R. (2002) *Faithlines: Muslim Conceptions of Islam and Society*. Kavachi: Oxford University Press.

Haynes, J. (1994) *Religion in Third World Politics*. Boulder, Colo.: Lynne Rienner.

Held, D., A. McGrew, D. Goldblatt and J. Perraton (1999) *Global Transformations: Politics, Economics and Culture*. Cambridge: Polity Press.

Heper, M. (1981) 'Islam, Polity and Society in Turkey: A Middle Eastern Perspective', *The Middle East Journal*, 35(summer): 345–63

Heper, M. (1984) 'Islam, Politics and Change in the Middle East' in M. Heper and R. Israeli (eds) *Islam and Politics in the Modern Middle East*. Sydney: Croom Helm.

Heper, M. (1985) *The State Tradition in Turkey*. Beverley: Eothen Press.

Heper, M. and A. Evin (eds) (1988) *State, Democracy and the Military – Turkey in the 1980s*. Berlin: Walter de Gruyter and Co.

Heper, M. and R. Israeli (eds) (1984) *Islam and Politics in the Modern Middle East*. Sydney: Croom Helm.

Heper, M. and J. Landau (eds) (1991) *Political Parties and Democracy in Turkey*. London: I. B. Tauris.

Hilmi, T. (2003) 'Amrika alati nabghad', *Al-Sha'b*, http://alarabnews.com/alshaab/GIF/17-10-2003/tareg.htm

Hiro, D. (2002) *War Without End: The Rise of Islamist Terrorism and Global Response*. London and New York: Routledge.

Hitti, P. (1962) *Islam and the West*. New York: Krieger Publishing Company.

Hodgson, M. G. S. (1974) *The Venture of Islam: Conscience and History in a World Civilization*, vol. 1–3. Chicago: The University of Chicago Press.

Huband, M. (1998) *Warriors of the Prophet: The Struggle for Islam*. Boulder, Colo.: Westview Press.

Huff, T. (2001) 'Globalization and the Internet: Comparing the Middle Eastern and Malaysian Experiences', *Middle East Journal*, 55: 439–58.

Huntington, S. P. (1993a) 'The Clash of Civilizations?' *Foreign Affairs*, 72(3): 22–49.

Huntington, S. P. (1993b) 'If not Civilizations, What? Samuel Huntington Responds to his Critics', *Foreign Affairs*, 72(5): 186–90.

Huntington, S. P. (1998) *The Clash of Civilizations and the Remaking of World Order*. New York: Simon & Schuster.

Huntington, S. P. (2000) 'Try Again: A Reply to Russett, Oneal and Cox', *Journal of Peace Research*, 37(5): 609–10.

Huntington, S. P. (2001) 'So, Are Civilisations at War?', *The Observer*, 21 October.

Huntington, S. P. (2004) *Who are We? The Challenges to America's National Identity*, New York: Simon & Schuster.

Ibrahim, S. E. (1980) 'Anatomy of Egypt's Militant Islamic Groups: Methodological Note and Preliminary Findings', *International Journal of Middle East Affairs*, 12: 423–53.

Ikegami, E. (1995) *The Taming of the Samurai: Honorific Individualism and the Making of Modern Japan*. Cambridge, Mass.: Harvard University Press.

Irfani, S. (1983) *Revolutionary Islam in Iran*. London: Zed Books.

Ismael, T. Y. and J. S. Ismael (eds) (1991) *Politics and Government in the Middle East and North Africa*. Miami: Florida International University Press.

Ispahani, M. (1989) 'Varieties of Muslim Experience', *Wilson Quarterly*, 13: 63.

Iveković, I. (2002) 'Nationalism and the Political Use and Abuse of Religion: The Politicization of Orthodoxy, Catholicism and Islam in Yugoslav Successor States', *Social Compass*, 49(4): 523–36.

Jameelah, M. (1975) *Islam and Modernism*. Lahore: Khan Publications.

Jáuregui, P. (2000) 'National Pride and the Meaning of Europe: A Comparative Study of Britain and Spain' in D. Smith and S. Wright (eds) *Whose Europe? The Turn Towards Democracy*. Oxford: Blackwell Publishers.

Jerichow, A. (1997) *Saudi Arabia: Outside Global Law and Order*. Richmond, Surrey: Curzon Press.

Juergensmeyer, M. (2003 [2001]) *Terror in the Mind of God: The Global Rise of Religious Violence*. Third edn, Berkeley: University of California Press.

Kadioğlu, A. (1996) 'The Paradox of Turkish Nationalism and the Construction of Official Identity', *Middle Eastern Studies*, 32: 177–93.

Kadioğlu, A. (1998) 'Republican Epistemology and Islamic Discourses in Turkey in the 1990s', *The Muslim World*, 38: 1–21.

Karpat, K. (1959) *Turkey's Politics*. Princeton, N.J.: Princeton University Press.

Kazamias, A. (1966) *Education and the Quest for Modernity in Turkey*. London: George Allen and Unwin.

Keane, J. (1991) *The Media and Democracy*. Cambridge: Polity Press.

Keane, J. (1995) 'Structural Transformations of the Public Sphere', *The Communication Review*. 1(1): 1–22.

Keddie, N. (ed.) (1983) *Religion and Politics in Iran*. London: Yale University Press.

Keddie, N. (1988) 'Ideology, Society and the State in Post-colonial Muslim Societies' in F. Halliday and H. Alavi (eds) *State and Ideology in the Middle East and Pakistan*. Basingstoke: Macmillan Education.

Keddie, N. (1994) 'The Revolt of Islam, 1700 to 1993: Comparative Considerations and Relations to Imperialism', *Comparative Studies in Society and History*, 36(3): 463–87.

Kedourie, E. (1980) *Islam in the Modern World*. London: Mansell.

Kedourie, E. (1992) *Politics in the Middle East*. Oxford: Oxford University Press.

Kepel, G. (2004) *Jihad: The Trail of Political Islam*. London: I. B. Tauris.

Keyder, C. (1988) 'Class and State in the Transformation of Modern Turkey' in F. Halliday and H. Alavi (eds) *State and Ideology in the Middle East and Pakistan*, Basingstoke: Macmillan Education.

Khalidi, R. (1997) *Palestinian Identity: The Construction of Modern National Consciousness*. New York: Columbia University Press.

Kidwai, M. (1959) 'Foreword' in A. Nabwi, *Islam and the World*. Lucknow: Academy of Islamic Research.

Kilminster, R. (1997) 'Globalization as an Emergent Concept' in A. Scott (ed.) *The Limits of Globalization*. London: Routledge.

Kilminster, R. (1998) *The Sociological Revolution: From the Enlightenment to the Global Age*. London: Routledge.

Köse, A. (1999) 'The Journey from the Secular to the Sacred: Experiences of Native British Converts to Islam', *Social Compass*, 46(3): 301–12.

Kostiner, J. (1997) 'State, Islam and Opposition in Saudi Arabia: The Post Desert-Storm Phase', *Middle East Review of International Affairs*, 1(2). http://meria.idc-ac.il/journal/1997/issue2/ju1n208.html.

Kramer, M. (1996) 'Fundamentalist Islam at Large: The Drive for Power', *Middle East Quarterly*, 3: 37–49.

Kramer, M. (1998) 'What You Should Know about Muslim Politics and Society' in P. Zelikow and R. Zoellick (eds) *American and the Muslim Middle East: Memos to a President*. Washington: Aspen Institute.

Kramer, M. (2001) *Ivory Towers on Sand: The Failure of Middle Eastern Studies in America*. Washington: The Washington Institute of Near East Policy.

Krauthammer, C. (1990) 'The New Crescent of Crisis: Global Intifada', *Washington Post*, 16 February.

Kurzman, C. (2002) 'bin Laden and Other Thoroughly Modern Muslims', *Contexts*, 1(4) (fall/winter): 13–20.

Landau, J. M. (1997) 'Arab and Turkish Universities: Some Characteristics', *Middle Eastern Studies*. 33(1): 1–19.

Laqueur, W. (2001) *The New Terrorism*. London: Phoenix Press.

Lerner, D. (1958) *The Passing of Traditional Society: Modernizing the Middle East*. New York: Simon & Schuster.

Lerner, D. (1964) *The Passing of Traditional Society*. New York: New York Publishers.

Levitt, M. A. (2002) 'The Political Economy of Middle East Terrorism', *Middle East Review of International Affairs*, 6(4): 49–65.

Lewis, B. (1990) 'The Roots of Muslim Rage', *Atlantic Monthly*, 266 (Sept.): 47–60.

Lewis, B. (2002) *What Went Wrong? The Clash Between Islam and Modernity in the Middle East*. New York: Perennial.

Lewis, G. (1974) *Nations of the Modern World – Turkey*. London: Ernest Benn.

Loimeier, R. L. (1996) 'The Secular State and Islam in Senegal' in D. Westerlund (ed.) *Questioning the Secular State: The Worldwide Resurgence of Religion in Politics*. London: Hurst & Co.

Louvish, S., A. Jamal and E. Fani (1994) *The Fundamental Question*. London: Broadcasting Support Services.

Lubeck, P. (2000) 'The Islamic Revival: Antinomies of Islamic Movements Under Globalization' in R. Cohen and S. M. Rai (eds) *Global Social Movements*. New Brunswick, N.J.: Athlone Press.

Lukes, S. (1973) *Emile Durkheim, His Life and Work: A Historical and Critical Study*. Harmondsworth: Penguin Books.

Lustick, I. S. (1996) 'Fundamentalism, Politicized Religion and Pietism', *MESA Bulletin*, 30: 26–32.

Lyotard, J.-F. (1984) *The Postmodern Condition*. Minneapolis: University of Minnesota.

Mabry, J. M. (1998) 'Modernization, Nationalism and Islam: an examination of Ernest Gellner's writings on Muslim society with reference to Indonesia and Malaysia', *Ethnic and Racial Studies*, 21(1): 64–88.

Macey, M. (1999) 'Class, Gender and Religious Influences on Changing Patterns of Pakistani Muslim Male Violence in Bradford', *Ethnic and Racial Studies*, 22(5): 845–66.

McLuhan, M. (1967) *Understanding Media*. London: Sphere.

McNeill, W. H. (1975) *The Rise of the West: A History of the Human Community*. Chicago and London: The University of Chicago Press.

McNeill, W. H. (1979) *A World History*. Oxford: Oxford University Press.

McNeill, W. H. (1980) *The Human Condition: An Ecological and Historical View*. Princeton, N.J.: Princeton University Press.

Maddy-Weitzman, B. and M. Litvak (2003) 'Islamism and the State in North Africa' in B. Rubin (ed) (2003), *Revolutionaries and Reformers: Contemporary Islamist Movements in the Middle East*. Albany, N.Y.: State University of New York Press.

Mahmoud, M. (1996) 'The Discourse of the Ikhwan of Sudan and Secularism' in D. Westerlund (ed.) *Questioning the Secular State: The Worldwide Resurgence of Religion in Politics*. London: Hurst & Co.

Mandaville, P. (2001) *Transnational Muslim Politics: Reimagining the Umma*. London: Routledge.

Mannan, M. A. (1986) *Islamic Economics: Theory and Practice*. Cambridge: Hodder and Stoughton, The Islamic Academy.

Mardin, Ş. (1989) *Religion and Social Change in Modern Turkey*. Albany, N.Y.: State University of New York Press.

Mardin, Ş. (1990) 'European Culture and the Development of Modern Turkey' in A. Evin and G. Denton (eds) *Turkey and the European Community*. Leske, Budrich: Opladen.

Marquand, D. and R. L. Nettler (eds) (2000) *Religion and Democracy*. Oxford: Blackwell Publishers.

Martin, D. (1978) *A General Theory of Secularization*. New York: Harper and Row.

Martin, D. (1991) *Tongues of Fire*. Oxford: Basil Blackwell.

Marty, M. E. and R. Scott Appleby (eds) (1991) *Fundamentalisms Observed*. Chicago: University of Chicago Press.

Marx, K. and F. Engels (1957) *On Religion*. Moscow: Progress Publishers.
Marx, K. and F. Engels (1968) *Selected Works in One Vol*. Moscow: Progress Publishers.
Marx, K. and Engels, F. (1983 [1848]) *The Communist Manifesto*. Harmondsworth: Penguin Books.
Mawdudi, S. A. A. (1983) 'How to Establish Islamic Order in the Country?', *The Universal Message*, May.
Mawdudi, S. A. A. (1986) *The Islamic Way of Life*. Leicester: The Islamic Foundation.
Mazlish, B. (2001) 'Civilization in a Historical and Global Perspective', *International Sociology*, 16(3): 293–300.
Meeker, M. (1991) 'The New Muslim Intellectuals in the Republic of Turkey' in R. Tapper (ed.) *Islam in Modern Turkey*. London: I. B. Tauris.
Mehmet, O. (1990) *Islamic Identity and Development – Studies of the Islamic Periphery*. London: Routledge.
Melucci, A. (1985) 'The Symbolic Challenge of Contemporary Movements', *Social Research*, 52: 789–816.
Melucci, A. (1989) *Nomads of the Present: Social Movements and Individual Needs in Contemporary Society*. London: Hutchinson Radius.
Mennell, S. (1990) 'The Globalization of Human Society as a Very Long-Term Social Process: Elias's Theory', *Theory, Culture and Society*, 7(2–3): 359–71.
Mennell, S. (1992) *Norbert Elias: An Introduction*. Oxford: Blackwell.
Mennell, S. (1996) 'Asia and Europe: Comparing Civilizing Processes' in J. Goudsblom, E. Jones and S. Mennell, *The Course of Human History: Economic Growth, Social Process and Civilization*. New York and London: M. E. Sharpe.
Mennell, S. (2001) 'The American Civilizing Process' in T. Salumets, *Norbert Elias and Human Interdependencies*. Montreal & Kingston: McGill-Queen's University Press.
Mennell, S. (2004) 'Not so Exceptional? State Formation Processes in America' in S. Loyal and S. Quilley (eds) *The Sociology of Norbert Elias*: Cambridge: Cambridge University Press.
Mernissi, F. (1989) *Women and Islam*. Trans. M. J. Lakeland. Oxford: Basil Blackwell.
Merton, R. K. (1957) *Social Theory and Social Structure*. New York: The Free Press.
Meyrowitz, J. (1985) *No Sense of Place*. Oxford: Oxford University Press.
Mezran, K. (2001) 'Negotiating National Identity in North Africa', *International Negotiation*, 6: 141–73.
Miller, J. (1998) *Interview with Osama bin Laden*, transcript at: abcnews.go.com/sections/world/DailyNews/miller_binladen_980609.html.
Mills, C. W. (1959) *The Power Elite*. New York: Oxford University Press.
Mitchell, R. P. (1969) *The Society of the Muslim Brothers*. New York: Oxford University Press.

Molokotos Liederman, L. (2000) 'Religious Diversity in Schools: the Muslim Headscarf Controversy and Beyond', *Social Compass*, 47(3): 367–81.

Moore, Jr., B. (1966) *Social Origins of Dictatorship and Democracy: Lord and Peasant in the Making of the Modern World*. Boston, Mass.: Beacon Press.

Mortimer, E. (1982) *Faith and Power: The Politics of Islam*. New York: Random House.

Moussalli, A. S. (1998) 'Globalization and the Nation State in the Arab World', *MESA Bulletin*, 32: 11–14.

Mozzafari, M. (ed.) (2002) *Globalization and Civilizations*. London and New York: Routledge.

Mudeiris, S. (2003) Transcript reported in MEMRI, http://www.memri.org/bin/opener_latest.cgi?ID=sr2403.

Munson, H. (1988) *Islam and Revolution in the Middle East*. London and New Haven: Yale University Press.

Murad, K. (1985a) *Sacrifice: The Making of a Muslim*. Leicester: The Islamic Foundation.

Murad, K. (1985b) *The Way of Justice*. Leicester: The Islamic Foundation.

Murphy, K. (1993) 'Have the Islamic Militants Turned into a New Battlefront in the US?', *Los Angeles Times*, 3 March.

Nabwi, A. (1959) *Islam and the World*. Lucknow: Academy of Islamic Research.

Nash, M. (1991) 'Islamic Resurgence in Malaysia and Indonesia' in M. E. Marty and R. Scott Appleby (eds) *Fundamentalisms Observed*. Chicago: University of Chicago Press.

Nasr, S. R. (1975) *Islam and the Plight of the Modern Man*. London: Longman Group.

Need, A. and G. Evans 'Analysing Patterns of Religious Participation in Post-communist Eastern Europe' *British Journal of Sociology*, 52(2): 229–48.

Newport, F. (2002) 'Gallup Poll of the Islamic World', http://www.gallup.com/poll/tb/goverPubli/20020226.asp?Version==p, 26 February.

Neyzi, L. (2001) 'Object or Subject? The Paradox of "Youth" in Turkey', *International Journal of Middle East Studies*, 33: 411–32.

Oneal, J. R and Russett, B. M. (2000) 'A Response to Huntington', *Journal of Peace Research*, 37(5): 611–12.

Özcan, Y. (1993), *A Quantitative Study of Mosques in Turkey*. Unpublished paper, Middle East Technical University, Ankara, Turkey.

Özdalga, E. (1998) *The Veiling Issue, Official Secularism and Popular Islam in Modern Turkey*. Richmond, Surrey: Curzon Press.

Paz, R. (2001a) 'Radical Islamist Terrorism: Points for Pondering', http://www.ict.org.il/articles/articledet.cfm?articleid=367.

Paz, R. (2001b) 'Programmed Terrorists: An Analysis of the Letter Left Behind by the September 11 Hijackers', http://www.ict.org.il/articles/articledet.cfm?articleid=419.

Paz, R. (2002) 'Middle East Islamism in the European Arena', *Middle East Review of International Affairs*, 6(3): 67–76.

Paz, R. (2003) 'Islamists and Anti-Americanism', *Middle East Review of International Affairs*, 7(4): 53–61.

Pedahzur, A., A. Perliger and L. Weinberg (2003) 'Altruism and Fatalism: The Characteristics of Palestinian Suicide Terrorists', *Deviant Behaviour*, 24(4) (July/Aug): 405–23.

Peretz, D. (1988) *The Middle East Today*. Fifth edn, New York: Praeger.

Peters, R. (1979) *Islam and Colonialism*. The Hague: Mouton Publishers.

Pew Global Attitudes Project (2003) 'Views of a Changing World', June 2003.

Pickthall, M. (1984) *The Meaning of the Glorious Koran*. New York: New American Library.

Pieterse, J. N. (1997) 'Travelling Islam: Mosques without Minarets' in A. Öncü and P. Wayland (eds) *Space, Culture and Power: New Identities in Globalizing Cities*. London: Zed Books.

Pipes, D. (1989) 'Fundamentalist Muslims in World Politics' in J. Hadden and A. Shupe (eds) *Secularization and Fundamentalism Reconsidered*. New York: Paragon House.

Pipes, D. and M. Stillman (2002) 'The United States Government: Patron of Islam?', *Middle East Review of International Affairs*, 6(1): 49–59.

Pollack, J. (2003) 'Anti-Americanism in Contemporary Saudi Arabia', *Middle East Review of International Affairs*. 7(4): 30–43.

Poppel, F. van and L. H. Day (1996) 'A Test of Durkheim's Theory of Suicide – Without Committing the "Ecological Fallacy"', *American Sociological Review*, 61(3): 500–7.

Potter, H. (2001) Why we are right to fight, *Observer*, 14 October.

Quasem, M. (1981) 'Psychology in Islamic Ethics', *The Muslim World*, 71(1): 213–27.

Qutb, M. (1964) *Islam: The Misunderstood Religion*. Cairo: Darul Bayan.

Ragin, C. and D. Chirot (1989) 'The World System of Immanuel Wallerstein: Sociology and Politics as History' in T. Skocpol (ed.) *Vision and Method in Historical Sociology*. Cambridge: Cambridge University Press.

Rahimi, B. (2003) 'Cyberdissent: The Internet in Revolutionary Iran', *Middle East Review of International Affairs*, 7(3): 101–15.

Rao, A. (1999) 'The Many Sources of Identity: an Example of Changing Affiliations in Rural Jammu and Kashmir', *Ethnic and Racial Studies*, 22(1): 56–91.

Raphaeli, N. (2003) 'Saudi Arabia: A Brief Guide to its Politics and Problems', *Middle East Review of International Affairs*, 7(3): 21–33.

Rashid, A. (2000) *Taliban: Islam, Oil and the New Great Game in Central Asia*. London: I. B. Tauris.

Reed, S. (1993) 'The Battle for Egypt', *Foreign Affairs*, 72(4): 94–107.

Reeve, S. (1999) *The New Jackals: Ramzi Yousef, Osama bin Laden and the Future of Terrorism*. London: André Deutsch.

Reuter, C. (2004) *My Life is a Weapon*. Princeton, N.J.: Princeton University Press.

Richmond, A. H. (2002) 'Globalization: Implications for Immigrants and Refugees', *Ethnic and Racial Studies*, 25(5): 707–27.

Robertson, R. (ed.) (1969) *Sociology of Religion*. Harmondsworth: Penguin Education.

Robertson, R. (1992) *Globalization: Social Theory and Global Culture*. London: Sage Publications.

Robertson, R. (1994) 'Globalization or Glocalization?', *Journal of International Communication*, 1: 33–52.

Robertson, R. (1995) 'Glocalization: Time–Space and Homogeneity–Heterogeneity' in M. Featherstone, S. Lash and R. Robertson (eds) *Global Modernities*. London: SAGE Publications.

Robertson, R. and F. Lechner (1985) 'Modernization, Globalization and the Problem of Culture in World Systems Theory', *Theory, Culture and Society*, 2(3): 103–18.

Robinson, M. (1977) *Islam and Capitalism*. Harmondsworth: Penguin.

Robinson, R. (1961) 'Mosque and School in Turkey', *The Muslim World*, 51: 107–10.

Rodinson, M. (1973) *Mohammed*. Harmondsworth: Pelican.

Roudometof, V. and R. Robertson (1995) 'Globalization, World-System Theory, and The Comparative Study of Civilizations: Issues of Theoretical Logic in World-Historical Sociology' in S. K. Sanderson (ed.) *Civilizations and World Systems: Studying World-Historical Change*. Walnut Creek, Calif.: AltaMira Press.

Roy, O. (1994) *The Failure of Political Islam*. London: I. B. Tauris.

Roy, O. (2004) *Globalised Isiam: The Search for a New Ummah*. London: Hurst & Co.

Rubin, B. (ed.) (2003) *Revolutionaries and Reformers: Contemporary Islamist Movements in the Middle East*. Albany, N.Y.: State University of New York Press.

Russett, B. M., J. R. Oneal and M. Cox (2000) 'Clash of Civilizations or Realism and Liberalism Déjà Vu? Some Evidence', *Journal of Peace Research*, 37(5): 583–608.

Rustow, D. (1965) 'Turkey: The Modernity of Tradition' in L. Pye and S. Verba (eds) *Political Culture and Political Development*. Princeton: Princeton University Press.

Ruthven, N. (1984) *Islam in the Modern World*. Harmondsworth: Penguin.

Saghieh, H. (2002) 'On suicide, Martyrdom and the Quest for Individuality', *ISIM Nwesletter*, 10(02): 9.

Said, E. (1978) *Orientalism*. Harmondsworth: Penguin Books.

Saikal, A. (2003) *Islam and the West: Conflict or Cooperation?* Basingstoke: Palgrave Macmillan.

Sakallıoğlu, U. (1996) 'Parameters and strategies of Islam-state interaction in Republican Turkey', *International Journal of Middle East Studies*, 28: 231–51.

Sakr, N. (2001) *Satellite Realms: Transnational Television, Globalization and the Middle East*. London and New York: I. B. Tauris.

Salib, E. (2003) 'Suicide terrorism: a case of *folie a plusieurs?*', *British Journal of Psychiatry*, 182 (June): 475–6.

Sanderson, S. K. (ed.) (1995) *Civilizations and World Systems: Studying World- Historical Change*. Walnut Creek, Calif.: AltaMira Press.

Sardar, Z. (1990) 'The Rushdie Malaise: A Critique of Some Writings on the Rushdie Affair', *Muslim World Book Review*, 10(3): 3–17.

Sayarı, S. (1984) 'Politicization of Islamic Re-traditionalism: Some Preliminary Notes' in M. Heper and R. Israeli (eds) *Islam and Politics in the Modern Middle East*. Sydney: Croom Helm.

Schäfer, W. (2001) 'Global Civilization and Local Cultures', *International Sociology*, 16(3): 301–19.

Seydi, S. (2001) *The Turkish Straits and the Great Powers from the Montreux Convention to the Early Cold War 1936–1947*. Unpublished PhD thesis, University of Birmingham.

Shakir, M. H. (trans.) (1988) *The Quran*. Elmhurst, New York: Tahrike Toursile Qur'an.

Shaw, S., and E. Shaw (1977) *History of the Ottoman Empire and Modern Turkey*. vol. II, Cambridge: Cambridge University Press.

Sidahmed, A. S. (1997) *Politics and Islam in Contemporary Sudan*. Richmond, Surrey: Curzon Press.

Sidanius, J., P. J. Henry, F. Pratto and S. Levin (2004) 'Arab Attributions For The Attack On America: The Case of Lebanese Subelites', *Journal of Cross-Cultural Psychology*, 35(4) (July): 403–16.

Simmel, G. (1966 [1955]) *Conflict and the Web of Group Affiliations*. Trans. Kurt H. Wolff and R. Bendix. New York: The Free Press.

Simms, R. (2002) ' "Islam is our Politics": A Gramscian Analysis of the Muslim Brotherhood (1928–1953)', *Social Compass*, 49(4): 563–82.

Sinclair, J., E. Jacka and S. Cunningham (eds) (1996) *New Patterns in Global Television*. Oxford: Peripheral Vision.

Sivan, E. (2003) 'Why Radical Muslims aren't Taking Over Governments' in B. Rubin (ed.) *Revolutionaries and Reformers: Contemporary Islamist Movements in the Middle East*. Albany, N.Y.: State University of New York Press.

Skocpol, T. (1979) *States and Social Revolutions: A Comparative Analysis of France, Russia and China*. Cambridge: Cambridge University Press.

Sofsky, W. (2002) *Zeiten des Schreckens. Amok, Terror, Krieg*. Frankfurt: Fischer.

Spier, F. (1994) *Religious Regimes in Peru: Religion and State Development in a Long-Term Perspective and the Effects in the Andean Village of Zurite*. Amsterdam: Amsterdam University Press.

Stack, S. (1990) 'New Micro-Level Data on the Impact of Divorce on Suicide, 1959–1980: A Test of Two Theories', *Journal of Marriage and the Family*, 55: 1018–24.

Stauth, G. (1997) 'Elias in Singapore: Civilising Processes in a Tropical City', *Thesis Eleven*, 50: 51–70.

Stenberg, L. (1996) 'The Revealed Word and the Struggle for Authority: Interpretation and Use of Islamic Terminology among Algerian Islamists' in D. Westerlund (ed.) *Questioning the Secular State: The Worldwide Resurgence of Religion in Politics*. London: Hurst & Co.

Stern, J. (2003) *Terror in the Name of God*. New York: Ecco.

Stone, N. (1989) 'We Need Russian Help Against Islam', *Daily Telegraph*, 19 February.

Sultàn, M. (1999) 'Choosing Islam: a Study of Swedish Converts', *Social Compass*, 46(3): 325–35.

Sumner, W. G. (1940) *Folkways: A Study of the Sociological Importance of Usages, Manners, Customs, Mores, and Morals*. Boston, Mass.: Ayer Company Publishers.

Sutton, P. W. and S. Vertigans (2002a) 'The Established and Challenging Outsiders: Resurgent Islam in Secular Turkey', *Totalitarian Movements and Political Religions*, 3: 58–78.

Sutton, P. W. and S. Vertigans (2002b) 'Islamic Movements Against Globalization? Political Opportunities and Action Repertoires in Turkey'. Paper presented at ISA XVth World Congress of Sociology.

Szakolczai, A. (2001) 'Civilization and its Sources', *International Sociology*, 16(3): 369–86.

Taji-Farouki, S. and H. Poulton (eds) (1997) *Muslim Identity and the Balkan State*. London: Hurst & Co.

Tapper, R. (ed.) (1991) *Islam in Modern Turkey*. London: I. B. Tauris.

Tessler, M. (2003) 'Do Islamic Orientations Influence Attitudes Toward Democracy in the Arab World: Evidence from the World Values Survey in Egypt, Jordan, Morocco and Algeria', *International Journal of Comparative Sociology*, (spring): 3–5.

Thabit, A. (2003) 'The Scapegoat has Something to Say and has Two Questions', *Al-Watan*, 1 September.

Thomas, W. I. (1928) *The Child in America*. New York: Alfred A. Knopf.

Thorlindsson, T. and T. Bjarnason (1998) 'Modelling Durkheim on the Micro Level: A Study of Youth Suicidality', *American Sociological Review*, 63: 94–110.

Tibi, B. (1988) *The Crisis of Modern Islam*. Salt Lake City: University of Utah Press.

Tiryakian, E. A. (2001) 'The Civilization of Modernity and the Modernity of Civilizations', *International Sociology*, 16(3): 277–92.

Toprak, B. (1981) *Islam and Political Development in Turkey*. Leiden: E. J. Brill.

Toprak, B. (1984) 'Politicization of Islam in a Secular State: The National Salvation Party in Turkey' in S. A. Arjomand (ed.) *From Nationalism to Revolutinary Islam*. London: Macmillan.

Toprak, B. (1996) 'Prejudice as Social Science Theory: Samuel P. Huntington's Vision of the Future', *Perceptions: Journal of International Affairs*, 1(1).

Touraine, A. (1981) *The Voice and the Eye: An Analysis of Social Movements*. Cambridge: Cambridge University Press.

Toynbee, A. J. (1934–61) *A Study of History*. 12 vols, Oxford and New York: Oxford University Press.

Toynbee (1972) *A Study of History*. Abridged edn, New York: Oxford University Press.

Trovato, F. and G. K. Jarvis (1986) 'Immigrant Suicide in Canada: 1971 and 1981', *Social Forces*, 65 (Dec.): 433–57.

Turan, I. (1991) 'Religion and Political Culture in Turkey' in R. Tapper (ed.) *Islam in Modern Turkey*. London: I. B. Tauris.

Turner, B. S. (1974) *Weber and Islam*. London: Routledge and Kegan Paul.

Turner, B. S. (1978) *Marx and the End of Orientalism*. London: George Allen and Unwin.

Turner, B. S (1993) *Max Weber: From History to Modernity*. London: Routledge.

Turner, B. S. (1994) *Orientalism, Postmodernism and Globalism*. London and New York: Routledge.

Turner, B. S. (2002) 'Sovereignty and Emergency. Political Theory, Islam and American Conservatism', *Theory, Culture and Society*, 19(4): 103–19.

Turner, B. S. (2003) 'Class, Generation and Islamism: Towards a Global Sociology of Political Islam', *British Journal of Sociology*, 54(1): 139–47.

Turner, B. S. (2004) 'Weber and Elias on Religion and Violence: Warrior Charisma and the Civilizing Process' in S. Loyal and S. Quilley (eds) *The Sociology of Norbert Elias*. Cambridge: Cambridge University Press.

United Nations Development Program (UNDP) (2001, 2002) *Human Development Report*. New York: UN.

van der Mehden, F. (1987) 'Islamic Resurgence in Malaysia' in J. L. Esposito (ed.) *Islam in Asia*. Oxford: Oxford University Press.

van Krieken, R. (1998) *Norbert Elias*. London: Routledge.

van Poppel, F., and L. H. Day (1996) 'A Test of Durkheim's Theory of Suicide – Without Committing the "Ecological Fallacy"', *American Sociological Review*, 61(3): 500–7.

Vertigans, S. (1999) *The Turkish Paradox: A Case Study of Islamic and Secular Influences on the Socialization of Turkish students based in Great Britain*. PhD thesis, University of Leeds.

Vertigans, S. (2003) *Islamic Roots and Resurgence in Turkey*. Westport, Conn.: Praeger Publishers.

Vertigans, S. (2004a) 'Socialising Terrorists in a Global Context'. Paper presented at the International Conference on Muslims and Islam in the 21st Century, Kuala Lumpur, 4–6 August.

Vertigans, S. (2004b) 'Social Barriers to Peace: Socialisation Processes in the Radicalisation of the Palestinian Struggle', *Sociological Research Online*, 9(3), http://www.socresonline.org.uk/9/3/vertigans.html.

Vertigans, S. and P. W. Sutton (2001) 'Back to the Future: Islamic 'Terrorism' and Interpretations of Past and Present', *Sociological Research Online*, 6(3), http://www.socresonline.org.uk/6/3/vertigans.html.

Vertigans, S. and Sutton, P. W. (2002a) 'Globalization Theory and Islamic Praxis', *Global Society*, 16(1): 31–46.

Vertigans, S. and Sutton, P. W. (2002b) 'Islam, *al-Qa'ida* and Globalization: An Established–Outsiders Perspective'. Paper presented at ISA XVth World Congress of Sociology.

Victor, B. (2004) *Army of Roses*. London: Constable & Robinson.

Volpi, F. (2003) *Islam and Democracy: The Failure of Dialogue in Algeria*. London: Pluto Press.

von Denffer, A. (1983) *Research in Islam*. Leicester: The Islamic Foundation.

von Grunebaum, G. E. (1946) *Medieval Islam: A Study in Cultural Orientation*. Chicago: University of Chicago Press.

Wallace, A. (1966) *Religion: An Anthropological View*. New York: Random House.

Wallerstein, I. (1974) *The Modern World-System: Capitalist Agriculture and the Origins of the European World-Economy in the Sixteenth Century*. New York: Academic Press.

Wallerstein, I. (1980) *The Modern World-System II: Mercantilism and the Consolidation of the European World-Economy, 1600–1750*. New York: Academic Press.

Wallerstein, I. (1983) *Historical Capitalism*. London: Verso.

Wallerstein, I. (1984) *The Politics of the World Economy*. London: Cambridge University Press.

Wallerstein, I. (1989) *The Modern World-System III: The Second Era of Great Expansion of the Capitalist World-Economy, 1730–1840s*. San Diego, Calif.: Academic Press.

Wallis, R. (1975) *Sectarianism*. New York: Wiley.

Warner, R. S. (1993) 'Works in Progress Toward a New Paradigm for the Sociology of Religion in the United States', *American Journal of Sociology*, 98 (March): 1044–93.

Waters, M. (1998) *Globalization*. London: Routledge.

Watt, W. M. (1968) *Islamic Political Thought*. Edinburgh: Edinburgh University Press.

Waxman, D. (1998) *Turkey's Identity Crisis: Domestic Discord and Foreign Policy. Conflict Studies*, Leamington Spa: Research Institute for the Study of Conflict and Terrorism.

Weber, M. (1966 [1922]) *The Sociology of Religion*. London: Methuen.

Weber, M. (1968) *Economy and Society*. New York: Bedminster Press.

Weber, M. (1970) 'The Social Psychology of the World Religions' in H. Gerth and C. Wright-Mills (eds) *From Max Weber: Essays in Sociology*. London: Routledge.

Weber, M. (1985) 'The Sociology of Religion' in K. Thompson (ed.) *Religion and Ideology*. Manchester: Manchester University Press.

Weber, M. (1992 [1904–05]) *The Protestant Ethic and the Spirit of Capitalism*. London: Routledge.

Wedeen, L. (2003) 'Beyond the Crusades: Why Huntington, and bin Laden, are Wrong', *Middle East Policy*, 10(2) (June): 54–61.

Weiker, W. (1991) 'The Republic of Turkey' in T. Y. Ismael and J. S. Ismael (eds) *Politics and Government in the Middle East and North Africa*. Miami: Florida International University Press.

Wendt, A. (2003) 'Why a World State is Inevitable', *European Journal of International* Relations, 9(4): 491–542.

Werbner, P. (2003) *Pilgrims in Love: The Anthropology of a Global Sufi Cult*. London: Hurst & Co.

Westen, D. (1985) *Self and Society: Narcissism, Collectivism and the Development of Morals*. Cambridge: Cambridge University Press.

Westerlund, D. (ed.) (1996) *Questioning the Secular State: The Worldwide Resurgence of Religion in Politics*. London: Hurst & Co.

Wilkinson, D. (1995) 'Central Civilization' in S. K. Sanderson (ed.) *Civilizations and World Systems: Studying World-Historical Change*. Walnut Creek, Calif.: AltaMira Press.

Williams, R. (1985) *Keywords: A Vocabulary of Culture and Society*. London: Fontana Paperbacks.

Williamson, B. (1987) *Education and Social Change in Egypt and Turkey*. Basingstoke: Macmillan.

Wilson, B. (1966) *Religion in Secular Society*. London: C. A. Watts and Co.

Wilson, B. (1975) 'The Secularization Debate', *Encounter*, 45: 77–83.

Wohlrab-Sahr (1999) 'Conversion to Islam: Between Syncretism and Symbolic Battle', *Social Compass*, 46(3): 351–62.

World Bank (2003) *Saudi Arabia at a Glance*. The World Bank Group: www.worldbank.org/data/countrydata/aag/sav_aag.pdf.

Wouters, C. (1990) 'Social Stratification and Informalization in Global Perspective', *Theory, Culture and Society*, 7(4): 69–90.

Wright, R. (1992) 'Islam, Democracy and the West', *Foreign Affairs*, 71(3): 131–45.

Zeidan, D. (2001) 'The Islamic Fundamentalist View of Life as a Perennial Battle', *Middle East Review of International Affairs*, 5(4): 26–53.

Zeidan, D. (2003) 'Radical Islam in Egypt: A Comparison of Two Groups' in B. Rubin (ed.) *Revolutionaries and Reformers: Contemporary Islamist Movements in the Middle East*. Albany, N.Y.: State University of New York Press.

Zogby (2003) News release dated 31 July 2003 available at http://www.zogby.com/news/ReadNews.dbm?ID=725>.

Zubaida, S. (1989) *Islam, the People and the State*. London: Routledge.

Zubaida, S. (2000) 'Trajectories of Political Islam: Egypt, Iran and Turkey' in D. Marquand and R. Nettler (eds) *Religion and Democracy*. Oxford: Blackwell Publishers.

ndex